THE HAMLYN HISTORY

OF AVIATION

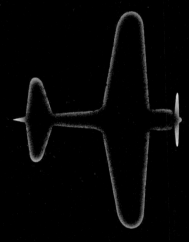

Editor: Dennis Baldry HAMLYN

First published in Great Britain in 1996
by Hamlyn
an imprint of Reed Consumer Books Limited
Michelin House, 81 Fulham Road,
London SW3 6RB
and Auckland, Melbourne, Singapore and Toronto

Copyright © 1996 Reed International Books Limited

ISBN 0 600 58994 3

A catalogue record for this book is available
from the British Library

Produced by Mandarin Offset
Printed in Hong Kong

INTRODUCTION

Almost invariably, the most difficult section to write of any book is the introduction. When the aim has been, from the outset, to create an all-embracing volume to cover the history of aviation, the task is even more complicated.

This is no place to tell you anything about the excitement that is an integral part of the aviation scene. This you can read for yourself in the pages which follow. Rather it would better that it is explained how you can use this book to find the answer to a particular question, or to expand your knowledge of aviation. This is not to suggest that you should not browse, or read through an entire section: but in so doing you may find a subject mentioned briefly and seek the short-cut to more detailed information.

In broad outlines, you can guide your reading by reference to the contents page. As you read through a particular section in the book you will find sub-headings which will help you keep you up to date as to where you are. Invariably, brief mention of indirectly related subjects will appear in most sections, but the index at the end of the should enable you to pinpoint the information you are seeking.

Of necessity, the aim to cover the history of aviation in a single, manageable volume, has imposed the need to condense the available material – written and illustrative – to key developments. Obviously, it has been as objective as possible in its selection, but inevitably a certain amount of disagreement will arise over some omissions. This is only to be expected, and in fact, is a sign of the dynamism of aviation.

Aviation knows no boundaries. Great contributions have come from all nations. In acknowledging the international nature of aviation the editor has been aided considerably by respected international consultants who have used their specialized knowledge to help maintain an equitable balance.

One other matter relating to an international readership is the need to give specification and performance details in both metric and Imperial notations. The metric equivalents used in this work are those in general use throughout the world, and which have been accepted internationally by common usage of the world's aviation press.

THE ORIGINS OF FLIGHT

From the earliest times the desire to fly has been a powerful human urge.

In vain attempts to realize their aim, many people strapped themselves to flimsy wings and threw themselves recklessly from roofs and cliff tops. However misguided and even comic these experiments may now seem, they had their own rational basis.

Flight of fantasy. The hinged paddles of this contraption appear to imitate the upstroke and downstroke of a bird's wings. The first 'bird-men' soon discovered that gravity is constant.

Attempts to fly were quite properly looked on as being dangerous, but the fears expressed were not always the same as those which one might expect today. In addition to the obvious hazards of crashing to the earth from a height, people in medieval and Renaissance times were often aware of dangers associated not so much with the act of falling as with the act of rising.

Aspects of both dangers are expressed in what is probably the best known of all the myths of attempted flight, that of Daedalus and Icarus. While they were trying to escape from the island of Crete, where they had been imprisoned, the famous inventor Daedalus designed a pair of wings for himself and for his son Icarus. Using eagle feathers, he and Icarus attached them to their arms with wax and prepared for flight. Before venturing into the air, Daedalus advised his son that, once away

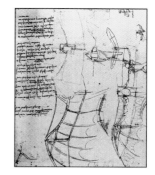

from the island, they should both fly at a very low level, close to the sea. Although the flight began successfully, Icarus soon grew so enchanted with the delights of this new freedom that he started to fly higher and higher. Eventually he rose so high that the wax melted from his wings, causing him to fall into the sea and drown.

Leonardo da Vinci

Leonardo da Vinci (1452-1519) is often described as one of the great forerunners of modern aeronautics. A professional engineer as well as a great painter, he was deeply interested in all scientific and mechanical matters and, as his notebooks show, was especially fascinated – even obsessed – with the problem of discovering how a man might fly. In common with nearly everyone else at the time, he put his faith in the imitation of birds and designed many machines with flappable wings. Some of these were to be operated by the arms alone, some required the use of arms and legs, while a number applied the power of the muscles through various systems of levers and pulleys. Realizing that the muscles of a man's arms are too weak to sustain him for long periods in the air, Leonardo designed his most elegant machines so that the powerful downstroke of the wings would be accomplished by the legs pushing against pedals, while the weaker upstroke would be carried out by the arms. On at least one occasion he thought of using a small motor operated by a powerful bow in which energy could be stored when the string was wound tight and which, after it had run down, could be rewound in flight.

As Leonardo's manuscripts remained virtually unknown until the end of the 19th century, he had no influence on the history of flight. Even if his ideas had been widely circulated, they would not have helped the advance of aerodynamic science.

A replica of Percy Pilcher's Hawk glider demonstrates how this intrepid Scot achieved partially controlled flight in 1896. The Hawk was towed into the air (either by willing helpers or a horse) and steered with a tiller, like a boat.

Models

Alongside the history of man's fruitless attempt to fly with wings is a parallel tradition of experiments with flying models. In medieval and Renaissance times the most commonly quoted example was the story of how Archytas of Tarentum (3rd century BC), a Greek mathematician and close friend of Archimedes, built a wooden dove which was reputed to have been powered by some kind of rocket engine or compressed air. If there is any truth at all in the story, Archytas probably succeeded in building a small wooden glider.

Whatever the facts behind the story of Archytas' dove, it cannot have been powered by gunpowder rockets, as these did not reach Europe from China until medieval times. By 1420, however, at least one man had thought of using rockets to propel a model bird. An interesting manuscript by a Venetian, Giovanni da Fontana, written early in the 15th century, describes a model dove with a rocket embedded in its body. Da Fontana's bird is designed along entirely practicable lines, and there is no reason to doubt that it could have been successfully flown.

An imaginative and serious, if also totally misguided attempt to build a flying machine with flapping wings was made in the mid-17th century by an ingenious Italian engineer, Tito Livio Burattini (1615-82). Burattini's machine, only a model of which was ever built, was designed to look like a fierce flying dragon. A kind of folded parachute attached by springs to the dragon's back was intended to allow a safe descent in the event of an accident. Burattini's flying machine caught the imagination of many 17th century scientists and did much to maintain an interest in the practical possibilities of flight.

The Birth of Aerodynamic Science

Compared with many other sciences, aerodynamics was slow to develop. Despite a good deal of empirical work in the mid-19th century, a correct formulation of basic aerodynamic principles did not emerge until the 1890s. The theory of flight is still developing, and even today there are aspects of the subject which are not at all well understood.

Sir George Cayley

The first fully thought-out aerodynamic experiments were undertaken early in the 19th century by Sir George Cayley (1773-1857), a meticulous worker whose interesting notebooks have survived and who

has been called 'the father of aerial navigation.' Pioneering a technique which was to be useful long after his death, he attached wing surfaces to the end of a rod which could be made to whirl horizontally and which enabled him to measure their lifting force at various angles of attack (the angle between the plane of the surface and the oncoming air stream). From 1804 to about 1809 he did useful work on some of the most crucial properties of aerofoils (wing surfaces).

When Cayley was only 11, two Frenchmen, Launoy and Bienvenu, made a small toy helicopter which was a development of a plaything common in medieval times. Two contra-rotating airscrews (made from feathers stuck into corks) were driven by a small bow-drill motor, powerful enough to make the toy fly into the air when the bow was released. Having encountered this little helicopter not long after its invention, Cayley built his own version in 1796. He kept thinking about the possibilities of rotary lift until, in 1809, he published a modified design of his own with a commentary on its function. This model flying machine became quite well-known in England, inspiring a number of other inventors and being rightly looked on as the origin of all subsequent rotorcraft development.

Cayley also undertook practical experiments both with fixed-wing models and with full-sized gliders. In 1804 he built a now famous little model glider, a replica of which may be seen in the Science Museum, London. About 1.5m (5ft) long, it consists of a small arch-topped kite attached to a pole, with a cross-shaped adjustable tail-unit at the rear. A sliding weight at the nose allowed Cayley to vary the position of the centre of gravity. The graceful descent of this glider when launched from the top of a steep hill inspired him to further work, with the emphasis sensibly placed on stability and control.

Although he remained interested in flight, it was not until towards the end of his life that Cayley returned to practical experiments. Having thought about multiplane structures since 1843, he built a triplane glider in 1849 and twice tested it in very short flights with a boy on board. In 1852 he returned to his

Right: Just like a modern hang glider pilot, German pioneer Otto Lilienthal controls his 1894 monoplane by body movements, swinging forward to restore the glider's natural centre of gravity.

Left: Percy Pilcher prepares to take off in the *Bat* at Eynsford, Kent, in 1897. This was self-launched by sprinting down a suitable slope or hilltop, the pilot touching down with his feet for landing.

early concern for monoplanes, designing (but not building) a graceful glider with large wide wings and incorporating many refinements of construction and flight control. Finally, in 1853, he built his most famous machine, a glider in which his coachman was reluctantly flown across a shallow valley. Although the flight ended without injury to the coachman, the poor man was so frightened by his experience that he immediately gave in his notice.

Fixed wings

During the middle part of the 19th century, the development of fixed-wing aircraft progressed sporadically. After Cayley the most serious work was carried out by William Henson (1805-1868), who designed an Aerial Steam Carriage. Although it was never built, it contained many prophetic features, including braced monoplane wings of 45.75m (150ft) span, twin pusher propellers, an enclosed cabin, and tricycle landing gear. Despite the inadequacy of the control system, such an aircraft could have flown if a sufficiently light and powerful engine could have been found.

Imaginative work was carried out in France in the 1850s by a naval officer, Félix du Temple, who in 1857 designed an elegant monoplane based on geometric principles and powered by a single tractor (puller) propeller. A model of this, tested in 1858, had the distinction of being the first heavier-than-air device to sustain itself in free flight.

A similar experiment, resulting in a powered hop followed by an immediate flop back to earth, was made in Russia in 1884 when a large steam-powered monoplane designed by Alexander F. Mojhaiski was launched. Three propellers were used, one tractor and two pushers, and like du Temple's hop, this can in no way qualify as a sustained and controlled flight.

Power Plants

During the second half of the 19th century, power plants underwent rapid improvement, tempting more and more experimenters to commit themselves to the air in barely controllable and totally untested machines. Among the most widely publicized of these was the remarkable looking *Eole* of Clément Ader (1841-1925). Powered by a very fine steam engine, this strange, bat-like aircraft had a semi-enclosed cockpit and a wingspan of about 15m (49ft). On 9 October 1890 Ader gained a minor place in history by becoming the first man to rise from level ground in a powered aircraft. Although the *Eole* managed only a brief flight of about 50m (165ft), the French military authorities were sufficiently interested to offer Ader a subsidy for further experiments.

Frenchman Alphonse Pénaud's (1856-80) contribution to aviation was sadly cut short by his death at 24. These drawings show his brilliance.

In the strong, steady winds sweeping across Kill Devil Hills south of **Kitty Hawk,** North Carolina, the Wright Brothers test their Glider No 3.

Further useful work was done in England by another original thinker, Horatio Phillips (1845-1924), who undertook a systematic series of experiments with aerofoils of widely differing shape. Having demonstrated that the greater part of the lifting force of a wing is contributed by the low pressure on top rather than by the high pressure below, he patented a series of aerofoils of various thicknesses and cambers. His findings were widely publicized and had considerable influence on later workers in the field. After further development, Phillips built and tested in 1893 a large powered multiplane which travelled around a circular track and demonstrated the validity of some of his theories of lift. This test-bed, affectionately referred to as 'the flying Venetian blind', consisted of a great many long, thin wings stacked one on top of the other.

Men Learn How to Handle Gliders

During the 19th century public enthusiasm for aeronautics kept growing. Colourful exploits in balloons attracted a great deal of attention, while at the same time a number of intrepid showmen tried to create an impression with flappers and gliders of various kinds. Among the most adventurous of these was the Frenchman Louis Letur, who built a curious,

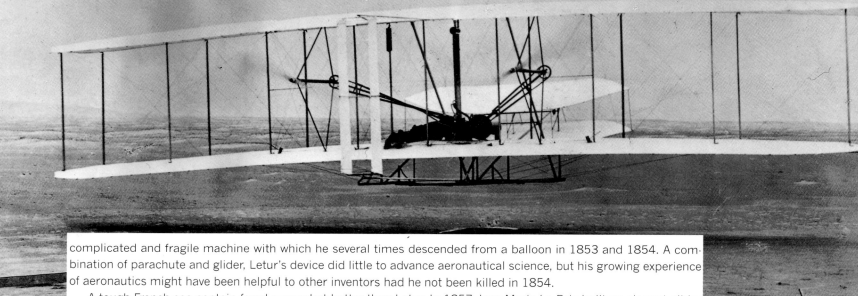

complicated and fragile machine with which he several times descended from a balloon in 1853 and 1854. A combination of parachute and glider, Letur's device did little to advance aeronautical science, but his growing experience of aeronautics might have been helpful to other inventors had he not been killed in 1854.

A tough French sea captain fared somewhat better than Letur. In 1857 Jean-Marie Le Bris built an elegant glider whose shape was based on the albatrosses he had seen. With Le Bris on board, the glider was placed on a farm cart which was then driven downhill until take-off speed was reached. A short glide resulted and encouraged Le Bris to continue. After the glider had again been launched downhill it once more carried Le Bris for a short distance through the air, but as he had no means of control he was unable to avoid a crash-landing in which he broke his leg.

Otto Lilienthal

In the late 1880s, gliding was at last put on a proper theoretical and practical footing by the efforts of one of the greatest of all pioneers of aviation, the German Otto Lilienthal (1848-96). Confident that success lay in a really careful study of control systems before applying power, Lilienthal embraced the old belief that the best procedure was to imitate the birds. He began with fixed-wing gliders which he flew so as to gain experience of the air. In the 1890s he built a series of 18 different types, all of them hang-gliders from which the pilot was suspended in a harness. Light, and necessarily somewhat fragile, the gliders were nevertheless structurally sound, being built with proper engineering principles in mind. For his earliest work he launched himself from natural heights, but in 1893, after he had had a hangar built to house his gliders, he flew from its roof. Finally he made an artificial mound 15m (50ft) high, from which he could fly in any direction and so launch himself directly into wind.

Lilienthal's gliders were built so that the pilot could support himself on his arms in the centre of the wings. With his hips and legs he could swing his body back and forth or even sideways, so adjusting the centre of gravity and controlling the glider's movement, a technique re-established by modern hang-gliders. Despite the inadequacy of the method of control, Lilienthal learned to manoeuvre with a remarkable degree of skill. Most of the gliders were monoplanes but in the hope of increasing the range of control he experimented for a while with biplanes.

European flying pioneer Alberto Santos-Dumont (a Brazilian) makes his record flight of 220m (720ft) in his grotesque canard-winged 14-*bis* on 12 November 1906.

Famous British aviator and designer Tommy Sopwith at the controls of his Howard Wright biplane which he flew from Kent to Belgium in 1910.

Orville Wright pilots the Wright Brothers' plane 'Kitty Hawk' on its momentous first 12-second flight on 17 December 1903.

On 9 August 1896, when Lilienthal was flying one of his monoplanes, he was thrown out of control by a sudden gust of wind. The glider suffered a 'wingdrop stall,' falling sideways out of control from a height of about 15m (50ft), giving Lilienthal insufficient time in which to recover. As a result of his injuries he died on 10 August. Lilienthal's publications, especially his book *Der Vogelflug als Grundlage der Fliegekunst* (Bird Flight as the Basis of Aviation), were based on meticulously kept records and provided valuable data for later experimenters.

Percy Pilcher

Inspired by Lilienthal's example, a young Scot called Percy Pilcher (1866-99) built his first glider in 1895. Pilcher had corresponded with Lilienthal and had twice visited him in Germany. On the-second occasion he had been allowed the rare privilege of flying one of his gliders. Retaining the basic hang-glider configuration, Pilcher introduced modifications of his own, including the use of wheeled landing gear and the development of a take-off technique using a tow-line.

Pilcher's somewhat naive enthusiasm may be gauged from his description of the early difficulties that he encountered. Despite Lilienthal's well founded assurance that a glider is controllable only if an adequate tailplane is fitted, Pilcher's first glider, the *Bat*, completed in the early part of 1895, had a vertical fin and a large degree of dihedral on the wings, but lacked horizontal tail surfaces. Finding in the event that Lilienthal had been correct, Pilcher modified the *Bat* which then became flyable, though only with difficulty. Two further gliders were tried before Pilcher built the *Hawk*, a famous machine which he flew from 1896 until his untimely death in 1899.

Pilcher was nevertheless much more than a slavish imitator, being prepared to consider many other approaches, including multiple wings. Although the Lilienthal glider which he had tried had been a biplane, he had begun with a prejudice against multiple wing surfaces, tending to rely on the monoplane. In 1897 he was nevertheless impressed by the limited success of a triplane glider being used in America by Octave Chanute, and began to make plans for a triplane or quadruplane (four-winged glider) of his own. The speed with which Pilcher worked, the interesting plans which he drew up, and the success of his engine all suggest that, had he lived, he might well have developed a controllable powered aircraft earlier than the Wrights. On 30 September 1899, however, while doing a demonstration flight in *Hawk* for Lord Braye of Stanford Hall, a bamboo rod in the tail assembly snapped when he was at a height of about 10m (33ft). The glider plunged out of control and Pilcher died two days later as a result of his injuries.

Octave Chanute

While Pilcher's main contribution to the history of aviation lay in his enthusiasm and in his further development of Lilienthal's ideas, Octave Chanute (1832-1910), whose active interest in flight began quite late in his life, made practical advances which materially assisted the Wright brothers to achieve their success. A French-born American, Chanute first expressed his fascination with the idea of manned flight in a series of articles which were collected together to form a classic book, *Progress in Flying Machines* (1894). By 1896, having been inspired by the example of Lilienthal, Chanute began building gliders. The first of these was a complex multiplane which underwent a strange series of modifications. To begin with it had six pairs of wings, but by July 1896 it had been converted into a five-wing machine, the original sixth wing now serving as a tailplane. A month later the number of mainplanes had been reduced to four, with one of the original wings still forming a tailplane. Although Chanute records that 'a great many glides were made, with the result of more than doubling the lengths previously attained,' the glider was growing a little worn and was abandoned in favour of something simpler. He next tried a triplane, which was also soon altered to become a biplane with cruciform tail unit. In its biplane form this was to remain the standard Chanute glider.

Chanute's gliders incorporated a number of structural refinements including in particular the light and rigid system of bracing which the Wright brothers were to adopt after the establishment of their friendship with Chanute in 1900. Now in his mid-60s he wisely considered himself too old to try flying himself. Instead, he employed a vigorous young engineer, A. M. Herring. Flying Chanute's biplane glider, which incorporated one or two ideas of his own, Herring made several successful flights in August and September of 1896.

Despite his attempts to find ways of manoeuvring his gliders, Chanute shared with most of his contemporaries an understandable concern for stability and safety. Indeed, he always gave absolute priority to stability, seeking, as he put it, 'exclusive equilibrium'. In this he differed fundamentally from the young men to whom he was to offer so much encouragement and support, Wilbur and Orville Wright.

The Wright Brothers

From time to time claims are made which attempt to show that the Wright brothers should not be considered the true inventors of the aeroplane. What the Wrights achieved, however, was something more significant: they designed and built a machine which, after rising from flat ground under its own power, could sustain itself in the air in level flight and could be controlled in all three dimensions of space.

Wilbur and Orville Wright (1867-1912 and 1871-1948 respectively), the sons of a bishop of the United Brethren Church, lived in Dayton, Ohio, USA. Having developed a successful business as bicycle manufacturers, they were familiar with machine design, skilled with their hands, and had at their disposal a modest amount of money and leisure time. In 1896 they learned of the death of Lilienthal, whose brave efforts so caught their imagination that they decided to embark on a methodical study of all the information they could find about experiments in flying. When they judged that their studies had given them sufficient preparation they began, in 1899, a rationally ordered sequence of experiments which led, four years later, to their much-deserved success.

Although the Wrights were a little secretive by nature and preferred to do much of their work in comparative isolation, they corresponded with many people, especially with Octave Chanute who recognized their talent and offered to help in a variety of ways. It was Chanute's example which led to their adoption of the biplane configuration and in particular to the light, rigid trussed structure which Chanute had managed to pioneer so successfully.

Following their initial correspondence with Chanute, the Wrights built a full-scale biplane glider which they flew during the autumn months of 1900. Needing to carry out their trials at a place where the winds were favourable and steady, they chose the sand dunes of Kitty Hawk, North Carolina. Their small glider, only 5m (17ft) wingspan, was equipped with a forward elevator which was to remain characteristic of all Wright machines for a decade. Although a few glides were made, with the pilot lying prone between the wings so as to reduce the

Leon Levavasseur's Antoinette is seen performing a low flyby at an early air pageant. This machine established features that were to become common on later aircraft. These included a mainplane in front of the tailplane and a tractor propeller.

drag, the Wrights mainly used this glider as an unmanned kite.

In 1901 they built a second and bigger glider, with a span of nearly 7m (22ft). Glides of well over 100m (328ft) were made when conditions were good, but the Wrights were beginning to experience control problems which led them to be suspicious of the findings of their predecessors. In the course of their work with this second glider, they found that although the wing-warping system produced the desired action of banking the wings, there was sometimes an alarming and unexpected tendency for the glider to begin to yaw, or turn horizontally, in the wrong direction. So if the left wing was lowered, with the idea of turning to the left, the glider would, when substantial warping was used, turn to the right instead. This turn against the direction of bank often led to the start of a spin and then to a crash.

Similar problems confronted the Wrights in 1902, when they built and flew their third glider. This had a still larger wingspan of about 10m (33ft), but it differed from its predecessors in a more important respect: for the first time vertical surfaces were used, in the form of a double fixed fin mounted behind the wings. The Wrights had introduced the fin in the hope of steadying the glider in the turn and so curing the yaw in the unwanted direction. The fixed fins did not, however, provide the necessary degree of correction and the problem was solved only when they took another vitally important step. The brothers had given a great deal of thought to the 'adverse yaw' and had puzzled over its cause. This led to their most important single insight and to what was probably their greatest contribution to the history of manned flight. When the wings were warped so as to vary the lift on the two sides of the glider, thereby making one wing rise while the other was lowered, the increase in lift on the up-going wing was accompanied by an increase in drag on the same side. As the wing was raised it was therefore also retarded by the drag, swinging the glider into a turn against the bank. Although the fixed fins

did not hold the glider against the turn, the Wrights realized that they could cure the problem by converting them into a movable rudder. This rudder now acted so that whenever bank was initiated to one side or the other, the tendency to yaw in the opposite direction was counteracted. The glider could then both execute balanced turns and roll back from a turn to straight and level flight without loss of control. They were now in a position to think about building a powered craft.

Having first applied for a patent for their glider, they set about tackling the problem of finding a suitable engine. Lightweight powerplants being scarce, they decided to design and build their own. Their efforts resulted in a 12hp petrol engine arranged to drive two pusher propellers which were also of their own design. For the *Flyer*, as they called their powered aircraft, they built a new biplane of 13m (40ft) wingspan, with forward biplane elevators and the double movable rudder at the rear. The light undercarriage consisted of skids which, for the take-off, were laid on a small wheeled truck running along a wooden rail.

In December 1903, the brothers were ready to experiment with power. After a minor accident on 14 December, which delayed them for three days, Orville made the first powered, sustained, and controlled flight at 10.35 on Thursday 17 December 1903. Although this lasted for only 12 seconds, it was followed by three others (the brothers alternating as pilot), the last of which covered 260m (852ft) in 59 seconds. The *Flyer* was not an altogether satisfactory

Louis Blériot derived much of his inspiration for his highly successful *No. XI* monoplane of 1909 from the Wright *Flyer III*, which he had seen displayed by its designers in France the previous year.

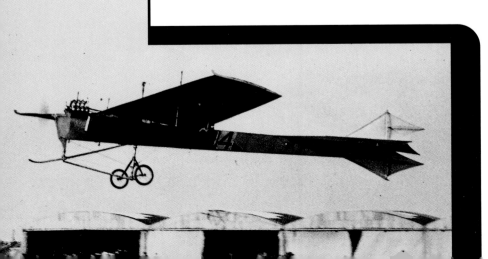

machine but it formed the basis for the aircraft with which they rapidly developed their flying skills over the next few years.

In 1904 the *Flyer II*, using a slightly more powerful engine, completed many successful flights, one of which lasted for more than five minutes. The Wrights, having become the world's first experienced pilots, flew from a 90-acre field eight miles from their home in Dayton, Ohio. About 80 flights were made, during one of which they executed a full circuit of the airfield, the first time such a manoeuvre had been carried out.

Following their pattern of using a new aircraft each year, they built the *Flyer III* for their 1905 season. Similar in size to the previous machines, but with the rudder and elevators placed further from the wings so as to increase their effectiveness, it used the excellent engine that had been installed in the *Flyer II*. Airspeeds of something like 55km/h (35mph) could now be achieved, but these faster aircraft created new problems. In this aeroplane, all three control surfaces – elevators, wing-tips, and rudder – could be moved independently, thus making the aircraft fully controllable about all three axes. With the modified *Flyer III* the Wrights could circle, perform figures of eight, and remain safely airborne for as long as half an hour.

After their successes of 1905 the brothers voluntarily grounded themselves while they tried to arrange

the sale of their invention. Only in 1908, when they had secured an agreement to have the *Flyers* built in France, and had arranged an official acceptance test with the US military authorities, did they emerge from obscurity. Using two-seater versions of the *Flyer III*, Orville flew in the USA while Wilbur went to France.

Early Powered Flight in Europe

Although most of the enthusiasm for aeronautics was centred in Europe, progress with the practical development of powered aircraft was slow in the early years of the century. In 1905, when the Wrights' fully controllable *Flyer III* was remaining airborne for half an hour and more, no European had managed a single sustained and controlled flight. Although within a few years inventors in Europe were developing aircraft which owed almost nothing to the Wrights, the first encouraging partial successes were undoubtedly the direct result of their influence.

French success

News of the Wright gliders had reached Europe not long after their work began and, despite many expressions of scepticism, a number of imitators were inspired to try similar machines. Among these was Captain Ferdinand Ferber, of the French artillery. In 1901 he was attempting to perfect a hang-glider built

Piloted by Captain Bertram Dickson, this Bristol Boxkite was the first used by the British Army for reconnaissance, during manoeuvres in September 1910.

on Lilienthal lines and, in search of guidance, began to correspond with Octave Chanute. After reading, on Chanute's advice, the text of a lecture which Wilbur Wright had delivered in Chicago on 18 September 1901, Ferber began experimenting with a glider based generally on the Wright configuration. This initially primitive aircraft was substantially modified and improved in the course of the next two or three years. By 1904 Ferber had, among other things, made one highly significant change which was to have an important influence on the history of aircraft design. While retaining the Wright-style forward elevator, he added a fixed horizontal tailplane at the rear.

In May 1905 Ferber added a 12hp motor to a glider built along these lines and attempted to fly it. Although it could not sustain itself, Ferber made a

later to exert a powerful influence on European aviation, Gabriel Voisin (1886-1973).

Abandoning this unsatisfactory machine, Archdeacon collaborated with Voisin to try something different, a large float-glider designed to include a high degree of inherent stability. The principles which they followed were those included in the design of the box kite, invented in Australia by Lawrence Hargrave (1850-1915). In the 1880s and 1890s, Hargrave, who kept in close touch with aeronautical progress in Europe, experimented with many gliders, flapping models, and kites. After trying a great variety of kite shapes, he perfected the simple, rectangular box kite in 1893.

The Archdeacon-Voisin float-glider, built in 1905, was the first significant aircraft to apply the Hargrave principle. Large box kite wings with four 'side-curtains' were attached to an open framework fuselage carrying a small double box kite tailplane. In June 1905 Voisin twice piloted this glider when it was

An accurate replica of the Blackburn monoplane departs Old Warden aerodrome in Bedfordshire. This aircraft forms an important part of the Shuttleworth Collection.

successful powered glide from an overhead cable, thus achieving a place in history as the first man in Europe to make a real free flight in a powered aircraft.

In 1903 the European aeronautical scene again experienced American influence when Octave Chanute paid a visit to France. In April he gave a lecture on flying machines to an audience which, as well as Ferber, included a wealthy Parisian lawyer, motor car enthusiast and devotee of flying, Ernest Archdeacon (1863-1957). Inspired by Chanute's accounts of the Wright brothers achievements, Archdeacon built a modified form of their No. 3 glider and tested it in 1904, the pilots being Ferber and a young colleague who was

towed off the Seine by motorboat and flown 'captive' as a kite. Two long hops of 150m and 300m (about 500ft and 1,000ft) were made without mishap.

A second float-glider was tried in the same year by Voisin, this time in collaboration with Louis Bleriot (1872-1936). Although built along essentially similar lines, it was distinguished from its predecessor by the sharp angling of the outer side-curtains on the wings, a modification which was intended to provide additional stability. Like the Archdeacon-Voisin float-glider, this also was flown captive in June 1905, but it crashed. After rebuilding, it was modified several times by Bleriot, who added a powerplant. Although he learned much from these trials, no real success was achieved with the glider in any of its forms.

Success of a qualified kind finally came when, in 1906, Alberto Santos-Dumont, a Brazilian living in

Paris and a highly enterprising designer of airships, tried his hand at heavier-than-air flight. Using the Hargrave box kite idea, he built a grotesque 'canard' machine, with forward box kite elevator, multiple box kite wings set at a sharp dihedral angle, and an enclosed rectangular fuselage. After trying the aircraft suspended beneath his airship, he undertook flights from the ground. When the need for lateral control surfaces became apparent, Santos-Dumont added large octagonal ailerons between the biplane wings. With this semi-controllable machine he managed to make a series of flights, the longest of which, lasting 21.2 seconds, covered a distance of 220m (720ft).

At about the same time, another expatriate living in Paris, the Romanian Trajan Vuia, experimented with two little aeroplanes which, although themselves unsuccessful, had a profound influence on the history of aviation. They were bat-like monoplanes with tractor propellers, the first driven by a carbonic acid motor and the second by a 24hp Antoinette. The pilot sat well below the wing on a framework to which a four-wheeled undercarriage was attached. Between March 1906 and March 1907 Vuia made several short hops from level ground using this first monoplane, and, although it could barely fly, it was destined to be the immediate ancestor of the many monoplanes which flourished in Europe until shortly before World War I.

Among the earliest of those to be influenced by Vuia was Santos-Dumont, who abandoned biplanes in favour of an elegant monoplane design known as the *Demoiselle* (dragonfly). The first of these had a wingspan of only 5m (17ft), weighed only 110kg (243lb), and used a 20hp 2-cylinder engine. Lateral control was achieved by the pilot leaning his body from side to side as he sat on the undercarriage frame.

The man who most firmly established the monoplane configuration was Louis Bleriot, who tried three machines of his own design in 1907. The last of these, his *No. VII.*, influenced the design of monoplanes for many years. It used a 50hp Antoinette engine to drive a tractor propeller, had a long, enclosed fuselage with landing gear consisting of two main wheels and a rear wheel, and was controlled by rear-mounted rudder and elevons.

Lindbergh made his historic solo crossing of the Atlantic in the *Spirit of St Louis*, a high wing Ryan NYP monoplane, in May 1927. He landed at Le Bourget airfield near Paris after two nights in the air.

For a time, however, the development of the biplane was to prove more important. Having started up a factory at Billancourt, Gabriel Voisin and his brother Charles standardized a configuration which was to dominate European aviation until 1910. Using their experience with the floatgliders of 1905, they built biplanes with box kite tails, pusher propellers, and forward elevators. It was in such an aircraft that Henry Farman, an Anglo-Frenchman, made the first fully controlled European flights. Tentative trials in September and October 1907 were followed by more adventurous flights, including a full circle on 9 November and a prize-winning kilometre circuit on 13 January 1908. A skilled and sensitive pilot, Farman used his experience to make many modifications to his aeroplane. In October 1908, having recognized the need for proper lateral control, he added four large ailerons which made his aircraft a great deal more manoeuvrable. On 30 October 1908 he was able to make the world's first real cross-country flight in a heavier-than-air machine, covering a distance of 27km (about 17 miles) in 20 minutes; the next day he established an official altitude record with a height of 25m (about 80ft).

The Aeroplane Comes of Age

If any year may be said to mark the final emergence of the aeroplane as a fully practical vehicle, it must be 1909. This year has a special place in aeronautical history because of the great encouragement provided by the first and most famous aviation meeting, held at Reims, France, from 22 to 29 August. The many contests were financially supported by the champagne industry, which offered handsome prizes.

In all, 38 aircraft were entered, though in fact only 23 took off. Over a period of 8 days, more than 120 take-offs were made and a number of records established. Of the 23 aircraft to fly, 15 were biplanes and 8 monoplanes. Top speeds of about 75km/h (47mph) were reached, the altitude record was 155m (508.5ft), and the greatest non-stop distance flown was 180km (111.8 miles), covered by Henry Farman in 3 hours 4 minutes 56.4 seconds. Although the spectators were disappointed by the Wrights' failure to attend, three of their aircraft were flown by French pilots.

The Reims meeting established the importance and viability of the aeroplane. Competitions, meetings, and races became popular and aircraft were produced in increasingly large numbers. Monoplanes and biplanes continued to flourish, with many manufacturers trying to outdo each other in improvements and refinements.

Aeroplanes began to be used in an ever greater variety of roles. The birth of the aircraft carrier may be said to have occurred on 14 November 1910, when an American, Eugene Ely, flew a Curtiss biplane from the cruiser *Birmingham* off Virginia, USA. The foredeck had been covered by a platform to give Ely a suitable runway, and the short take-off performance of the aeroplane may be judged from the platform's length,

which was only 25m (82ft). The first float-plane was flown in 1910, and in the same year bombing trials were made over targets marked-out like ships. The first mid-air collision also occurred in 1910, when an *Antoinette*, dived into a *Farman* near Milan. Both pilots survived, though one was seriously injured.

From about 1912, when designers and governments alike were giving increased attention to the aeroplane's military potential, the biplane configuration with tractor propeller began to predominate. In view of the technology this is not surprising, since it was a good deal easier to build strong and compact biplane wings, especially if they had to support the weight of twin engines. This trend was nevertheless unfortunate in slowing down the development of the monoplane which, as early as 1911, had appeared in beautifully streamlined form when Levavasseur introduced his Latham design.

Three Great Flights Across Water

During the first 25 years of the aeroplane's existence as a practical vehicle, many exciting pioneer flights were made. Among the most courageous were those in which pilots used fragile and unreliable aircraft to cover considerable distances with minimal navigational aids, very poor weather information, and no established search-and-rescue system. Flights over water were particularly dangerous, since over reasonable terrain a forced landing was a much safer proposition than a ditching.

The Crossing of the English Channel

Before 1909 the Channel had been crossed several times, but only in balloons. Among the many prizes put up by the London newspaper the *Daily Mail* to promote the development of heavier-than-air flight was the sum of £1,000 for the first crossing of the English Channel in an aeroplane. During the summer of 1909 a number of well known pilots, including Wilbur Wright, contemplated trying to win it, with the the Anglo-Frenchman Hubert Latham nearly succeeding on 19 July 1909. Flying an *Antoinette IV*, he was less than half way across when the engine failed and Latham had to ditch. Both he and the aircraft were rescued by a French destroyer.

The Channel crossing was finally achieved six days later by Louis Blériot, who had recently collaborated with Raymond Saulnier in the design of a new and highly successful monoplane. Known as the *Blériot XI*, it had a wingspan of about 8m (26ft), could make a top speed of 60km/h (37mph), and included a number of interesting features giving it a comparatively modern appearance. The pilot sat over the braced monoplane wings in a partially enclosed fuselage of rectangular section. A 25hp, 3-cylinder Anzani engine drove a wooden two-bladed tractor propeller fixed directly to the crankshaft. The now familiar stick and rudder bar were used to operate the control surfaces, consisting of warped wingtips, hinged tailplane tips acting as elevators, and a large all-moving rudder.

Although confident that his *No. XI* could manage the crossing, Bleriot needed first class conditions and good luck if he were to succeed. Despite some discomfort which he suffered as a result of a crash a little while before, he set off from Les Baraques, near Calais, at 04.41 on 25 July 1909. The morning was calm but misty, and Blériot, who had no compass or other navigational instruments, had to navigate by visual reference and fly 'by the seat of his pants.' Official timekeepers recorded

A Vickers Vimy bomber is being readied for a record breaking flight to Australia in November 1919.

the duration of the flight as 37 minutes 12 seconds at the end of which Blériot made a heavy landing on a grassy hillock in Northfall Meadow near Dover Castle. The distance covered over the surface was about 38km (23.5 miles).

The First Non-stop Crossing of the Atlantic

Like the Channel crossing, the first non-stop flight across the Atlantic was promoted by the *Daily Mail*, which offered the generous prize of £10,000. After World War I, which delayed serious thought of so hazardous an undertaking, many teams began planning flights, and several hastily organized attempts ended in crashes. Success was eventually achieved in June 1919 by two British pilots, John Alcock and Arthur Whitten Brown. The aircraft chosen by Alcock and Brown was the twin-engined Vickers *Vimy*, a large biplane bomber first flown in 1918. The *Vimy* was fitted with extra fuel tanks for the long journey. Essentially a wooden aeroplane, it was entirely fabric covered. The four-bladed propellers were powered by Rolls-Royce V12 engines. It had a biplane tail with twin fins and rudders, and powerful aerodynamically balanced ailerons on both upper and lower wings.

As the prevailing wind across the Atlantic blows from west to east, Alcock and Brown began their flight from Newfoundland. On 14 June 1919, in very poor weather, they took off. The aircraft was so overloaded with fuel that it could only just climb away, and, once airborne, the pilots had to contend with reduced visibility because of fog and drizzle. These conditions are ideal for the formation of ice, and for about four hours the whole of the *Vimy* was coated in frozen sleet. Most dangerous of all was the icing-up of the engine air intakes which would have led to engine failure unless cleared. In order to do so, Brown climbed out along the wings to clear each engine in turn. On one occasion the poor visibility caused the pilots to lose control of the aircraft, which entered a spin from which they recovered just a matter of feet above the surface of the

An ignominious end
for the Vickers
Vimy in which
Alcock and Brown
made the first
non-stop crossing
of the Atlantic in
June 1919.

water. Despite the difficulties of navigation, they maintained a good course to Ireland, flying at about 1,200m (about 4,000ft) and covering the distance of 3,041km (1,890 miles) in 16 hours 27 minutes. Their landing in Ireland was rather anticlimatic for the field which they had chosen proved to be so soft that the four-wheeled undercarriage dug in and the aircraft nosed over. In recognition of their courageous flight, Alcock and Brown were knighted by King George V.

The First Solo Crossing of the Atlantic

One of the most astonishing flights in history, requiring not only an outstanding pilot but also an aircraft of unusual endurance and reliability, was the first solo crossing of the Atlantic by Charles Lindbergh on 20-21 May 1927. Before Lindbergh achieved the crossing which won him a prize of $25,000, several pilots had failed in the attempt, and six had

died. To prepare himself for the many hours that he would spend alone in his aircraft, Lindbergh undertook a number of long flights to develop his own endurance.

Lindbergh's famous *Spirit of St Louis* was a highwing Ryan monoplane equipped with the then recently-developed Wright Whirlwind radial engine, which for its day was highly efficient and reliable. The aircraft had nevertheless to undergo substantial modification before the flight was possible. Extra fuel tanks had to be installed and these not only made the aircraft extremely heavy on take-off but also obscured the forward visibility. In order to see ahead Lindbergh had either to look obliquely forward through the side windows or use a specially-installed periscope.

The take-off, early on the morning of 20 May 1927, was a delicate matter. Rain had softened the field, further slowing down the acceleration of the already sluggish aeroplane so that it only just managed to get airborne. The long, demanding trip across the Atlantic was flown with minimal navigational equipment which obliged Lindbergh to descend, on one occasion, almost to surface level to watch the waves and spray so that he could check his estimates of wind speed and direction. One of his greatest problems was to try and keep awake, and once lost control of the aircraft. However, he finally reached Paris after two nights in the air, but large crowds at Le Bourget airfield added to his problems by impeding his touch-down. The journey of 5,810km (3,610 miles) took 331 hours at an average speed of 173km/h (107.5mph).

Lindbergh's aircraft, which was only flown by him, now hangs in the National Air and Space Museum in Washington DC.

Throughout the short <u>history</u> <u>of</u> <u>aviation</u>, one constant factor has been relied upon to spur advancement in aircraft design – conflict. Through two World Wars and subsequent decades of uneasy peace, aircraft have been viewed with increasing esteem as the <u>ultimate</u> <u>weapons</u> <u>of</u> <u>power</u> <u>projection</u>.

AIR WARFARE

2

Reconnaissance Aircraft

Prior to World War I few national or military leaders gave much thought to the possible use of aeroplanes in war. This was to some degree understandable because war in the air was a completely novel idea that seemed best fitted to the pages of science fiction, and the weak and flimsy aeroplanes of the day had enough difficulty getting into the air, without having to operate in a war. The only task which the flying machine might be suited was reconnaissance. This was because for over 100 years observers in balloons had proved that they could usefully watch the enemy from their lofty position and report his movements in a way impossible from ground level.

Even before the outbreak of World War I in August 1914 there had already been numerous combat missions by aeroplanes, most of them concerned with reconnaissance. The first took place on 23 October 1911 when Capt Piazza of the Italian Army took off in his Blériot XI and spent an hour writing details of the movements of the Turkish forces between Tripoli and Aziziyah. On 10 January 1912 the first 'psychological warfare' mission showered Arabs with leaflets urging them to support the Italians, and from 24 February aerial cameras were used for the first time. Further photographic missions were flown in the Balkan War later the same year.

On 22 August 1914 the German airship SL2 penetrated 480km (300 miles) into Russian territory on the world's first long-range reconnaissance mission. The best machine for short-range reconnaissance over the battle area proved to be a two-seater aeroplane with an 'observer'. In the summer of 1912 Britain had held trials to find the best military aeroplane, the only duty considered being reconnaissance. The only good competitor was the B.E.2 tandem-seat biplane, but as this had been designed at the government's own Royal Aircraft Factory at Farnborough it was barred from taking part. Despite this, the B.E. was adopted as the standard aeroplane of the Royal Flying Corps, and was produced in large quantities through the first three years of warfare. Though outwardly a serviceable and efficient machine, the B.E. in fact was destined to cause the deaths of more British airmen than any other World War I aircraft.

One of the basic requirements when it was designed by Geoffrey de Havilland in 1912 had been that it should possess powerful natural stability, so that it could safely be left to fly by itself while both crew-members carried out reconnaissance duties. This stability made it very hard to manoeuvre, and, as recounted later, once enemy aircraft began to come after the B.E.s with machine-guns there was little the

With no threat from enemy aircraft, an unescorted B.E.2 of the Royal Flying Corps makes a visual reconnaissance of front-line trenches in the early months of World War I. By late 1915, B.E.2s had become 'Fokker Fodder'.

Last of the Spitfire photo reconnaissance variants, the Griffon-engined PR.19 had a top speed of 740km/h (460 mph) and its 13,100m (43,000ft) service ceiling put it beyond the reach of the first jet fighters.

The high-speed, long-range Mosquito was an obvious candidate for the PR role. The PR.34 carried six oblique cameras and a single vertical camera.

luckless Brits could do about it. The observer in the B.E. was foolishly put in the front cockpit, and when in self-defence he was given a Lewis machine-gun there was no way he could fire this without the struts and wires around it getting in the way. The sky did not become deadly until the late summer of 1915, and by that time all the army commanders on the Western Front had learned the value of aerial reconnaissance. In fact, the quick evolution of the fighter was not to shoot down other fighters but to shoot down enemy reconnaissance aircraft. In fact many of the armed combat aircraft were themselves intended for reconnaissance and were called fighting scouts, or just scouts.

By 1915 most air reconnaissance was being done with specially designed cameras, which were either mounted vertically in the floor of the aircraft or held by the observer over the side – no easy job with frozen fingers, 'archie' (anti-aircraft) shellbursts and the drag of the massive camera in the slipstream. Gradually the cameras became more reliable and automatic in operation, so that frozen fingers in heavy gloves did not have to do 10 or 11 distinct tasks between exposing each glass plate. Likewise, the aircraft got better, and France, Britain and Germany all produced excellent specially designed reconnaissance machines able to hold their own against individual enemy aircraft. By the time of the final German offensive in March 1918 the Idflieg (Imperial German air force) was taking about 4,000 photographs a day on the Western Front alone, while the newly formed RAF had no fewer than 9,000 cameras in action.

A related duty was artillery observation. Gunners on the ground could seldom see accurately where their shells were falling; the aerial observer soon fulfilled this extra task. The standard method was the 'clock code': the air crew were told the position of the target and placed a transparent sheet over a map, centred on this position and arranged like a clock but with added circles at different radii from the target. Each shell-burst was then quickly related to the position on the 'clock' so that the result could be sent to the gunners (often by Aldis lamp using Morse code) as a simple letter/number code. This 'spotting' duty was to remain an important one for co-operating with both armies and navies until after World War II.

In the 20 years between the world wars there was gradual progress in the design of aerial cameras, in detailed mapping and aerial survey and in the aircraft themselves. From its birth in March 1935 the Luftwaffe concentrated strongly on reconnaissance, and about one-fifth of its strength comprised specially equipped reconnaissance machines such as the Hs 126 and Fw 189. German photographic coverage of British military installations was complete by the end of the 'phoney war' on 10 May 1940, and thousands of missions had also been flown over Poland, Norway and France. But once battle was joined in earnest the German crews had little time for reconnaissance. Tremendous efforts were made to build better strategic reconnaissance aircraft, but Allied command of the air denied them any opportunity until, in the closing months before VE Day, the twinjet Ar 234B and Me 262A appeared in reconnaissance versions that no Allied fighter could catch.

In contrast the Allies had thousands of reconnaissance aircraft airborne daily. The RAF pioneered the PR (photo-reconnaissance) fighter, using the Allison-Mustang for low-level work and such superb camera platforms as the Spitfire PR.XI for high-

Captured intact in May 1945, this Ar 234 was one of
about 300 Blitz (lightning) jets produced at the
Alt Lonnewitz plant on the Czech border.
The Ar 234B-1 reconnaissance version had two large
cameras and provision for a 300 litre (66gal) drop
tank under each engine nacelle. The reflector sight
above the cockpit was used to aim the pair of
MG151/20 cannon, which were fixed in the bottom of
the rear fuselage.

level sorties. The PR.XI had several times the fuel capacity of most fighter Spitfires and could cover targets as far as Berlin or Prague in daylight. Another valuable PR aircraft was the Mosquito. The RAF PR aircraft took many millions of photographs all over Europe on which appeared countless Nazi secrets like the first V-1 flying bomb and V-2 rocket. Meanwhile the US Army and Navy used camera-equipped versions of many famous fighter and bomber aircraft, while the Japanese consistently accorded reconnaissance the honour of calling for purpose-designed aircraft rather than mere versions of combat types. The best-known were the twin-engined Mitsubishi Ki-46 of the army and the carrier-based Nakajima C6N of the navy. Both were outstanding in performance, and generally superior to Allied counterparts, which was not the case with combat aircraft.

A factory-fresh 1954 Canberra PR.7, one of 71 built for the RAF by English Electric. Carrying the same camera load as the Mosquito PR.34, the PR.7's speed and altitude performance was world class.

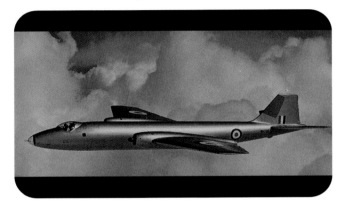

An aspect of reconnaissance that might be overlooked is Elint (electronic intelligence). From its earliest days, it was thought that radar and military electronics would become an important branch of warfare, with nations doing their best both to find out about enemy equipment and interfere with its operation. A instance occurred on 22 February 1941 when an RAF Spitfire raced at tree-top height past a German radar station to bring back the first pictures. This was traditional reconnaissance, but true Elint began on 3 December 1942 when a specially equipped Wellington succeeded in luring up radar-equipped night fighters.

Before being shot to ribbons it radioed back full details of the German radar, including the vital wavelength and pulse-repetition frequency.

The Lockheed U-2 spyplane, originally designed to a CIA specification, is still in operation, helping monitor peace in places like Bosnia.

Ever since, Elint has been one of the most vital reconnaissance tasks of all service arms, and, during the 1950s, the USAF and USN sent out aircraft packed with Elint equipment to bring back details of the radars, communications and other installations round the Soviet Union. Some of these aircraft, operating from bases in Britain and other NATO countries, are known to have made deep penetrations into Soviet airspace. Though not yet officially admitted, the RAF is also thought to have carried out similar reconnaissance flights, initially with PR Mosquitoes and later with Canberra jet bombers, the latter carrying Elint receivers and other special equipment. Over the years more than a few USAF and USN aircraft were quite legitimately shot down, their fate often sealed by the very ground-based radars they were sent out to detect.

In the face of increasingly effective Soviet early-warning systems and swarms of supersonic MiG fighters, existing USAF and USN reconnaissance aircraft were unable to photograph targets deep within the USSR. This was not good enough for the US Central Intelligence Agency (CIA), who were acutely interested in Soviet nuclear weaponry and ballistic missile developments. The CIA secretly funded the development of an aircraft specifically designed for ultra-high overflights of the USSR – the Lockheed U-2. The combination of a powerful jet engine and a sailplane-like wing gave the U-2 a remarkable rate of climb, a maximum ceiling of about 22,250m (70,000ft) and a very long range. By 1959 Russian radar operators had become accustomed to tracking the U-2, but no fighter could reach it. Flying from various bases in countries along the Soviet border (and from Britain, sometimes with RAF pilots) the existence of the U-2 was no longer a secret, but only a few people knew exactly what it was up to. A cover story explained how the aircraft was being used for 'upper-atmosphere research'.

On 1 May 1960 (the May Day date was specially chosen), CIA pilot Gary Powers took off from Pakistan, intending to take photographs and Elint recordings all the way across the USSR before landing in Norway, 6,440km (4,000 miles) away. Near the Siberian city of Sverdlovsk he was shot down by a new V750VK surface-to-air missile (SAM). The U-2 was no longer immune from interception, although flights over China continued for some time. During the 1991 Gulf War U-2s employed a variety of sensors to track the battle. The progress of brutal civil war in the former Yugoslavia has also been monitored by U-2s based in the UK. Refurbished with new mission avionics and more powerful engines, the latest U-2s are more than a match for the air defences of most countries.

In response to the threat from surface-to-air missiles (SAMs), the Lockheed SR-71 was designed to fly even higher than the U-2 and sustain speeds in excess of Mach 3. Designed at the height of

Gears travelling, a Lockheed SR-71 of Detachment 4, 9th Strategic Reconnaissance Wing, blasts off on a Baltic mission from RAF Mildenhall in the UK in 1988

the Cold War, this fantastic aircraft entered service in 1968 and carried out global strategic reconnaissance missions at speeds comfortably exceeding 3,218km/h (2,000mph) at heights in the order of 24,624m (80,000ft). No other air-breathing vehicle (as opposed to rocket-engined craft, which can fly outside the Earth's atmosphere), has approached the SR-71's sustained speed and altitude performance, or surpassed the tremendous feat of design and construction needed to achieve it. Even now, some 30 years after its first flight, the shape of the SR-71 still looks incredibly futuristic.

When fitted with SLAR (side-looking aircraft radar) and highly sensitive Elint or infra-red equipment, the SR-71 could obtain the information required (eg, whether or not a Russian nuclear submarine had put to sea or the location of a new missile site) from the safety of international airspace. The SR-71's optical cameras were of incredibly high resolution, enabling the aircraft to return with amazingly sharp photographs of whole battlefronts, or a specific building or object – all while travelling a mile every two seconds at a height of 38km (15miles). This type of mission often required the 'Blackbird' to overfly hostile territory, but in any event its combination of Mach 3 speed and extreme altitude, together with stealthy radar-absorbing materials and defensive electronic systems, made it virtually invulnerable. Indeed, the presence of an SR-71 would often go completely unnoticed by both airborne and ground-based radars. Soviet MiG-25s (and the odd Swedish JA37 Viggen) attempted to

intercept SR-71s over the Baltic – in international airspace – but none succeeded. The SR-71 yielded intelligence of the highest importance until it was prematurely retired by the USAF in 1990, leading some to speculate that it had in fact been replaced by a secret hypersonic vehicle.

Today nearly all reconnaissance is performed by multi-role tactical combat aircraft fitted with quickly attached pods, and visual-light cameras are no longer enough. Other cameras are needed with film sensitive to IR (infra-red, or heat) radiation. Others use films sensitive to other parts of the EM (electro-magnetic) spectrum, so that when all the photographs of each target are compared the results defeat all enemy attempts at camouflage. Further pictures are taken by IR linescan, which records the 'picture' even further into the infra-red to indicate such things as the place where a car was parked a few minutes before. SLAR is another valuable sensing tool, carried by most advanced combat aircraft to search for scores of miles on either side of the flight path and bring back pin-sharp photographs showing a vast amount of detail invisible in pictures taken by optical or IR cameras. Elint accounts for a further burden of 'black boxes' that must today be carried by the specialised aircraft.

The list of tasks for reconnaissance platforms is seemingly endless. In 1962 photographs taken over Cuba showed Russian ballistic missiles and triggered a near-nuclear crisis. For the next ten years thousands of reconnaissance aircraft operated in south-east Asia, many of them of a new type called the RPV (remotely piloted vehicle) which contains no human pilot but,

The USAF's unarmed RF-4C Phantom II featured a redesigned nose with forward and side-looking radars as well as comprehensive camera and high frequency communications systems. This Alconbury-based example has everything down and dangling for landing.

as its name suggests, is flown by a pilot in another aircraft far away, or on the ground. Today the RPV is an integral part of battlefield surveillance and general intelligence gathering. Its miniature TV/infra-red cameras and other sensors can provide 'real time' target information for special forces, artillery, attack helicopters, strike aircraft and warships. Powered by a compact piston engine driving a propeller or ducted-fan, RPVs are very small and extremely quiet, which makes them difficult to spot and shoot down. Most go about their business undisturbed.

The vast majority are launched from ramps mounted on vehicles or set up on the ground nearby, but they can also be flown off fast patrol boats and other warships. When its mission is complete, the RPV is recovered by parachute. Israel has used its RPVs very imaginatively in planning punitive raids against unfriendly forces beyond its borders. Supposedly secret enemy camps in southern Lebanon were located and then discretely observed without risking the lives of aircrew and ground troops. The resulting air strike would come as a complete surprise. Israel has also used RPVs against Syria, notably during the big air battles over the Bekaa Valley in Lebanon in May 1982. Fitted with radar reflectors to impersonate full-size attack aircraft, RPVs fooled the Syrians into activating their mobile SAM batteries. Orbiting Elint platforms were then able to detect the location of the batteries and the operating frequencies of their guidance radars. Electronic warfare aircraft used this information to make sure the Syrian radars were blinded while the real strike force destroyed the missiles. With the SAM threat all but eliminated, Israeli F-15 and F-16 fighters concentrated on destroying the MiGs sent up to meet them.

More recently, RPVs were used extensively in the 1991 Gulf War with Iraq, where they helped to pinpoint enemy defensive positions in and around Kuwait City. RPVs also kept watch on Republican Guard formations in the open desert, some of which were later routed by the American 1st Armoured Division at Medina Ridge. In September 1995, the success of the devastating NATO air strikes against Bosnian Serbian positions around Pale and other areas of Bosnia owed much to the countless RPV flights made over the former Yugoslavia in the preceding months. Pictures taken by RPVs of alleged mass graves in Bosnia may be used as evidence in any future trials for war crimes.

Today the Balkans is just one area of the world where perhaps the most important class of reconnaissance aircraft is hard at work – the AEW (Airborne Early

Warning) aircraft. The best known is the Boeing E-3 Sentry, more popularly known by the acronym that describes its mission: AWACS (Airborne Warning And Control System). The E-3 is based on the 707-320 jetliner but has a large rotodome (housing a powerful radar antenna) mounted above the fuselage and carries many tons of electronics and a crew of up to 24 to a height of seven miles or more. This flying battle station can remain airborne for 12 hours (or even longer with inflight refuelling) and is able not only to intently study friendly and hostile airspace but can direct all military effort, both defensive and offensive, in a way never before possible.

This capability was clearly demonstrated during the 1991 Gulf War with Iraq, when E-3s co-ordinated hundreds of aircraft performing every kind of mission from combat air patrols to rescue operations deep behind Iraqi lines. The USAF took delivery of its first E-3A in March 1977 and currently operates a total of 34. NATO has an 18-strong E-3A fleet, while Britain, France and Saudi Arabia each have seven, four and five (plus eight KE-3 tankers) respectively. Boeing closed the 707 production line after delivering the last E-3D Sentry AEW.1 to the RAF. In December 1991 the company announced the 767 AWACS, a military version of its twinjet 767 airliner.

An airliner also provided the platform for the Soviet Union's 'Awacski', the Tu-126, which was based on the Tu-114. Tupolev faired the radar into a deep rotodome carried on a single broad pylon above the rear fuselage. The A-PVO (air defence force) received the first of nine Tu-126s in 1965, but its AEW performance was disappointing, partly due to the interference caused by the aircraft's 32 propellers! The Beriev A-50, an AEW conversion of the Il-76 jet transport, replaced the Tu-126 in 1984. This is a vastly more capable aircraft, but its computer processing systems are much less compact than those fitted to the E-3 and their bulk limits take-off fuel load, making inflight refuelling essential for long missions. Nevertheless, the A-50 is able to guide interceptors against difficult targets such as low-flying cruise missiles over sea or land.

The most numerous AEW type is the Grumman E-2 Hawkeye, operated by the USN since the early 1960s. Though still a large and extremely expensive aircraft, the Hawkeye is much smaller than the E-3 due to the size restrictions imposed by the need to operate from carriers. In its latest E-2C form the Hawkeye's radar system is capable of fully automatic overwater and overland target detection and tracking. More than 150 E-2Cs were delivered to the USN between 1972-1993, and land-based versions are in service with Egypt, France, Israel, Japan, Singapore and Taiwan. Interestingly, the USN pioneered AEW after being subjected to attacks by Japanese *kamikaze* suicide aircraft in World War II. Shipborne radars were unable to give adequate warning of incoming raids, for despite constant fighter patrols and intense anti-aircraft fire many *kamikaze* succeeded in penetrating the defences by approaching at wavetop height, putting several US carriers out of action and sinking more than 200 ships. Grumman's first AEW aircraft was a version of the Avenger torpedo bomber fitted with a large radar under the belly, whereas in the Hawkeye the radar is mounted inside a rotodome or 'frisbee' atop the fuselage like the Boeing E-3.

Bombers

The idea that flying machines might drop bombs has been written about for centuries in what was then mere science-fiction. Once man began to travel above ground in powered airships and aeroplanes the bomber was only a matter of time. The first effective bombers were airships, and the Zeppelin, Schutte-Lanz and Parseval ships of the Imperial German Navy and, to a slightly lesser degree, Army, were engaged in practice bombing before the start of World War I.

The first heavier-than-air bomber was nothing more than a prank by high-spirited young officers in the US Army in 1910 using two live bombs dropped them from a Wright Flyer. On 1 November the following year Gavotti of the Italian Army dropped a Cipelli heavy grenade on Turkish troops at Ain Zara, near Tripoli. Nearly a year later, in the Balkan war, specially designed aerial bombs were dropped in fair numbers. But the methods were still crude, most being thrown out by hand.

Gradually methods were made less rough and ready. Bombs began to be hung from specially designed racks, at first along the side of the fuselage outside the cockpit and later from the underside of the fuselage or wing, with the bombs carried horizontally to reduce air drag. Release was effected by pulling a wire or string. Having the bombs already fused to explode on impact was dangerous; they might be jolted free on take-off. Some had safety pins which could be withdrawn by the pilot pulling another string, while from 1915 properly designed bombs came into use with good aerodynamic and ballistic properties, so that they fell accurately point-first, with a small fan driven by the slipstream to unscrew a safety device and make the fuse live.

More important even than developing bombs was learning how to aim them. The first person to make a bomb sight was Riley E. Scott, an American, who constructed a device involving a pivoted telescope and tables of figures. Finding no interest in the United States he took it to France and in 1912 won the first-ever bombing contest. His crude sight was the starting point for those of almost all other air forces.

As already related, most officials doubted that aeroplanes could serve any useful purpose in war except as reconnaissance platforms. Yet a few far-sighted manufacturers proposed 'combat aircraft', and some constructed machines capable of carrying a significant bomb loads. The pioneers were Russian and Italian.

General officers of the Imperial Russian Army with the second Ilya Muromets, which made an epic 30 hour 30 minute return flight between St Petersburg and Kiev in 1914.

Pride of place must be accorded to Igor Sikorsky. He designed a giant biplane, the world's first four-engined aeroplane. Completed in May 1913, it flew with complete satisfaction. The second example, flown in December 1913, became the prototype of the famed IM class of giant warplanes which not only equipped the world's first heavy-bomber unit – the EVK, Squadron of Flying Ships, formed in December 1914 – but pioneered the concept of strategic bombing. Though apparently flimsy, they proved tough and serviceable, making long bombing missions lasting up to six hours. Defensive armament was increased until later models carried eight machine-guns and sometimes a 50 mm cannon. Self-sealing fuel tanks were introduced, for the first time on any aircraft, and the lower part of the pilot's cabin and the backs of the seats were armoured.

Italy's pioneer was wealthy industrialist Count Gianni Caproni. He built the Ca 32, which had three 100hp Fiat water-cooled engines. It was put into immediate production and 164 were built for the Corpo Aeronautica Militare. Entering service from July 1915, they were courageously flown on long bombing missions across the Alps and other hazardous obstacles against Austro-Hungarian strategic targets. From the Ca 32 stemmed many later Capronis for bombing, torpedo dropping and other duties. .

The brothers Voisin, pioneers of aviation after the Wrights, were among the chief suppliers to the French Aviation Militaire. In 1914 four squadrons were equipp-ed with the Type L pusher biplane, which though puny (80hp, carrying up to 60kg [132lb] of small bombs) was strongly made in steel, and proved itself able to take punishment. Voisins flew the first bombing mission of World War I on 14 August 1914, but it was May 1915 before proper missions were organized. Subsequently Voisin gradually gave way to the equally slow but more powerful Breguet-Michelins and then the excellent Breguet XIV tractor machine.

In Britain there were no bombers at the start of the war, and the Royal Flying Corps had no thought of such machines; but the Royal Naval Air Service was more awake. The Admiralty Air Department issued a specification in 1914 for a bomber with two engines and able to carry six 50.8kg (112lb) bombs. Frederick Handley Page responded with the O/100, first flown on 18 December 1915. Powered by two 250hp Eagle II engines, it carried double the requested bomb load at 129km/h (80mph), with defensive armament of up to five machine-guns. Then came the O/400 with more powerful engines and speed nudging 161 km/h (100mph). These great bombers carried bombs of up

to 748kg (1,650lb), the maximum load being 907kg (2,000lb). At the end of the war the much larger V/1500 was entering service with the RAF's Independent Air Force. The V/1500 had four engines and could carry a bomb load of 3,402kg (7,500lb).

Even the V/1500 was beaten by the largest of the Staaken 'Giants' built for the German Idflieg (air force). Known as the R series, these were the greatest bombers of World War I. The most important model was the R.VI, with two tandem pairs of engines, 18 wheels, a crew of seven, and a load of 18 bombs of 100kg (220.5lb). The Giants were well equipped, with radio navigation direction-finder, oxygen, comprehensive flight instruments and even a simple autopilot. The wing span of 42.2m (138ft 6in), largest of any service bomber until the B-29 Superfortress 30 years later.

Between the Wars

Between the two world wars bombers developed in tune with improved engines, new kinds of structure and

A 'Bloody Paralyser', the Handley Page 0/400 entered squadron service in the spring of 1918 and gradually became the backbone of the RAF's Independent Force.

advances such as flaps, retractable landing gear, variable-pitch propellers and the power-driven gun turret. Throughout the 1920s most nations progressed slowly, with metal structures instead of wood but still braced with wires and covered with fabric. Only in the Soviet Union was there dramatic change, and this was because of the setting up by the German

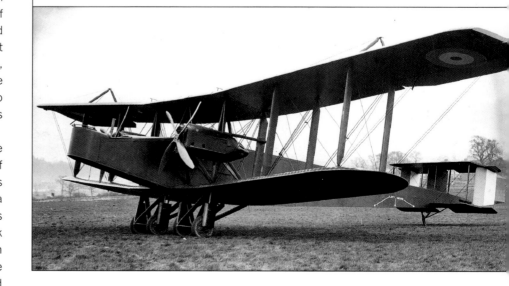

First flown in September 1934, the Hawker Hind was the last biplane light bomber to equip regular RAF bomber squadrons. A star attraction of the Shuttleworth Collection, this Hind is resplendent in the colours of No 15 Sqdn.

Juicy targets for Russian fighters, JU87Ds (Stuka dive bombers) maintain tight formation over the Eastern Front in the summer of 1942.

The Handley Page Halifax shared the brunt of RAF Bomber Command's offensive from 1942 onwards. Though never as good as the Lancaster, the Hercules-powered B Mk III of 1944 was a big improvement.

Obsolete as a day bomber by 1940, the 'long nose' Blenheim IV, with a navigator/bomb aimer forward of the pilot, was highly vulnerable to fighter attack.

The maximum load for this Vickers Wellington Mk III a 1,816kg (4,000lb) 'Cookie high-capacity blast bomb.

Equivalent to the Mosquito, the Junkers Ju 88 was one of the outstanding combat aircraft of World War II.

Junkers company (which could not build in its own country) of an aircraft plant at Fili, near Moscow.

This was an example of what is today called 'technology transfer'; the new Soviet government found itself possessed of the ability to build large cantilever monoplanes with all-metal construction. The leader of the team to put the Junkers technology to use was Andrei N. Tupolev. In 1925, his bureau produced an excellent twin-engined bomber, the ANT-4, put into service by the Soviet air fleet as the TB-1. Powered by 500 hp M-17 water-cooled engines, it was noteworthy for its completely unbraced all-metal wing.

Only a month after the TB-1 first flew, the government issued a specification for a bomber with even greater capability, with engines totalling 2,000hp. Tupolev did the obvious: he doubled the number of engines to produce the first four-engined cantilever monoplane. The ANT-6 was first flown in December 1930. It was basically a scaled-up TB-1, with a monster all-metal wing, tandem-wheel landing gears and no fewer than five machine-gun stations. Normal bomb load was 2,200kg (4,850lb), but for overload missions some versions could be burdened with 5,800kg (12,800lb), greater than any other bomber of the period. In the mid-1930s they were used as pioneers of mass use of paratroopers, carried the first airborne tanks, and landed on skis at the North Pole.

In the United States the most significant advance of the inter-war period was the Martin 123. By 1930 German development of stressed-skin structures, which unlike the Junkers/Tupolev technology did not suffer the drag penalty of a corrugated skin, had sparked construction of truly modern aircraft in the US. Boeing's B-9 bomber unfortunately appeared a

few weeks ahead of Martin's 'dark horse' which had not been designed to an official specification. Martin put into the Model 123 every new feature, including the 600hp Cyclone engine driving the new Hamilton propeller. Even in its original form the Martin reached a speed of 317km/h (197mph), which exceeded that of any single-seat fighter in the Army Air Corps!

By this time Boeing had flown the Model 299, a startlingly large and advanced aircraft with four engines and so many gun positions a newspaperman called it the Flying Fortress, a name which stuck. Because of its geographical position the United States judged that its only bomber targets might be a hostile fleet. Boeing chose four engines purely for greater over-target height and speed. At this time the Army Air Corps strongly believed in unescorted mass attacks in

daylight at the greatest height possible. The Norden bombsight promised unprecedented accuracy, and the General Electric turbocharger greatly increased power at heights as high as 9,000m (29,530ft). Gradually the impressive Boeing, which was ordered with both the new devices in 1937 as the B-17, became the focal point of an entirely new kind of air power in which attacks were made from the stratosphere.

Germany's reborn Luftwaffe had the misfortune to lose its first Chief of Staff, General Wever, in a crash in June 1936. With him died plans for four-engined strategic bombers. His successor, Kesselring, believed in smaller twin-engined bombers for tactical support in a Blitzkrieg campaign. So the Luftwaffe equipped itself exclusively with medium bombers, the biggest being the broad-winged He 111, the lightest the twin-finned Do 17 and the newest the Ju 88. The first two saw action in Spain and, because they encountered no determined modern fighters, left the Germans satisfied that their bombers were adequate for any future war despite their light defensive armament. The Luftwaffe also put into service the Hs 123 biplane and then the Ju 87 monoplane as purpose-designed dive bombers, able to put down heavy bombs with considerable precision in dives as steep as 80°.

The electrically powered Bendix 'chin' turret of the B-17G increased defensive armament to 13 0.5in machine guns. Flying Fortresses dropped more than 640,000 US tons of bombs on European targets.

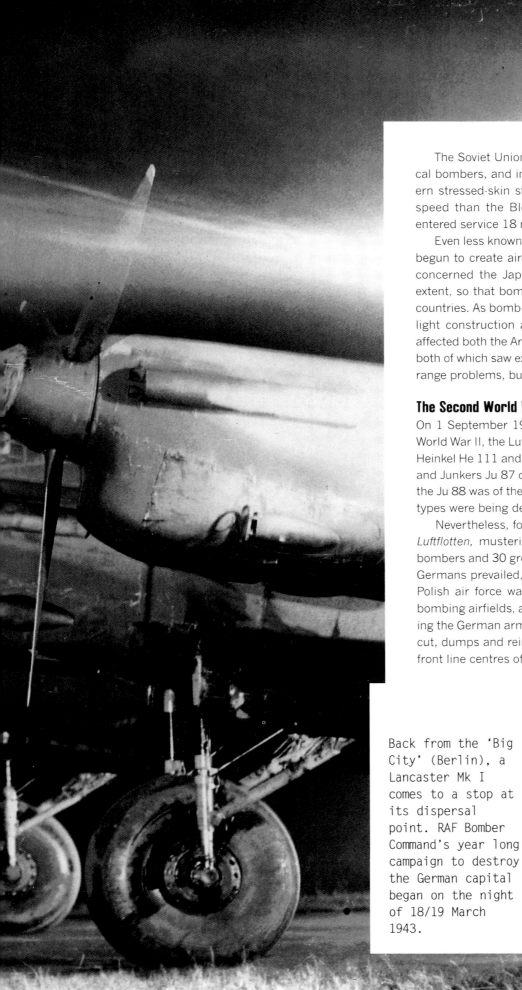

The Soviet Union likewise decided to concentrate on smaller tactical bombers, and in the Tupolev SB-2 had one of the best, with modern stressed-skin structure, and both heavier bomb-load and higher speed than the Blenheim, the RAF's first modern bomber, which entered service 18 months after the SB-2.

Even less known by the world outside, Japan had by the mid-1930s begun to create aircraft of outstanding quality. Where bombers were concerned the Japanese were confronted by a war theatre of vast extent, so that bomber range tended to be twice as great as in other countries. As bomb-load and speed were vital the penalty tended to be light construction and lack of armour or fuel-tank protection. This affected both the Army Ki-21 and the otherwise remarkable Navy G3M, both of which saw extensive action in China in the late 1930s. Both had range problems, but pushed the available technology to the limit.

The Second World War

On 1 September 1939, when the German invasion of Poland started World War II, the Luftwaffe was fairly well equipped with Dornier Do 17, Heinkel He 111 and Junkers Ju 88 level bombers, and Henschel Hs 123 and Junkers Ju 87 dive-bombers. Notable, though, is the fact that only the Ju 88 was of the very latest design, and that replacements for these types were being developed only as a very low priority.

Nevertheless, for the Polish campaign, the Luftwaffe deployed two *Luftflotten,* mustering between them 648 level bombers, 219 dive-bombers and 30 ground attack aircraft. Strategically and tactically the Germans prevailed, though only as a result of fairly heavy losses. The Polish air force was effectively destroyed in the air or grounded by bombing airfields, allowing the bombers to turn their attentions to aiding the German army without hindrance. Lines of communication were cut, dumps and reinforcements attacked, headquarters bombed, and front line centres of resistance crushed at the request of the army.

As a result of Germany's invasion of Poland, France and Great Britain declared war on Germany. Afraid that an attack on land targets would bring retaliation from bombers, each of the combatants refrained from all bombing except that which was directed against naval installations and ships. In this way the Royal Air Force on 4 September sent a force of Bristol Blenheims and Vickers Wellingtons to attack Wilhelmshaven: pounced on by German fighters, the British bomber force lost five Blenheims and two newer Wellingtons, indicating that in daylight raids bombers were incapable of warding off the attentions of fighters.

The RAF high command decided that in future losses of this magnitude would have to

Back from the 'Big City' (Berlin), a Lancaster Mk I comes to a stop at its dispersal point. RAF Bomber Command's year long campaign to destroy the German capital began on the night of 18/19 March 1943.

be expected in daylight raids against Germany, and so night bombing, less accurate but also less costly, was decided upon as the RAFs operational norm.

Operations during the early stages of the battle for France and Belgium made it apparent that day bombing, with its far greater accuracy could be a decisive weapon only when total air superiority was assured. On 11 May, for example, the Belgian air force committed almost all its Fairey Battle light bomber force, with fighter escort, in an attempt to destroy the vital bridges over the Albert Canal in the vicinity of Maastricht: German fighters and AA guns shot down nearly all of them.

What could be achieved in a situation of air superiority was demonstrated on 13 May, when the Luftwaffe's II and VIII *Fliegerkorps* unleashed 310 level bombers and 200 dive-bombers in a number of waves against the French artillery defending the west bank of the Meuse river in the Sedan sector, chosen as the spot where the main German armoured thrust was to divide the Allied defences and push on to the coast. There were few defending fighters and AA defences were almost non existent.

At about the same time, the old quarter of Rotterdam was razed in an attack by 86 Heinkel He 111 medium bombers just as the Dutch capitulated. The threat of such bombing was intended to scare the Dutch into surrender, but failure in the German communication system caused the threat to be implemented, confirming opinion that the Germans were advocates of 'terror bombing'.

During the Battle of Britain in the summer of 1940, the Germans were forced to learn the lesson they had themselves inflicted on the Poles, Norwegians, Dutch, Belgians, French and British: that without air superiority over the target, daylight bombing is a expensive business. After the last day raid against London on 27 September, the Luftwaffe concentrated its efforts on night bombing of London and other industrial cities, the so-called 'blitz'.

A new type of bomber battle began that was to continue throughout the war: on the one side, bombers tried to find their targets in the dark and inflict serious damage; on the other side, ground defences attempted to conceal targets by decoys and used ever more sophisticated methods to jam or distort the attackers' electronic aids, so that the enemy bombers could be destroyed by AA guns and potent night-fighters fitted with radar. Throughout the winter of 1940 and 1941 the German bombers attacked targets in southern and central England, the most significant being that of

Technically the most advanced
aircraft of World War II,
the Boeing B-29 Superfortress

14 November 1940 when the pathfinder force led 437 other bombers to Coventry, whose centre was devastated. RAF Bomber Command was unable to respond, for the number of aircraft available rarely exceeded 100, and the electronic navigation devices pioneered by the Germans were not yet available to the British.

While the US Army painfully developed the B-17 and its later partner the B-24 Liberator, Britain built a comprehensive range of two- and four-engined bombers without a clear idea of how they should be used. The best of the early twins was the Vickers Wellington – it remaining in production until after the end of the war when the total of 11,461 exceeded that of any other bomber in Europe. Though Wellingtons flew over 180,000 missions, the RAF decided to concentrate on four-engined heavy bombers for its main strategic attacks. There were three types, the Short Stirling, Handley Page Halifax and Avro Lancaster. By far the best of them was the Lancaster, a four-engined derivative of the unsuccessful twin-engined Manchester. It had an excellent performance at all altitudes and was simpler to make and maintain.

With the appointment of Air Marshal Arthur T. Harris in February 1942 as its commander-in-chief, Bomber Command was gradually transformed into a force which made the German bomber fleet look puny in comparison. Between February 1942 and March 1944, Bomber Command dropped some 195,000 tons of bombs on German cities, and lost 4,285 aircraft – the effectiveness of their raids was not all that had been hoped for, since the Germans learned to live with the bombing, and their industries were removed to less accessible or bomb-proof sites. Nevertheless, the growing might of the bomber offensive had forced Germany to divert a significant proportion of its industrial capacity into building up anti-aircraft defences at the expense of hard-pressed front-line forces. The raids also weakened the German war machine by disrupting communication links as well as power and water supplies.

One of the milestones in the campaign was the first '1,000-Bomber raid,' against Cologne on 31 May-I June 1942, using the new bomber stream tactics to concentrate the aircraft over the target and give the defence forces as small a target as possible to aim at; earlier tactics had allowed pilots to approach the target over a course of their own choosing, but the individual crews had provided the line of German night-fighter defences with ideal targets. Also notable were the devastating raids on

Essen and Bremen during June. Thereafter Bomber Command entered into a see-saw competition with the German nightfighter arm as first one and then the other gained a measure of superiority, to be counterbalanced only by improvements in the other side's tactics or electronics.

Another milestone at this time was the first raid launched by US heavy bombers from England, the precursor of a great effort by the USAAF's 8th Air Force. Disbelieving the British assessment of the dangers of day bombing, the Americans were convinced that the tight boxes of Boeing B-17 and Consolidated B-24 bombers could protect each other from determined fighter attacks. So the double offensive against Germany was begun, the RAF bombing cities and whole industrial areas by night, and the USAAF striking at pinpoint targets by day.

The main objectives for the US effort at the beginning of 1943 were U-boat construction yards and pens, and aircraft factories. The RAF's main objectives were still German cities. However, the efficiency of the RAF's effort was greatly improved by the introduction of a new navigation aid, 'Oboe,' new centimetric airborne radar (H2S), and special bombs to mark the target area. Between March and July 1943 Bomber Command launched 43 major raids in the Ruhr, but failed to disrupt the output of the area significantly. Some 18,000 sorties were dispatched, but losses amounted to 872 lost over Germany and 2,126 damaged, Bomber Command's heaviest losses of the war. However, Bomber Command came closest to success in late July and early August 1943, when a large proportion of Hamburg was razed in four raids, the second of which caused the first 'firestorm', in which some 40,000 people died.

The 8th Air Force, meanwhile, had suffered its first major reverse in an attack on Bremen in April 1943, when 15 of 107 bombers were lost, and another 48 damaged. However, the threat of the US effort, which was still in its infancy, caused the Luftwaffe to call back to the Reich fighter units from other fronts, easing the task of the Allies in those areas.

Another major US raid was the double attack on Schweinfurt and Regensburg on 17 August 1943. Considerable damage was caused but 59 of the 363 bombers dispatched were lost, and very many others

Laden with bombs, the Ar 234B-2 was slower that Allied fighters – hence the Ar 234C with four BMW turbojets. Had the war continued, the C-series would have been the standard production version.

were severely damaged. The USAAF had already begun to appreciate the need for fighter escorts to accompany the bombers, but as yet these were limited to the Lockheed P-38 Lightning and Republic P-47 Thunderbolt, neither of which had the range to roam deep into Europe.

Harris now tried to seal his success in the Battle of Hamburg with the Battle of Berlin, which saw 16 main raids between 18 November 1943 and 24 March 1944 against the capital. Harris believed that if Bomber Command and the 8th Air Force could devastate Berlin, the Nazis would be forced to sue for peace. The 'Big City' was the target every bomber crew dreaded. Berlin was deep in the heart of the Third Reich and the long journey across Germany gave the city's awesome flak and fighter defences plenty of warning. The extreme range of the target required extra fuel, which meant that fewer bombs could be carried. Berlin failed to buckle under the onslaught.

At the beginning of 1944, the USAAF embarked on an offensive to destroy the Luftwaffe as an effective weapon: while the heavy bombers eliminated aircraft production facilities, their escort fighters would destroy the Luftwaffe's fighter arm as it tried to intercept the heavy bombers. The campaign got off to an inauspicious start on 11 January 1944, when the bomber and escort forces failed to link up, resulting in the loss of 60 out of 667 bombers attacking targets in the Brunswick area. However, the 'Big Week' between 20 and 26 February was far more successful, 26 factories being attacked, for the loss of only 228 of the 3,800 sorties dispatched. US fighter losses were only 28, but the Luftwaffe lost 355 of its 1,100 fighters.

At the end of March 1944 the strategic forces of Britain and the US came under the control of Eisenhower for the final run-up to the invasion of France, which took place on 6 June 1944. Only after this had clearly succeeded did the strategic forces revert to their previous 'owners'. After the strategic bombers had returned to their original tasks, the Luftwaffe's decimation at the hands of the USAAF continued until Germany was all but defenceless in the air, despite the introduction of new fighters. Germany's power supplies and oil production installations became the primary targets, and so effective were the heavy bombers that Germany's armies were starved of fuel by the beginning of 1945.

The most advanced bomber of World War II was without doubt the B-29 Superfortress. In every respect the B-29 thrust ahead into new areas. It was defended by electrically driven gun turrets armed with heavy machine guns and cannon, aimed from manned sighting stations via a complex control system which enabled gunners to control whichever turrets

Top: Huge drop tanks and twin 20mm tail cannon identify the B-47E Stratojet, the most numerous nuclear bomber in the United State's Strategic Air Command (SAC) with more than 1,400 delivered between 1953 and 1957.

Above: The first Canberra B.2s went to No 101 Squadron at Binbrook, Linconlshire, in May 1951. The improved B.6 of 1954 had more powerful Avon engines.

they most needed; the turrets themselves were exceptionally small and offered little drag. All crew compartments were fully pressurized, for comfort and unimpaired efficiency at cruising heights of not less than 10,000m (32,000ft). Fuel capacity was, by any previous standard, enormous.

The strategic bombing war in the Pacific was exclusively an American affair. Both sides made extensive use of medium bombers for tactical support, as had all parties in the European war, but only the Americans had the technological expertise and production capabilities, coupled with the determination, to use strategic bombing in the war against Japan. During 1942-3 it was only from China that a beginning could be made against Japan's cities and industries, with the main part being played by the 14th Army Air Force. However, with the advance across the central Pacific by the forces under the command of Admiral Chester W. Nimitz, islands from which the new Boeing B-29 Superfortress bombers could operate against Japan fell into American hands during 1944.

The first B-29 arrived on Saipan in the Marianas on 12 October 1944, and it is from this date that the true air offensive against Japan may be dated. Based in the Marianas was the 21st Bomber Command, part of the 20th Army Air Force, whose other formation, the 20th Bomber Command, was in India for operations in South-East Asia. The scale of operations was soon built up, and the B-29s made their first decisive raid on 19 January 1945, when the Kawasaki factory near Tokyo was hit, reducing Japan's output of aircraft engines by a staggering 12½ per cent and that of aircraft by almost 20 per cent.

The performance of the 21st Bomber Command was generally inadequate until Major-General Curtis LeMay diagnosed that night raids with incendiaries, flown at low altitudes, would produce better results than high-explosive raids by day at high altitude. The diagnosis and remedy were borne out by the results of the raid on Tokyo on 9-10 March 1945: 334 bombers dropped napalm and incendiaries, burning out 16 square miles of the city, killing 124,000 people and making another one million homeless. Thereafter the B-29s, in ever increasing numbers, devastated Japan's cities, food production, power system, transportation network, and industrial areas, making it all but impossible for Japan to sustain her war effort.

However, despite the success of these conventional

Together with the Valiant and Victor, the Vulcan formed the RAF's V-force deterrent in the 1960s. Later switched to the non-nuclear role, the Vulcan B.2 remained in service until 1982, bombing the runway at Port Stanley during the Falklands War.

attacks, it was to take a new weapon to put an end to the war. On 6 August 1945 the port and industrial city of Hiroshima, hitherto only lightly touched, fell victim to the first atomic weapon used in anger: some 47 square miles of the city were destroyed, 71,400 people killed, and another 68,000 injured. A similar fate befell Nagasaki on 9 August, although the geography of the city, built on hilly ground, prevented the damage from being so devastating.

By combining resources of many companies B-29 production got into its stride in 1944 and by VJ-day deliveries totalled 3,667. Subsequently the B-29 was developed into the even more powerful and efficient B-50, while in 1946 Convair flew the world's biggest-ever bomber, the gigantic B-36, designed in 1941 to bomb Germany after the possible defeat of Britain. Originally powered by six 3,000hp Pratt & Whitney R-4360 Wasp Major piston engines, the B-36 was in 1950 boosted by the addition of pods under the outer wings each containing two J47 turbojets, which added speed and height.

Vulnerability was still a problem, and protracted experiments were made with parasite fighters carried inside the bomb bay. McDonnell made the grotesque little XF-85 Goblin fighter to defend the B-36, but difficulties were such that the idea never became operational. The F-84F fighter-reconnaissance aircraft was also hung under the B-36, and towed from the wingtips, in further attempts to reduce the monster's vulnerability by allowing it to stand-off at a safer distance from its targets.

The Cold War and Jet Bombers

By the end of World War II it was obvious the future lay with the gas-turbine engine. Germany had actually built jet bombers and got them into action: the purpose-designed Ar 234B and the Hitler-inspired Me 262A-2a.

By 1945 a whole range of much larger jet bombers were on the drawing boards in the US. The conventional North American B-45 Tornado entered service with the

Using water injection to boost its eight J57 turbojets, a B-52G Stratofortress of the 2nd Bomber Wing makes a typically smoky departure from Barksdale Air Force Base, California, in 1989.

In production for 38 years, the Tu-95 was Russia's counterpart to the B-52. This is the final new-build variant, a Tu-95MS-6 long-range missile carrier, the last of which was delivered to the CIS Air Armies in 1992.

newly created USAF in 1948. and was followed by the dramatically unconventional Boeing B-47 Stratojet. This introduced swept wings and tail, podded engines, bicycle landing gears on the centreline and a radar-directed tail turret.

Over 2,000 of these impressive bomber, reconnaissance and electronic-warfare aircraft were delivered, in what in monetary terms was probably the largest manufacturing programme in history to that time. The B-47 also briefly introduced another concept, the strategic stand-off missile. In 1943 the Luftwaffe had used two types of radio-guided missile, the Hs 293 and FX 1400, in attacks on ships and other important targets. Other nations did not develop

such weapons until much later, and by the 1950s the need was not only to hit the target accurately but also to allow the bomber to stand off outside the heavy target defences.

This new requirement caused cancellation of Britain's first precision-guided bomb, the Blue Boar, and its replacement in 1953 by the long-range winged Blue Steel. Until a few years previously it had been believed that a bomber flying at 16,000m (52,500ft) at Mach 0.9 would be safe from AA guns and almost immune to interception, and three types of 'V-bomber', the Valiant, Vulcan and Victor, were built to drop free-fall nuclear and conventional bombs.

By 1953 it was very clear that a stand-off missile such as Blue Steel would be needed to help deliver nuclear warheads to heavily defended targets, though the quest for greater speed and height persisted. New versions of the Vulcan and Victor were produced with greater power and larger wings.

In the United States the giant eight-engined B-52 likewise appeared with much more powerful engines, and considerable effort was also put into developing supersonic bombers. First was the USAF's Convair B-58 Hustler, an outstanding technical achievement, able to fly over 8,000km (5,000 miles) without air refuelling and to exceed Mach 2. France built the much smaller, shorter-ranged Mirage IVA, which is still in service as the upgraded IVP armed with the ASMP nuclear cruise missile.

In the Soviet Union one of a series of large strategic bombers from the Tupolev bureau was the Tu-95, in which the apparent impossibility of securing adequate range with turbojets was answered by using four giant turboprops. Built in many different versions, including the redesigned Tu-142 for the AV-MF (naval aviation), the Tu-95 first flew in November 1952 (six months later than the Boeing B-52) and by 1959 about 150 were in service with the ADD (long-range aviation). A distinctive aircraft with swept wings and tail, the Tu-95 still serves in a number of different versions for strategic reconnaissance, ASW and electronic duties.

The last of the high-speed high-altitude bombers, the gigantic American Mach 3 B-70 Valkyrie was cancelled in 1964. Powered by six General Electric YJ33-3 turbojets, the technology and flight performance of the B-70 remains awe-inspiring. In July 1965 the second B-70 (which was tasked with sonic boom research for NASA), gave a sobering demonstration of its potential by maintaining Mach 3.08 for 33 minutes during a flight across eight Western States. One legacy of the B-70 programme is the MiG-25, which Mikoyan produced as a countermeasure. It was soon recognized that in order to penetrate defended airspace the bomber now had to hug the ground, to try to evade detection and accurate plotting by enemy radar. Though the B-70, like the B-58, was good on low-level missions it was inferior to aircraft designed specifically for them.

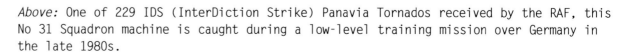

Above: One of 229 IDS (InterDiction Strike) Panavia Tornados received by the RAF, this No 31 Squadron machine is caught during a low-level training mission over Germany in the late 1980s.

Left: A nearly perfect plan view of an early F-111A with mid-sweep selected for its variable geometry wings. In 1968, F-111As were bombing Vietnam at night with greater accuracy than other bombers could manage by day.

From the Ground Alert
'Cocked' position,
Strategic Air Command's
B-58 Hustlers could be
airborne inside five
minutes.

Despite its fighter designation, the General Dynamics F-111 was in fact a bomber, and gradually overcame a long list of design faults and numerous other problems to become an outstanding low-level strike aircraft. The F-111A pioneered automatic terrain-following with radar and its variable-geometry (swing-wing) configuration influenced the design of the Sukhoi Su-24 and Panavia Tornado.

After more than a decade of study the Rockwell (North American) B-1 was finally flown in 1974 as the next bomber for the USAF. The gap of more than 20 years since the B-52 was the longest in history between successive generations of aircraft, and the B-1 was designed for specific purposes. Its main need was to carry a nuclear deterrent that could unfailingly strike back after a Russian attack by missiles on the United States. Such an attack could knock out America's own missiles, which dared not be fired on the mere appearance of what looked like Russian warheads on American radar screens. But the B-I, designed to start engines and take off within two or three minutes of an enemy attack being detected, could get away from its airfields into the safety of the sky. From there it could hit back, should the Russian attack prove to be real. Cancelled in 1977, the B-1 programme was reinstated in 1980. Redesigned solely for the low-level mission, today's B-1B Lancer can fly intercontinental missions at tree-top height with its variable-sweep wings at their most acute angle.

Cruise missiles have formed an integral part of America's offensive capability since the early 1980s and can be launched from land, sea and air. Fitted with conventional warheads, Tomahawks fired from USN warships were used to attack targets in and around Bagdad during the Gulf War in 1991. The modern cruise missile is more sophisticated and can take evasive action, shelter behind ECM (electronic countermeasures) and try to protect itself with various decoys against missiles sent to shoot it down. Stealth technology has made the latest US cruise missiles even more difficult to detect, let alone destroy, especially when launched from the B-2 Spirit stealth bomber.

All modern bombers are packed with defensive electronics, which were designed into the B-IB and are an integral part of the latest Russian strategic platform, the Tupolev Tu-160, called 'Blackjack' by NATO. Earlier aircraft, such as the B-52, Vulcan, and Mirage IVA have had to be progressively modified and updated with systems to give warning of hostile radars; emitters to interfere with hostile communications; and

An F-15E Strike
Eagle showing off
its bombs – it
can carry up
to 11,113kg
(24,500lb) of
ordnance.

A Tupolev Tu-22MS thunders down the runway at the start of its memorable 1992 Farnborough display.

a mass of other 'penaids' (penetration aids) such as chaff, flares and active jammer payloads. Chaff, the American name for what the RAF called Window in World War II, comprises billions of small pieces cut from thin strips of metal foil which is used to confuse the enemy's radar.

For all except the longest strategic missions there is no need for purpose-designed bombers. Modern fighters such as the F-15E Strike Eagle can carry such heavy weapon loads that they can fly all the required attack missions, backed up by certain specialised close-support or anti-tank aircraft.

Stealth Bombers

Since the invention of radar aircraft have been vulnerable to detection, whether flying at night, in cloud, or hundreds of miles away from their intended targets. Most aircraft have plenty of flat surfaces, which make excellent reflectors for the electromagnetic waves produced by powerful radar transmitters. The desirability of reducing radar cross-section (RCS) was largely ignored until the early 1970s, when Lockheed Advanced Development Projects, the so-called 'Skunk Works' responsible for the U-2 and SR-71, began to develop what we know today as stealth technology for an 'invisible' combat aircraft.

The Rockwell B-1B Lancer maintains the airborne leg of America's nuclear triad.

Apart from being visible on radar, jet-powered aircraft (especially supersonic designs which use afterburning) can easily betray their presence to highly sensitive infra-red detectors. By mid 1978 the first of up to seven (the exact number has yet to be revealed) XST (experimental stealth technology) aircraft had flown, these being simplified scale models of the future F-117A low-observable (LO) attack aircraft. At least two XSTs were lost in accidents, but because the stealth programme was top secret the outside world remained ignorant of their true identity and purpose.

During the course of many flights against various air-defence systems (including captured Soviet radars), the XSTs revealed that if the external shape of an aircraft is made up of carefully angled flat surfaces, incoming radar waves are scattered in such a way that only a tiny amount is reflected back to its source. This technique is called faceting. When used in conjunction with radar absorbent materials, jet inlet screens (engines are highly reflective on radar) and specially treated cockpit

Outwardly similar to the the B-1B, the Tu-160 is much bigger and, according to its designers, far superior in every department.

The Northrop B-2 Spirit is ultra stealthy in a way yet to be revealed. What has been revealed is the cost – over $2 billion per aircraft.

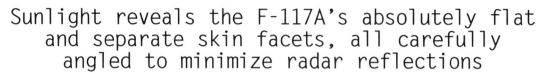

Sunlight reveals the F-117A's absolutely flat and separate skin facets, all carefully angled to minimize radar reflections

transparencies, RCS is reduced to extremely low values. Stealth design compromises the aerodynamic efficiency of the F-117A to such an extent that powerful flight-control computers (and long runways) are needed just to get it off the ground, though once airborne the software makes the aircraft smooth to fly and quite manoeuvrable.

Infra-red emissions are minimized by using non-after-burning turbojet, the hot gases of which are mixed with cool air in the jetpipe before being dispersed via a thin horizontal nozzle. The lack of afterburner (and consequent lack of supersonic performance) hardly matters when your aircraft is virtually undetectable. Even so the F-117A is no slouch, having a maximum speed at sea level of 1,100km/h (684mph) or Mach 0.9.

In daylight, nothing could be done to mask the 'Black Jet' from short-range anti-aircraft guns and missiles, which can be directed optically, and for this reason the aircraft makes its attacks nocturnally – hence its official name Nighthawk. As external stores would massively increase RCS, the aircraft has two internal weapon bays arranged side-by-side in the lower part of the centre fuselage. The usual weapon load is two 907kg (2,000lb) LGBs

(laser-guided bombs), but IR or laser-guided Maverick missiles can also be carried.

So as not to show up on radar the weapon bay doors flip open and shut in a fraction of a second. Most importantly, the Nighthawk's navigation systems and attack sensors are entirely passive (receiving, but not emitting). The primary navaids are inertial and GPS, while an advanced FLIR (forward-looking infra-red) system allows the pilot to search, identify and then attack the target. Once the pilot has selected the aimpoint and locked on, the weapon release system takes over. The weapon will home on automatically and is usually guided by the aft-firing laser under the nose of the aircraft, which illuminates the target with an invisible beam.

The F-117A made its first flight in June 1981 and entered service with in October 1983, initially with the 4450th Tactical Group at Tonopah Test Range, Nevada. The unit was subsequently redesignated as the 37th Tactical Fighter Wing in October 1989. A total of 59 Nighthawks were delivered to the USAF, the last just six months before the 37th TFW deployed to Saudi Arabia in December 1990 for Operation *Desert Storm*.

Fast and armed with two machine guns, the Albatros D III gave the Germans complete command of the air in early 1917.

The French Spad 13 was issued to the US Army Air Service and was the favourite mount of Eddie Rickenbacker, the first American ace.

With a Lewis gun mounted at the front of the one-man nacelle, the D.H.2 pusher gave the RFC a fighting chance against the Fokker E-III monoplane.

Fighter and Attack Aircraft

This section deals with the third type of warplane to be developed. Some of the earliest of this class were called fighting scouts, or just scouts, because they also often had to fly scouting (reconnaissance) missions in between dog-fighting with the enemy. Another duty was bomber or reconnaissance-aircraft escort, and by the 1930s some fighters had been specially designed for long-range escort duties. Another name is the pursuit, but this was just the common American term for a fighting aeroplane until after World War II. Night fighters usually differed from other fighters only in detail until World War II when the invention of airborne radar led to a class of large multi-seat radar-equipped night fighters which would have been of little use in a daytime dogfight.

The interceptor was at first a fast-climbing fighter to protect home targets, and today this term describes all fighters used in a defensive role. Today's interceptors all carry radar and are both day dog-fighters and night fight-ers rolled into one. To add even further complexity, almost all modern fighters can carry many tonnes of bombs or

missiles and may frequently be called upon to strike at surface targets.

A few far-sighted people thought through the possibility of air warfare several years before World War I and came up with proposals for fighters, to shoot down the aircraft belonging to enemy nations. Seven or eight inventors proposed 'synchronization gear' with which a machine gun could be interlinked with an aeroplane engine in such a way that it could safely fire straight ahead, the bullets passing between the revolving blades of the propeller. Others proposed pusher aircraft, in which the problem of mounting a machine gun disappeared. The early Wright Flyers were pushers, and it was one of these which in June 1912 may have been the first aircraft to complete official firing trials with a machine gun. Two months later the British FE.2 had a Maxim gun in the nose of its pusher nacelle, and in France two aircraft carried guns before 1912 was out, one of the guns being a shell-firing cannon. There arose a growing number of novel schemes for fitting aircraft with guns, not necessarily for use against other aircraft, but when World War I broke out there was no such thing as a fighter, a fighter pilot or any accepted doctrine for air combat.

Two-seaters soon began to carry such weapons as rifles, carbines and revolvers, fired by the observer, and on 5 October 1914, a French Voisin III shot down a German aircraft, the first aerial victory. The Voisin was not a fighter but an obser-

Thanks to its forward-firing machine gun and propeller interupter gear, the Fokker E-III shot down Allied aircraft at will in the autumn and winter of 1915. The 'Fokker Scourge' lasted until April 1916.

vation and bombing aircraft which happened to carry a machine-gun. This event spurred the already widespread attempts to produce an aeroplane specially suited to shooting down other aircraft. The ideal appeared to be a small single-seater able to fire a machine-gun straight ahead. The pusher machines had a decided advantage in this respect, because there was no propeller in the way. But it was still a new field in which most things had to be learned by painful experience. Capt de Havilland designed the D.H.2 as a true single seat fighter but still provided the pilot with left and right mountings on which he could mount a Lewis machine-gun. His problems in a deadly combat can be imagined, for he had to work the rudder pedals, control column, throttle, aim the gun, work the trigger and change magazines, whilst looking through the gunsights.

Inventors, aircraft manufacturers and squadron pilots all sought the most effective armament. One aircraft had two rotary engines side by side with guns in the centre. A second had one engine with guns on each side, firing beyond the tips of the propeller blades. A third had guns inclined outwards to miss the propeller, but this was difficult to aim. A fourth had two rotary engines mounted fore-and-aft on each side of the nose, driving a central propeller through the centre of which fired a 37mm cannon. A fifth had five Lewis guns fixed to the landing gear. A sixth had a 37mm cannon, almost 3m (10ft) long, mounted obliquely, firing up through the centre of the upper wing, loaded by the observer in the rear cockpit. A BE.2c carried Lee Prieur rockets, another anti-aircraft darts and a third the frightening Fiery Grapnel device, a kind of explosive anchor dropped on enemy aircraft. Meanwhile a few crack shots, such as Lanoe G. Hawker of the Royal Flying Corps, kept on shooting down enemies though armed with nothing but a single-shot Martini rifle.

Before 1914 was out several pushers had appeared with guns fixed to fire straight ahead, thus leaving the pilot free to fly the aircraft, and aiming the gun by aiming the whole aircraft. Later, in 1915, this seemingly obvious answer partly solved the problem of the British D.H.2. But the thread of development that led to the main stream of fighters began in France. Before the war began three French aircraft constructors, Deperdussin, Esnault-Pelterie and Saulnier, had all independently invented methods of safely firing a machine-gun through a revolving propeller disc. Saulnier's famed demonstration pilot, Roland Garros, joined the Aviation Militaire, but could get no official to show interest in Saulnier's invention. As a second-best solution he personally spent months

developing and refining steel channel-shaped deflectors on his propeller blades, and from November 1914 until early 1915 overcame one difficulty after another. Eventually he received permission to try his deflectors in action, and after prolonged bad weather at last saw a German aircraft on 1 April 1915. Garros shot it down in flames, and he shot down more Germans on 15 and 18 April. Later on the 18th he went out to bomb Courtrai railway station but was shot down and captured.

Like the tank, an idea of the very greatest military importance had been allowed to fall into the enemy's hands prematurely, without any advantage having been taken of it except on an unimportant and purely local scale. The Germans quickly assessed Garros's deflectors and asked their Dutch aircraft constructor, Anthony Fokker, to copy it. Fokker did better: his German engineers designed an interrupter gear which linked the engine and a fixed Parabellum machine-gun so that the latter could fire only when there was no propeller blade in front of the gun barrel. In three days Fokker had developed, tested and perfected an installation for a forward-firing gun on one of his M.5 monoplanes, generally known as E-types from *eindecker,* German for monoplane. By chance the Fokker monoplane was a direct copy of a pre-war Morane-Saulnier type, the Model H, which could in fact have been in service, with Saulnier's own gun-firing gear, before the outbreak of war.

What happened next was the first phase of organised air warfare, and it was a particularly bloody one. The little Fokker was just sufficiently faster and more manoeuvrable than the early aeroplanes of the Allies to have the latter completely at its mercy. Moreover, some of the pilots of the German Idflieg (Imperial Air Force) were outstandingly gifted and far-sighted officers, who devoted their working hours not only to seeking out the enemy but also to working out how best the new breed of fighting aeroplanes should be used. Oswald Boelcke was the leader, and his chief assistant was Max Immelmann (though the first actually to shoot down an Allied aircraft was Kurt Wintgens). Using their little 100hp monoplanes they worked out much of the basis of air tactics, deflection shooting, how to work in pairs with a wingman, how to avoid being 'jumped' from behind and many other totally new ideas. Usually the Fokker E-types had a single Spandau (Parabellum 08) on the centreline, but a few had two guns and Immelmann once tried three. Some pilots fitted a headrest to assist in accurate aiming, Garros having fitted a forehead rest in front (which in a crash might have killed him).

Top: Manfred von Richthofen scored most of his 80 victories in Albatros fighters, but will always be associated with the blood-red Fokker Dr-I triplane.

So heavy were Allied casualties that newspapers wrote of 'the Fokker Scourge', calling Allied pilots 'Fokker fodder'. Gradually it was realised the little Fokker was really quite primitive. Even the D.H.2 and FE.2b could beat it, and when such purpose-designed Allied fighters as the Nieuports, the Sopwith Pup, Bristol Scout, Hanriot and Spad designs came into use the Fokker swiftly faded. In its place Germany uniformly relied upon biplanes with six-cylinder water-cooled engines, and fighters of this layout dominated the German and Austro-Hungarian air forces for the remainder of the war.

But at the end of 1916 the Sopwith company produced a triplane (three superimposed wings) which did well in combat. It caused such a stir on the German side that copies were immediately started, and the Fokker Triplane, the Dr.I, was actually made in greater quantity than the British machine. Triplanes were at least equal to contemporary biplanes with regards to climb and manoeuvrability, and the greatest ace of the war, Baron Manfred von Richthofen, was flying one when he was killed in April 1918. But they were only a temporary phenomenon.

The most successful fighter of World War I was the British Sopwith Camel, which shot down more than

Introduced in April 1917, the superb Bristol F2B Fighter had the performance and agility of a single-seater but with the protection of a rear gunner.

3,000 enemy aircraft, a score far in excess of that achieved by any of its contemporaries. The Camel was a tricky biplane, rather short and hunchbacked and powered by a 130hp rotary engine over which fired two Vickers guns in most versions. But the old-fashioned rotary engines were having their final fling, and were incapable of being developed to give the powers of 300 or 400hp that were being demanded. One of the best Allied engines was the Hispano-Suiza of 250-300hp. and this was used in a superb British fighter, the SE.5a, but its unreliability, especially when fitted with a reduction gear to the propeller, caused severe delays and casualties. Greater power meant

higher speed and more rapid climb to greater altitudes, and instead of staggering off the ground with one gun, and being sluggish with a big pilot, fighters were by late 1917 climbing purposefully to over 6,000m (20,000ft) with two guns and a heavy load of ammunition. Many of the best fighters were two-seaters. The first was the versatile but curiously named Sopwith 1 1/2-strutter, the first aircraft to have a properly thought-out scheme providing for synchronized fixed guns for the pilot, rear guns aimed by the observer and bombs. Upgraded to twice the horsepower, the Bristol Fighter of late 1916 was an out-

Probably the best single-seat fighter of World War I, the Fokker D-VII was rushed into service in the spring of 1918.

standing type which could behave as a single-seater at the front while the observer shot down additional aircraft from the rear.

In the immediate post-war years there were few changes in fighter design, apart from elimination of rotary engines and general consolidation on more reliable engines of 400hp and above. Two fixed machine guns remained common armament, and though most of the guns were reasonably reliable 'stoppages' of various kinds were still common. It was therefore almost universal to mount the guns close enough to the cockpit for the pilot to reach them and, using a mallet if necessary, clear the offending round, re-cock the gun and rejoin combat. Having to clear a stoppage

The Gloster Gladiator came into production at the end of 1936 and was the RAF's last biplane fighter. In 1940 the Gladiator saw action in Norway and throughout the Middle East.

during combat was often fatal, but it was still important to be able to attempt it.

From 1916 fighters had also increasingly to take on various missions against ground targets, and these often became accepted fighter duties. One was close support of friendly troops, using the fixed guns against hostile land forces. Several important types of ground-attack fighter were built, notable for their heavy frontal firepower and considerable armour protection, which of course had to be gained at the expense of reduced performance. In Germany the Junkers company built both cantilever monoplane and cantilever biplane attack aircraft of all-metal construction, known by

The Fiat CR 42 was a good match for the Gladiator but was outclassed by the monoplane fighters.

such names as 'Tin Monkey' and 'The Furniture Van' but nevertheless strong enough to stand up to severe front-line missions. Between the two world wars many fighters had to fly ground-attack missions, both in major wars and in policing colonial empires. In the latter duty flight performance became relatively unimportant, the dominant requirements being supreme reliability and versatility when operating in remote areas in possibly very harsh climates.

Two new factors in the 1920s were, first, the emergence of naval fighters and, second, the emergence of new air forces. The mighty United States had been unprepared for war in 1917 and filled its air squadrons with types bought, borrowed or given by France and Britain, and later made under licence. But in the 1920s its growing home industry began to flex its design muscles and produced increasingly competitive fighters, at first with water-cooled in-line engines and then almost exclusively with air-cooled radials. Almost all had all-metal structures, and after 1930 the American designers led the trend towards stressed-skin metal covering. The American Browning machine gun also existed in two sharply differing sizes, a 7.62-mm (0.30in) and 12.7-mm (0.5in), and the bigger gun increasingly began to supplement or replace the rifle-calibre weapon. A common American fighter armament was one gun of each calibre.

Japan at first relied totally upon imported designs and designers, but after 1930 was sufficiently confident to produce totally original fighters, the first of which were water-cooled biplanes, and then, from 1935, came air-cooled radial monoplanes. Like Italy, Japan willingly sacrificed almost everything to the attainment of the highest possible manoeuvrability. The two leading fighters of the late 1930s, made in very large numbers, were the Army Ki-27 and Navy A5M. Very alike in design, they had just two rifle calibre guns, and were lightly built, but could make a tighter turn inside every foreign fighter they met – even the Soviet 1-15 biplane.

Russian designers tried more contrasting designs of fighters than those of any other nation. Water and air cooling, single and twin engines, biplanes and monoplanes and a fantastic variety of armament

schemes were all to be found on Russian fighters of the 1930s. The Russian gun designers produced the 7.62-mm ShKAS and later the 12.7-mm Beresin and 20-mm VYa, all of them guns of outstanding quality and exceptional performance. Despite this extensive experiments were made with large-calibre recoilless weapons, usually of 75mm (2.95in) calibre, which probably owed much to the recoilless Davis and the Vickers (Crayford) rocket guns used to a limited extent in the larger fighters of World War I. Russian designers also produced reliable and accurate rocket projectiles which are very effective against armoured vehicles and similar 'hard' targets, and though these were used in large numbers at public manoeuvres from 1935 onwards they still managed to surprise both Allies and enemy in World War II.

Many fighter pilots continued to insist long after 1935 that a fighter had to be a biplane with an open cockpit, in order to offer the best possible all-round view and the greatest possible manoeuvrability. Many countries, especially the Soviet Union, conducted prolonged comparative trials, and the Russians deliberately kept the I-15, I-15bis and I-153 in production long after the I-16 monoplane was in service in numbers. The I-16 was the first cantilever monoplane fighter with retractable landing gear to go into service with

First of the RAF's eight-gun fighters, the Hurricane was the Spitfire's senior partner in the Battle of Britain, equipping 38 Fighter Squadrons and shooting down more enemy aircraft than all the other defences combined.

Settling back on the runway, this black-painted Hurricane night fighter/intruder was the personal mount of Sqn Ldr D.C. Smallwood who led No 87 Squadron during the winter of 1941-42.

North African-based Spitfire VC fighter-bombers fly in support of the allied invasion of Sicily in November 1942. Armed with up to four 20mm cannon, the Mk VC could also carry a 227kg (500lb) bomb under the fuselage or (as here) two 250-pounders under the wing.

any air force, and though tricky and only marginally stable longitudinally, its outstanding speed and fire-power made it a formidable opponent (though in the Spanish Civil War it was badly flown because of rigid Russian political control). In fighting against Japan, however, the agile Japanese monoplanes beat the I-16 and put fresh impetus behind advanced I-15 biplanes such as the 1,100hp I-153 with retractable landing gear. The Russians even built a biplane fighter which could retract the lower wing into the upper! (During World War II Britain built a version of the monoplane Hurricane with a biplane upper wing which could be jettisoned if necessary.)

By 1934 the British Air Ministry had satisfied itself that in a future war the time available for shooting down enemy bombers might be as little as two seconds of accurate shooting, and the belief that an average of 250 rifle-calibre bullets would be needed naturally led to a search for armament capable of scoring 250 hits in two seconds. (Curiously, no calculations appear to have been done on the effect of different larger calibres, such as the 20mm cannon that was finally adopted.) The answer, translated into about 8,000 shots per minute, appeared to be eight machine-guns. The Vickers that had served the RFC and RAF so faithfully was basically a 19th-century gun, and after looking for a more modern weapon the British chose the American Browning (which was only slightly later in origin but far more reliable). New fighters with eight Brownings of 7.7mm (0.303in) calibre were going to need at least 1,000hp, and several suitable engines were available; British designers mainly chose the liquid-cooled Rolls-Royce Merlin, which later proved eminently suitable for development to give greater power at all altitudes. Around this engine Hawker Aircraft produced the Hurricane, with its eight guns in compact groups. This fighter, flown in 1935, was a traditional fabric-skinned machine of rather large dimensions, but it was tough, manoeuvrable and available in large numbers in the nation's dire hour of need in 1939-40. Supermarine produced the Spitfire, considerably smaller and of stressed-skin construction. Few of these were available in 1939, but it was to become by far the most important British fighter of World War II.

Germany's leading World War II fighter had a most inauspicious beginning, its designer, Willi Messerschmitt, being unpopular with the Nazis and totally discounted as a fighter designer. His Bf 109, flown in 1935, was even smaller than a Spitfire, and likewise a modern stressed-skin machine. Fitted with powerful slats and flaps it managed to use a wing far smaller than those of the British fighters, and it was continuously developed until 1945 with more powerful engines and devastating armament. But, unlike the Spitfire, later Bf 109 versions of the G series (popularly called Gustav) were even more full of shortcomings than the early models had been. At low speeds they were excellent, but the controls tightened up with increasing speed until at really high speeds the manoeuvrability was very poor, further handicapped by the attitude of the pilot and difficulty of applying large forces to the control column to roll the aircraft. The best feature of the 109 was its weaponry, which included outstanding guns of 7.92, 13, 15, 20 and 30mm calibre. In many versions a shell-firing cannon was mounted on the engine to fire through the hub of the propeller, an arrangement pioneered by the Hispano-Suiza company from World War I. From 1942 most versions of 109 could carry *Rüstsätze* (field modification kits) for a wide variety of different extra guns and other devices, such as rocket launchers or extra fuel tanks which could be jettisoned when empty (so-called drop tanks). This fighter was also one of the first to be used as a bomber. Despite its shortcomings, the Bf 109 shot down more aircraft than any other fighter in history by a large margin.

In fact the chief pioneers of the fighter-bomber were the US Navy, as explained in the section on carrier-based aircraft. On land airfields the pressure to make one aircraft do two or more jobs may have been less intense, and until well into World War II there was a general rather cosy belief that first-line land combat aircraft could be divided into specialised bombers and specialised fighters. A few of the new breed of monoplane bombers were at first thought so fast and manoeuverable as to be capable of fighting other aircraft, but actual experience soon swept away this notion. There remained, however, the notion of the twin-engined long-range escort fighter, while the

reborn Luftwaffe became polarised around the *Zerstörer* (destroyer), which was a similar machine but used not so much to escort bombers as to penetrate enemy airspace and destroy aerial opposition. It was recognised that large twin-engined machines could not manoeuvre as tightly or quickly as small single-engined types, but they were expected to compensate for this by their heavy armament and good all-round performance.

Many nations built these big fighters, which all had two engines and a crew of at least two. Two of the earliest were the Bristol Bagshot and Westland Westbury, built in Britain in 1927, mainly for shooting down bombers. These big multi-seat machines each carried two of the enormous Coventry Ordnance Works 37mm cannon, aimed by hand or fixed at an oblique angle and aimed by the pilot from below and behind the target. (This method of shooting was extensively explored in Britain in the late 1920s, but was never used operationally by British aircraft in World War II – though it was by her enemies.) These lumbering machines were aberrations, as were the succession of 'multiplace de combat' (multi-seat warplanes) built in France which were supposed to be large bombers that were also fighters. By 1935 many countries were building small, powerful twin-engined

Built in 1940, this Spitfire Mk IIA survived the war (though patches cover the bullet holes in her wings) and is today one of many 'Spits' maintained in pristine airworth condition.

aircraft as fast as the other new fighters, but Britain showed no interest until near the start of World War II when, suddenly recognizing the omission of a long-range fighter, urgent conversions were made of the Blenheim bomber which proved grossly deficient in speed, manoeuvrability and firepower. The purpose-designed twin-engined fighters included the Bf 110, Fw 187, Potez 63, SE 100, Breguet 690, Fokker G.I, PZL Wilk, Lockheed P-38 and Bell XFM-1. The last-named was the strangest of all, for it had the new nosewheel landing gear, two pusher engines in large over-wing nacelles and a gunner with a 37mm cannon in the nose of each nacelle. The P-38 was also unusual in having the tail carried on twin booms, mainly in order to find somewhere to put the rear wheels of the nosewheel landing gear, the engine cooling radiators and the turbochargers to give power at altitude. The armament of one 37mm cannon, two 12.7mm guns and two rifle-calibre guns was grouped in the nose ahead of the single seat. Britain's Westland Whirlwind also had two engines and guns in the nose – the very heavy armament of four 20mm cannon – but this machine had low-powered and unreliable engines and accomplished little.

In the Battle of Britain in 1940 the Bf 110 came up

Fallen eagle. The Messershmitt Bf 109 shot down more aircraft than any other fighter in history, but this 'Emil' came off second best to the RAF in the Battle of Britain.

The twin-boom P-38, named Lightning by the British, was used as a long-range fighter in Europe and the Pacific.

against the RAF's Hurricanes and Spitfires, and quickly suffered heavy casualties. Within two weeks it was recognised by the Luftwaffe that their big twin-engined fighter, the pride and elite of the nation, could not even survive in combat with modern single-engined fighters flown with skill and determination, and for the rest of World War II the Bf 110 was never again used for dog-fighting in daylight except in the few theatres where opposition was weak. Another shock, this time to the RAF, was the realization that a fighter with its guns in a power-driven turret was if anything even easier meat. The RAF had devoted immense effort to turrets in the late 1930s, and by 1940 not only had large numbers of Defiant turret-armed fighters coming into service but also planned a series of bigger fighters with monster turrets armed with four 20mm cannon. When it met the Luftwaffe the Defiant was apparently often mistaken for a Hurricane and attacked from above and behind, with disastrous results for the enemy. When it was recognised however, it was attacked from below or ahead, and as it could not

Originally designed for long-range bomber escort, the Messerschmitt Bf 110 Zerstörer (destroyer) was re-employed as a fighter-bomber and nightfighter.

rival the Bf 109's performance and manoeuvrability it was shot down. None of the projected turret fighters entered service, though later the US Army P-61 night fighter often carried a turret· however, the results of this change did not come up to the original expectations.

In 1940 the fighting in Europe caused American designers to tear up their fighter plans and instead double the horsepower. Vought had already built the Corsair XF4U prototype for the US Navy, with the 2,000hp Double Wasp engine swinging a four-blade propeller larger than any previously fitted to a fighter. Despite its great size this prototype in 1940 became the first American aircraft – even including racers· to reach 644km/h (400mph). Republic built the P-47 Thunderbolt and Grumman followed in 1942 with the F6F Hellcat, all using the Double Wasp engine which grew to 2,300, 2,500 and finally 2,800hp in war emergency condition with water injection. With such power these large fighters could out-fly their opponents despite having heavy fuel loads, heavy armament and considerable armour protection. They were produced in great numbers; there were over 12,000 Hellcats, over 12,000 Corsairs and over 15,000 Thunderbolts.

At first their enemies were much smaller and lighter. The Japanese Navy mainstay was the Mitsubishi A6M, popularly called the Zero, and despite having barely 1,000hp it could out-fly all its rivals in 1941-42 and destroy them with cannon and machine guns. A special quality of the A6M was its very long range. which enabled it to conquer vast areas of the Pacific and south-east Asia even when operating from very distant airstrips. Only gradually was it realised that, far from being invincible, it was actually deficient in flight performance (compared with the less-obsolete fighters the Allies eventually supplied to the Pacific theatre) and ill-protected, so that it was easy to shoot down. The corresponding Army fighter, the Nakajima Ki-43, was even more manoeuvrable but totally lacking in everything else and usually carried only two machine guns. By 1942 most Allied fighters either had six 12.7mm or four 20mm guns, which could blow the Japanese fighters apart. Gradually the Japanese saw the need for a complete rethink. A generation of fighters totally unlike their predecessors, with small wings and everything sacrificed to performance and firepower (examples were the Ki-44 and J2M) were unimpressive, and only near the end of the war were such excellent machines as the Ki-84 and Ki-100 produced – and then it was too late.

In Europe the Luftwaffe produced ever-greater quantities of successive versions of the Bf 109, despite

Fitted with a four-gun turret behind the pilot, the Boulton-Paul Defiant proved unable to take on the Luftwaffe's fighters in daylight and survive.

the fact it had in 1941 introduced a vastly superior machine of completely new design, the Fw 190. This was one of the most outstanding fighters of the war, with unsurpassed technology and engineering design, cleverly packaged with a 1,700hp radial engine into an extremely compact airframe. It had no deficiencies, and its fantastic capability is shown by the ability of later versions to carry torpedoes and bombs weighing up to 1,800kg (3,968lb). By 1943 the Fw 190 was by far the chief tactical attack machine of the Luftwaffe, replacing the Ju 87 'Stuka' dive bomber and serving on all European fronts in large numbers. Like many of today's attack aircraft the Fw 190 served as an offensive carrier of bombs, mines, rockets, heavy cannon and even guided missiles, but with absolutely first-class qualities in the quite different role of dog-fighter. Russian designers rated the Fw 190 highly. They consistently kept their own fighters small, despite the development of more powerful engines, and put every ounce of effort into achieving greater performance and manoeuvrability even at the expense of firepower. Despite having engines of around 1,600hp, the 1943-44 crop of Soviet fighters seldom had more than one cannon and two heavy machine guns.

One thing all Russian fighters lacked was radar. This had been pioneered in Britain, and the saving grace of the Blenheim fighter was that it could carry the clumsy early airborne radar equipment. In the late fall (autumn) of 1940 it was followed by a greatly superior machine, the Beaufighter, with Hercules sleeve-valve engines of almost double the power and the devastating armament of four 20mm cannon and six machine guns. This became the most widely used Allied night fighter, with the RAF and USAAF, and though a little on the slow side its range and firepower fitted it for long attack missions with guns, rockets and torpedo in all European theatres. Another outstanding aircraft was the Mosquito, conceived as an unarmed bomber but soon modified as the greatest Allied night and long-range fighter. Much faster than the Beaufighter, it had four

The Mitsubishi A6M5 Zero-Sen, Japan's most successful fighter, was fast, heavily armed and highly manoeuvrable.

Lined up at RAF Duxford, USAAF P-47D Thunderbolts of the 78th Fighter Group. A powerful fighter, they were long-range escorts for bombers on daylight raids.

20mm cannon (the first fighter version had four machine guns as well) and also carried bombs or rockets with enough range to hit the furthest areas in the Balkans or Scandinavia. Special versions carried a 57mm (2.24in) gun, various radars and extended wing-tips for use at extreme altitude. In the United States the complex P-61 was the main night fighter, with powerful radar and four 20mm cannon (often plus four heavy machine guns in a turret), while even the small carrier-based single-seaters often carried new radars which operated on very short wavelength.

Luftwaffe night fighters were at first modified Bf 110, Do 17 and Ju 88 aircraft, later joined by the big Do 217. Despite being burdened by cumbersome aerial arrays the later night-fighter Bf 110 and Ju 88 versions were able to inflict extremely heavy losses on the RAF bombers, largely because the latter did all they could to help; they broadcast radar signals continuously, so that night fighters could home on the bombers automatically, and were totally devoid not only of defensive armament underneath but lacked even a window that could look down and to the rear. Increasingly the night fighters were armed with oblique upward-firing guns, basically like those tried by the RAF 15 years previously, which offered a perfect no-deflection shot. Purpose-designed night fighters generally failed to see service, the exception being the outstanding He 219 Uhu (owl).

By mid-1944 jet propulsion was fast opening up new horizons in aircraft performance, and especially relevant to fighters. First to reach the squadrons was the radical German Me 163 Komet, which was a tail-less rocket interceptor with very short endurance. Though superb to fly (much better than a Bf 109G) it was designed to take off from a jettisoned trolley and land on a skid, and this, coupled with the danger of its highly reactive fuels, made it exceedingly tricky and dangerous. The bigger Me 262 was an even

One of the greatest fighters of World War II, the Focke-Wulf Fw 190 became the the Luftwaffe's top ground attack aircraft.

more formidable aircraft, a conventional twinjet with 900kg (1,984lb) thrust Jumo 004 engines and armament of four 30mm (1.18in) cannon, the heaviest then flown. Roughly 161 km/h (100mph) faster than Allied fighters, the 262 was impossible to catch unless it could be 'bounced' (taken by surprise) while taking off or landing. Near the end of the war in Europe the little He 162 was put into production as a 'volksjäger' (people's fighter) to be built at the rate of 4,000 a month and flown by the hastily trained Hitler Youth. Though potentially formidable, and far in advance of other nations in its concept, with multiple rocket launchers and X-4 wire-guided missiles backing up the heavy cannon, this desperate last-ditch measure merely showed Germany had lost the war.

In fact the first jet fighter actually to become operational with regular squadrons was the RAF's Gloster Meteor (616 sqn, July 1944), but few of these saw action. After the war the Meteor was given much more powerful engines, gaining a world speed record in full fighting trim, and also became a stop-gap night fighter. Far more significant was the American XP-86 (later F-86) Sabre. This was designed by North American Aviation, which in 1940 had been asked by the British to build the old Curtiss P-40 fighter and instead built a better fighter of their own, the Mustang. When fitted with the British Merlin engine the

Mustang became the leading Allied fighter, combining outstanding performance at all heights with enough range to escort bombers from England to Berlin or Czechoslovakia. There were nearly 15,000 P-51 Mustangs, and they did more than any other aircraft to defeat the Luftwaffe even over the heart of Germany. It was natural to use it as the basis of a jet, but in fact the result (the Navy FJ-1 Fury) saw only limited production. The key to the XP-86 was swept wings. German documents captured in 1945 showed how speed could be increased, typically from 900 to 1,100km/h (560 to 680mph), by sweeping back the wings and tail like an arrowhead. The XP-86, flown in October 1947, was the first all-swept fighter.

In June 1950 war broke out when North Korea invaded South Korea, and soon various Allied fighters were in use helping the South Koreans. The jets were handicapped by their inability to use short rough airstrips or carry heavy bomb loads and fly long distances at low levels, because early turbojets burned fuel very rapidly. Such machines as the Mustang and carrier-based Skyraider and Sea Fury came back into prominence as attack aircraft, with bombs and rockets, and jet combats lagged until suddenly the North Koreans appeared with advanced swept-wing jets. These were the MiG-15s, quickly produced in the Soviet Union in 1947 as a result of a British Government free shipment of the latest jet engines. At once the tables were turned, and though the F-86 Sabre in improved versions achieved ascendancy over the MiG-15 this was mainly because of better Allied pilot skill and aggressive tactics, allied with superior shooting. Subsequently the MiG bureau, which had taken a back seat in World War II, produced an outstanding succession of advanced fighters. The MiG-19 twinjet was one of the first supersonic fighters, and its outstanding manoeuvrability makes it formidable in close combat to this day. The

A home grown Soviet fighter, the Yakovlev Yak 3, which entered service in 1944, was fast and widely used as an escort for ground attack aircraft.

Although more thought of as a bomber and high altitude reconnaissance platform, the de Havilland Mosquito was also pressed into service as an effective long-range escort fighter.

Russian bureau Yakovlev's workhorse fighter of the latter part of the war was the small but fast Yak-3A.

automatically so that it could shoot the enemy down, at first with guns, then with a battery of rockets and finally, from 1956, with air-to-air guided missiles.

These developments revolutionised fighter design and operation. By the mid 1950s it could be seen that there was little point in regarding the radar-equipped night fighter as a special class; all fighters were going to need radar. The last examples of the old-style night fighter were the gun-armed British Javelin and Russian Yak-25, both quite large twin-jets of the mid-1950s. By this time the US Air Force was receiving the Convair F-102 Delta Dagger, a supersonic delta with automatic fire-control and guided-missile armament. Since then the developments have merely been ones of degree, in particular (through advances in electronics) easing the workload of the crew.

On 27 May 1958, a two-seat, twin-jet carrier-borne interceptor named the Phantom II made its first flight from St Louis. This was the US Navy XF4H-1 built by McDonnell and for the next 20 years (at least) it provided the yardstick for all other jet combat aircraft. What made the F-4 Phantom so special was its outstanding all-round performance – in nearly every respect it exceeded the capability of existing specialist attack or fighter aircraft. This was immediately recognized by the United States Air Force, who swallowed their pride and took the landmark decision to order a minimum-change version of the Navy F-4B for Tactical Air Command in 1961.

Fully variable inlets and supersonic nozzles gave the

delta-winged MiG-21 has been built in enormous numbers as a small multi-role attack fighter. In 1995, developments of both the MiG-19 and -21 were still in production in China as the A-5 and F-7 respectively. The much later MiG-23 is a swing-wing fighter and interceptor (fully automatic in the MiG-23P sub-type), and the MiG-27 is the corresponding tactical attack version bristling with advanced sensors and weapons. Designed in the early 1960s to combat the XB-70, the MiG-25 is the fastest interceptor in service, with a maximum speed at height of 3,000km/h (1,864mph, Mach 2.82) and immensely powerful radar and long-range missiles for destroying aircraft at a distance; it is in no sense a dogfighter. The two-seat MiG-31 is a thorough redesign of the MiG-25 with digital avionics, improved acceleration and climb performance as well as better sensors and armament for engaging targets at any altitude from sea level to more than 22km (70,000ft).

Of the profusion of new jet fighters built in the ten years after World War II the most innovatory were the interceptors of the US Air Force. These carried totally new radar fire-control systems by the Hughes Aircraft Company, in which powerful radars, auto-pilots and computers were linked to steer the aircraft automatically to shoot down intruders at night or in bad weather, without the pilot of the fighter even having to see the enemy. Previously fighters had invariably tried to get on the tail of their opponent, but these new interceptors used the collision-course technique from the side. The enemy aircraft could be seen better by the radar from the side, and the computer could steer the aircraft

Phantom Mach 2-plus capability and this was soon demonstrated when a specially prepared F-4A established an absolute speed record of 2,584km/h (1,606mph) and broke every time-to-height record in the book. Even more remarkable was Project Sageburner, which produced a low level speed record of 1,453km/h (903mph) that stood until the mid 1970s.

Handling the F-4, which was as heavy as fully-loaded World War II four-engined bomber but vastly more complex and capable, was considered too difficult for a single pilot. The title given to the 'guy in back' (GIB) depended on the operator. In the US Navy he was called a Radar Intercept Officer (RIO), while his USAF equivalent was given the title Weapons System Operator (WSO or 'Whizzo'). The RAF simply prefered navigator. Former single-seat fighter pilots initially regarded their backseaters as excess baggage, but the benefits of a 'scope dope' soon became obvious in the confusion of combat. A second pair of eyes always helps and the backseater would sometimes be the first to spot incoming SAMs or enemy aircraft. And arriving back on the carrier (which pilots found more stressful than meeting MiGs) was made that much safer when you had someone

Best known of all the Mustang variants is the Merlin-engined P-51D, which gave the Luftwaffe a particularly hard time in 1944-45. Col. J.J. Christian lost his life in this aircraft, a P-51D named LOU IV of the 8th Air Force's 361st Fighter Group.

With its 850km/h (528mph) top speed and four 30mm cannon, the Messerschmitt Me 262 would probably have made American daylight bombing missions untenable had it been available in large numbers.

to help with the pre-landing checklist (fuel state, radar on standby, weapons on safe, slats and flaps deployed, gear down and locked, approach speed, etc).

Most Phantoms could carry four medium-range radar-guided Sparrow AAMs (carried semi-submerged in the fuselage to minimise drag) and four short-range infrared (IR) Sidewinder AAMs. Its ability to carry eight AAMs in addition to a heavy load of ordnance remains impressive even today, and is one reason why the last F-4s are unlikely to be retired before the year 2000. Sparrow's semi-active seeker homed on to the radar energy reflected back from the target, which had to be 'locked on' using the sharpened beam from the parent aircraft from launch to impact. In theory this gave the Phantom a beyond visual range (BVR) capability, but this was seldom achieved when the aircraft went to war in Southeast Asia.

Operation Bolo on 2 January 1967 was significant in being one of the few occasions when Sparrow was employed in its intended BVR role. In this set-piece mission, USAF F-4s commanded by World War II veteran Col. Robin Olds shot down seven MiGs after flying in a formation normally associated with bombers, thereby fooling

The Me 163 rocket fighter had a terrific rate of climb but had serious operational problems. On landing, unspent fuel could explode or even dissolve the pilot.

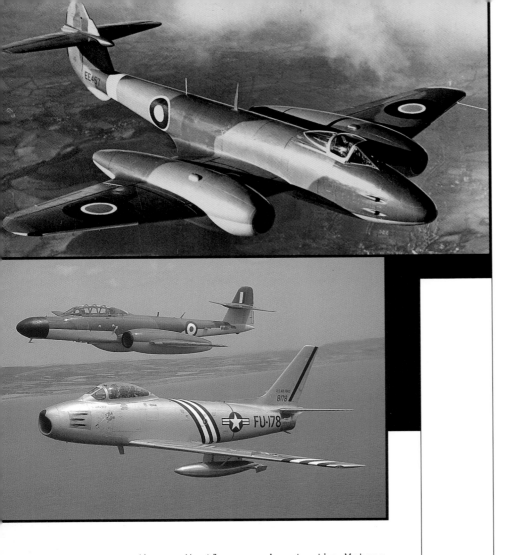

the Vietnamese GCI (ground control interception) radar operators into sending in their fighters at a tactical disadvantage.

Early versions of Sparrow and Sidewinder were notoriously unreliable, often failing to guide toward the target and sometimes remaining stubbornly attached to the launch aircraft. The situation improved when technical reps from the missile companies visited US Navy carriers in the Gulf of Tonkin and pointed out that sensitive missiles could hardly be expected to perform as advertized after being left on the aircraft for weeks on end in a salty environment or being rolled across the deck prior to loading · guidance fins do not respond well to such treatment! But the big problem was the restrictive rules of engagement, which insisted that the target had to be positively identified as hostile before being engaged. That meant closing to visual range, negating the Phantom's 'long arm' and enabling the small and agile MiGs (especially the MiG-17) to escape or turn the tables by using their superior manoeuvrability.

More than 100 Phantoms were lost trying to tangle with MiGs, often as a result of pilots pulling too hard to bring the sight on to a hard-turning target and stalling the aircraft, which then usually went into a spin – an irrecoverable situation which left little time to eject if the combat had occurred at low level over the jungle.

The cure was improved air combat training – 'Top Gun' for Navy crews and the Fighter Weapons School at Nellis AFB for their Air Force equivalents – and the introduction of improved versions of Sidewinder and Sparrow. The scanner of the powerful Westinghouse APQ-72 fire-control radar was also modified to prevent it from toppling under G-loads, a serious shortcoming in the heat of battle. Not before time, leading-edge manoeuvre slats first appeared on the USAF F-4E in June 1972. The extra lift of the slats enabled the Phantom to turn much more tightly at all altitudes and prevented many irrecoverable stall/ spins. Although the extra drag of the slats made the F-4 a sub-Mach 2 aircraft, this had little or no effect on its operational performance. Much more important was that in afterburner the engines still provided the supersonic acceleration to impart maximum energy when launching air-to-air missiles.

Even though the vast majority of Phantom kills in Vietnam were scored by Sidewinder, pilot pressure for a more reliable short-range weapon gave the F-4E an M61 six-barrel 20mm gun under the nose, the 640-round ammunition drum being located ahead of the cockpit. The proximity of the gun meant that the solid-state APQ-120 fire-control radar had to be protected against vibration. The vast majority of new-build Phantoms were fitted with two General Electric J79 turbojets, those fitted to the F-4E being rated at 8,100kg

Above: Vastly superior to the Meteor but matched by the MiG-15, the F-86 Sabre re-established Allied air superiority during the Korean War. In the background is a Meteor NF Mk 11 night fighter.

Top: Powered by 910kg (2,000lb) thrust Welland engines, Meteor F Mk IIIs began replacing earlier variants in No 616 Sqn in December 1944. Later versions remained in front-line RAF service until 1957.

(17,900lb) thrust. British Phantoms for the Royal Navy (F-4N) and RAF (F-4K) were powered by two Rolls-Royce Spey turbofans of 9,300kg (20,500lb) thrust. Despite the extra poke, these Phantoms were only marginally faster than slatted versions, being limited to Mach 1.9 by a combination of extra drag under the rear fuselage (the Spey was bigger than the J79) and engine temperature restrictions.

The 5,201st and final Phantom was an F-4EJ built by Mitsubishi and delivered to the 303rd Fighter Squadron of the Japan Air Self-Defence Force on 21 May 1981. Since then Japan has joined several foreign Phantom operators in updating its fleet. The Super Phantom produced by Israel Aircraft Industries is a virtually remanufactured F-4 with P&W 1120 turbofans and completely new avionics. German F-4Fs have been fitted with Hughes APG-65 radars from the Hornet as part of a major weapon/avionics upgrade to keep them in service until the Eurofighter 2000 becomes operational. Today the only remaining Phantoms in US service are special test aircraft and QF-4 supersonic targets.

An even more impressive interceptor was the huge Avro CF-105 Arrow, which first flew two months before the Phantom on 25 March 1958. This had a giant radar scanner and a cavernous internal weapon bay with no fewer than 11 missiles for long-range combat. Unfortunately, the Arrow fell victim to the belief that interceptors could be replaced by much cheaper 'push button' ground-based missiles, though nobody seemed able to explain how such a missile could intercept and escort unfriendly aircraft in peacetime or identify stray airliners. The decision proved to be a costly fiasco; the Bomarc missiles did not work and Canada had to make do with second-hand F-101 Voodoo interceptors from the USAF instead.

In April 1957 Britain went one better than Canada and produced a Defence White Paper which announced that all manned fighters and bombers were obsolete. This must have come as a surprise to America and the Soviet Union, who were busy spending huge sums on the design and manufacture of a new generation of combat aircraft. The English Electric Lightning had 'unfortunately gone too far to cancel', and consequently survived to become the first and only truly supersonic fighter of British design and manufacture to see operational service with the RAF. More than a decade before the F-15 Eagle, the Lightning pioneered high thrust/weight ratios (better than unity with a light fuel load) and moderate wing loading. Interestingly, the two afterburning R-R Avon turbojets were arranged one above the other in a deep fuselage and were fed by a circular nose inlet with Ferranti AI.23 radar in the conical centrebody. The RAF joined the Mach 2 club when No 74 (Tiger) Sqn received their first F.1 single-seat all-weather interceptors in 1960.

The Lightning immediately established a reputation as a pilot's aircraft with exemplary handling and searing performance. The rate of climb exceeded 400m/sec (45,000ft/min) and the aircraft was supersonic without afterburner. The ultimate RAF version, the F Mk 6, usually carried a built-in armament of two 30mm cannon in an enlarged ventral tank (the Lightning never had enough fuel) and a pair of Firestreak or Red Top IR-guided missiles. Until the early 1970s, the warhead and sensor performance of Red Top was more than a match for Sidewinder and, together with improved AI.23B radar, gave the Lightning a head-on attack capability. Delays to the Tornado ADV (which has an inferior climb rate, service ceiling, and top speed, but is much faster at low level and totes a much heavier weapon and fuel load), kept the Lightning in service until 1989, the last two squadrons being Nos 5 and 11 at RAF Binbrook in Lincolnshire.

Top: Designed as a bomber destroyer for the RAF, the Hawker Hunter later excelled at ground attack.

Middle: The evergreen MiG-21 is the world's most widely used jet fighter. A Slovakian MiG-21bis prepares for landing.

Above: The MiG-23/27 family has been built in greater numbers than any other swing-wing aircraft. This MiG-23 is operated by the Czech air force.

Stepped up neatly for the
camera, these early F-100A
Super Sabres were proclaimed
as the world's first supersonic fighters.

Lockeed's 'missile with a man in it', the
F-104A Starfighter was the first US
fighter to be armed with the M61 six-
barrel 20mm cannon. Sidewinders added
lift to the incredibly thin wing.

Britain's other potential Mach 2 fighter, a development of the Fairey Delta 2 world speed record breaker, was cancelled in the 'missile madness' of 1957. But this exquisite design inspired the Dassault Mirage III, a tailless delta of identical layout with scaled-up dimensions. Powered by a single SNECMA Atar turbojet, the Mirage IIIC was initially built for the French air force as a single-seat all-weather interceptor and could be fitted with a SEPR rocket pack to boost climb and altitude performance. Initially Marcel Dassault refused to have the lines of his beautiful Mirage spoiled by bombs, but the later Mirage IIIE was given a useful ground attack capability. The Mirage IIICJs supplied to Israel played a leading role in the pre-emptive strikes against Egyptian and Syrian air bases which began the 1967 Six Day War and rapidly gained ascendancy over the few MiGs that survived. The Mirage III became an international symbol of French prestige and with its combat credentials firmly established, 1,412 were built for customers in 20 countries. After being refused further supplies for political reasons (despite having paid for the aircraft in cash), Israel produced its own version of the improved Mirage 5 strike fighter as the Kfir (Lion Cub). Built in total secrecy by Israel Aircraft Industries, the Kfir was powered by a J79 turbojet (as used by the F-4) and much of the weapons system was of Israeli manufacture. Compared to the Atar-powered 'cooking' version, the Kfir offered improved flight performance and combat radius.

The MiG-25 interceptor, evocatively called 'Foxbat' by NATO, was cleared for Mach 2.8 and had a fire-control radar of unprecedented power.

In 1965 the USAF requested funding for a new fighter programme, the FX. This was a direct response to the apparent threat posed by the Soviet MiG-25 'Foxbat', although the main problem was the inability of the F-4 to deal effectively with the supposedly inferior MiG-17, -19 and -21 in close combat. In Southeast Asia the USAF was never seriously challenged by the much smaller North Vietnamese air force, but in central Europe it faced the prospect of being overwhelmed by thousands of MiGs operated by the Soviet Union and Warsaw Pact.

McDonnell won the FX contest on 23 December 1969, and the first F-15A flew on 27 July 1972. Named Eagle, the F-15 was designed purely as an air-superiority fighter, combining a formidable medium-range multiple kill capability with the exceptional manoeuvrability and acceleration needed for visual range 'dogfighting'. Outwardly the F-15 appeared similar to the MiG-25, with a high wing, twin-engines fed by fully variable wedge inlets on each side of the forward fuselage and a twin-fin tail mounted on long beams, which also carried the slab tailplanes. But the Eagle could not have been more different.

The deceptively simple wing was a masterpiece, optimized for maximum high-subsonic turning performance yet coping easily with Mach 2.5 and low-speed flight. Plain, two-position flaps were carried inboard of the wing and traditional ailerons outboard, there being no high-lift devices or spoilers. With its large, lightly-loaded wing and twin Pratt & Whitney F100 afterburning turbofans of nearly 10,890kg (24,000lb), the F-15 set the standard for specific excess power (the ability to regain energy by climbing or accelerating); sustained turn rate (maximum turn rate without loss of speed); and instantaneous turn rate (maximum achievable turn rate with transient loss of speed). In practical terms this meant that the F-15 could out-manoeuvre any combat aircraft in the world.

The F-15 employed the same Sparrow/Sidewinder missile combination as the F-4, but the M61 gun was located in the starboard wing root (where it would not interfere with the radar) and fed by a belt passing over the right inlet duct from a 940-round drum in the fuselage. Fire-control was provided by the Hughes APG-63 radar, which could automatically track up to 24 targets at long-range and prioritize those which needed the most urgent attention. Alternative modes included look-up, shoot-up for high altitude targets such as the MiG-25R reconnaissance

Identified by the larger intakes for its Rolls-Royce Spey turbofans, an RAF Phantom FGR.2 (F-4M) poses with power and deflected slats and flaps.

USN F-4B Phantom of VF-111 'Sundowners' from the USS *Coral Sea* releases its bombload under radar control during the Vietnam War.

aircraft and look-down, shoot-down for low flying targets. The preferred tactic against the opposition was to 'shoot 'em in the face'. This involved setting up a medium-range Sparrow shot against a head-on target at closing speeds approaching Mach 3 (faster including the missile) giving the enemy pilot little time to react, even if alerted by on-board radar warning receivers (RWR). APG-63 could maintain lock on a manoeuvring target far more effectively than preceding radars. Having loosed off a couple of Sparrows and maintained target lock until impact, the F-15 then had the option of turning back to re-attack any surviving aircraft in the enemy formation with further Sparrows or closing in to kill with Sidewinders if the odds were favourable.

The pilot enjoyed a commanding all-round view thanks to a high seating position and large teardrop canopy. Having been originally designed for two crew members, there was already adequate room for the second seat later added to the operational trainer and Strike Eagle versions. Single pilot operation of this sophisticated aircraft was made feasible with the first HOTAS (Hands On Throttle And Stick) system, in which the vital 'switchology' for the radar and weapons came literally to hand instead of being scattered around the cockpit.

Since the F-15A entered USAF service in November 1974, the already exceptional APG-63 radar system has been massively upgraded in terms of signal processor capability (digital), computer memory and

software. The F-15C and two-seat F-15D introduced in 1979 have APG-70 radar and can carry a conformal low-drag fuel tank on each side of the fuselage for 5,678 litres (1,248 gal) of extra fuel. When the F-15 was being designed the USAF had been adamant:'NOT A POUND FOR AIR-TO-GROUND!' But now, in addition to the extra fuel, up to 12 bombs of 454kg (1,000lb) or four of 910kg (2,000lb) can be hung under the conformal tanks as well as various reconnaissance or day/night surface attack sensors.

The dual-role F-15E Strike Eagle has an even heavier ordnance load. Apart from APG-70 and its related avionics, the other major improvement in the Eagle's air-to-air capability has been advent of the AIM-120 AMRAAM which, unlike Sparrow, enables the F-15 to break away immediately after launch and avoid the risk of being hit by missiles fired by opposing fighters. Structural improvements also allow the F-15C/D to pull 9G at maximum weight.

The F-15 has probably shot down more aircraft than any other jet fighter in the last 25 years, Israeli Eagles having scored heavily during the big air battles with Syrian MiG-21s and MiG-23s over the Bekaa Valley in Lebanon in May 1982. More recently, USAF F-15Cs of the 36th Tactical Fighter Wing, normally based at Bitburg in Germany, destroyed about two-thirds of the 40-plus Iraqi aircraft lost in air combat during the 1991 Gulf War. On 19 January 1991 two MiG-25s fell victim to the Eagle, while in another early dogfight six F-15Cs shot down three MiG-29s using

Sidewinders. With AWACS aircraft able to confirm the targets as hostile, on 27 January 1991 two F-15Cs from the 53rd Tactical Fighter Squadron 'splashed' three MiG-23s and one Mirage F.1 in a look-down, shoot-down attack using AIM-7M Sparrows and AIM-9M Sidewinders. An F-15C of the Royal Saudi Air Force scored the first double kill of Operation Desert Storm, when on 24 January 1991 two Mirage F.1EQs, which were believed to be attempting an Exocet anti-ship attack, were shot down with Sidewinders.

Ten years after the F-15 came the Soviet Mikoyan MiG-29 and Sukhoi Su-27. Both were designed to defeat the F-15, but in terms of performance, agility, weapons and sensors the larger Su-27 is regarded as probably the world's best air combat fighter. Yet as first flown in T-10 prototype form on 20 May 1977, this aircraft was in serious trouble and went on to claim the lives of two test pilots before being completely redesigned into a fighter of stellar quality. The transformation included a new wing, a new fuselage with larger radar radome, a revised twin-tail shape with vertical underfins, revised inlets and a new large dorsal airbrake *a la* F-15. Much later in development than the Eagle, the Su-27 incorporated fly by wire from the start. The quality of the aerodynamics was demonstrated by test pilot G. Pugachyev, who gave his name to the jaw-dropping Cobra manoeuvre first seen in the West at the 1989 Paris Air Show.

Modern fighters tend to fall into one of two groups, the first being relatively large twin-engined machines such as the McDonnell Douglas F-15 Eagle and Sukhoi Su-27, and the second being the smallest single-engined aircraft that can carry the required radar and

Afterburner and a sharp turn immediately after takeoff was the Viggen's party piece at air shows. In war, the low-speed agility of this canard/delta would enable it to operate from specially designated public roads.

weapons, such as the F-104 of the 1950s, the MiG-23 of the 1960s, the F-16 of the 1970s, the Mirage 2000 of the 1980s and the JAS 39 Gripen in the 1990s. Exceptions in the latter category include the F-A/18 and MiG-29 of the late 1970s, where designers have opted for two engines to provide more power as well as increased safety in the event of engine failure, which could be caused by a malfunction or battle damage. Thanks to sustained development of jet engines, notably the high-pressure afterburning turbofan, today's fighters no longer suffer from the limited endurance and weapon load of the Korean War period. Even the smallest can use short airstrips, carry five tonnes or more of bombs or missiles and fly a four-hour mission. Equipment always includes an ejection seat, comprehensive ECM and other defensive decoys, and a flight-refuelling probe giving almost unlimited endurance.

First flown in YF-16 prototype form on 2 February 1974, the General Dynamics F-16 Fighting Falcon was a landmark in fighter design . Originally conceived as a lightweight fighter to complement the more costly F-15 Eagle, the F-16 has grown

The Tornado Air Defence Variant will remain the RAF's standard interceptor until the introduction of the Eurofighter, in about 2002.

from a lightly-armed clear weather dogfighter into a potent multi-role combat aircraft. It was the first production fighter with artificial stability and fly by wire, setting new standards for manoeuvrability (its near-instantaneous 9G turns became the bane of F-4 drivers) and ease of operation.

The cockpit was one of the first to incorporate a head-up display (HUD) and the pilot uses a force-sensing sidestick rather than a position-sensing conventional stick. The ACES ejection seat is reclined at a comfortable 30 degrees not to improve the pilot's G-tolerance (a task performed by the G-suit), but simply to fit it inside the YF16's relatively shallow forward fuselage.

A plain, fixed inlet under the nose feeds a single P&W F100 turbofan and gives the F-16 a shark-like appearance. Since 15 March 1995, production of the F-16 at the giant Fort Worth plant in Texas has been controlled by Lockheed Martin, which delivered the 3,500th Fighting Falcon the following month. The current F-16C can carry the full range of USAF tactical weapons and the LANTIRN (Low-Altitude Navigation and Targeting Infrared for Night) sensor/attack pod. Compared to the pathetic air-to-air armament of early F-16As (two wingtip-mounted IR-guided Sidewinders), the F-16C can tote up to six AMRAAMs (advanced medium-range air-air missiles), giving the aircraft a formidable beyond visual range (BVR) kill capability.

The latest fighters such as the Eurofighter 2000 and Dassault Rafale are light (due to the extensive use of composite materials); highly agile in all axes (thanks to artificial stability with fly by wire, and canard/delta wing configuration); and incorporate ultra-fast computers and advanced sensors for either air-to-air or air-to-surface missions. Linked to the electronic flight control system (EFCS), these computers enable the pilot to fly the aircraft to its aerodynamic and structural limits irrespective of weapon load or other factors without fear of entering an uncontrollable manoeuvre such as a spin.

Integrated with a helmet-mounted sight or other weapon-aiming modes, the EFCS also allows the aircraft to point at a target displaced from its flightpath, enabling the pilot to rapidly engage a short-range (ie, visual) target approaching from near head-on with either guns or missiles. Alternatively, for ground strafing, (eg, 'walking' rounds towards a truck travelling along a road) the gun can be kept continuously on target when the pilot fires, achieving maximum effect with the minimum expenditure of ammunition .

Helmet-mounted sight systems (HMSS) have been used by MiG-29 pilots since 1979, forming part of an integrated fire-control system which includes Fazotron multi-mode radar, infra-red search and track (IRST) and a laser ranger. Using MiG-29s inherited from the former East German air force, Luftwaffe evaluation pilots were tremendously impressed by the Russian fighter, most especially its ability to engage targets at large off-boresight angles (ie, highly displaced from the aircraft's flightpath) using the HMSS and laser ranger to aim and fire short-range missiles or put every round from its 23mm twin-barrel cannon unerringly on target.

The first Western fighter with HMSS/IRST is expected to be the Eurofighter 2000, which is scheduled to enter service with the RAF, Luftwaffe, Italian and Spanish air forces from about 2002. In the case of EF2000, the pilot designates the target

Below: Top-scorer in the 1991 Gulf War with 29 kills, the F-15 Eagle air superiority fighter has been the best in the West for more than 20 years. The Su-27 is its Russian rival.

Bottom: The F-16B two-seater retains the combat capability of the single-seater and the longer canopy actually reduces drag.

Below: The Spanish air force is a major operator of the Hornet multi-role fighter, receiving the last of its 60 EF-18As and 12 EF-18B two-seaters in 1990.

simply by looking at it, then calls up the appropriate weapon (gun or missile) either by direct voice command (eg, 'Select ASRAAM') or by pressing a button on the throttle. In automatic mode computers do the rest, firing the missile at the optimum range, but the pilot may opt to fire the weapon manually by pulling the trigger on the control stick.

The combination of HMSS, the 'pointing' ability conferred by the EF2000's electronic flight control system and the tremendous manoeuvrability of ASRAAM enables the pilot to engage an enemy fighter from virtually any angle, even one that is relatively close alongside (say, within 1,000m). The missile's infra-red seeker automatically acquires the target by being slaved to the pilot's line of sight. After launch, ASRAAM (advanced short-range air-air missile) is capable of accelerating rapidly and can turn through almost 180° before exploding within lethal distance (at least 25m) of the target. (All AAMs use proximity fuses to increase their chances of success a direct hit is relatively rare.) Engaging targets in this way limits an opponents' options for evasive action and leaves the launch aircraft clear of any debris from the victim. Alternatively, as with the MiG-29, gunfire can be directed so accurately that only a very short burst is required, one or two rounds being sufficient to cripple an opposing fighter.

Top: Powered by a Volvo RM12 turbofan, Saab claims business-jet operating costs for the Gripen, here in air defence configuration with two AMRAAMs and four Swedish-made Sidewinders.

Designed to defeat the Su-27 and MiG-29 at long-range and in close combat, the Eurofighter 2000 will also have a full air-to-surface capability.

Like all today's highly agile fighters, the Dassault Rafale is designed

Perhaps surprisingly, the USAF has not specified any HMSS for its new Lockheed Martin F-22 Lightning II, which is expected to replace the F-15 Eagle in the air-superiority role from 2002. Named after Lockheed's twin-tailed P-38 pursuit ship of World War II, the F-22 is the world's first true stealth fighter and has been carefully designed to ensure a low radar cross-section (RCS). It is also the first fighter designed to cruise and manoeuvre supersonically. Conventional Mach 2 fighters spend only 0.1 per cent of their service lives at supersonic speeds; external weapon carriage increases drag (and RCS) and prolonged use of afterburner for combat acceleration and manoeuvring consumes fuel at an alarming rate.

The F-22 carries all its missiles (up to eight AMRAAMS) in fuselage weapon bays, the doors of which flip open and shut in a fraction of second when a round is fired. The inlets for its two Pratt & Whitney F119 engines are highly stealthy (at the expense of a significant reduction in thrust) and vectoring nozzles

provide outstanding supersonic manoeuvrability. The F-22 is able to find, track and destroy multiple targets automatically while remaining undetected by enemy fighters. Its own radar is an advanced phased array, which sends target data to the pilot's multi-function displays (MFDs) and the inertial guidance system carried by each AMRAAM via one of the fastest digital computers yet devised. Avionics account for 50 per cent of the cost of each F-22, easily the highest proportion in the history of fighter design.

Most of the missions flown by 'fighters' in the past 30 years have been against surface targets, the Gulf War in 1991 being the latest example. In World War II a few special attack aircraft were built, such as the Il-2 Stormovik for the Russian Air Force and the Hs 129 of the Luftwaffe. These had poor flight performance but thick armour and a heavy gun for knocking out tanks. Such machines tended to be forgotten in the 1950s (though a few significant prototypes were built, such as the French Potez 75 with its pioneer

to cope with a wide variety of air-to-surface missions.

wire-guided anti-tank missiles) but the simmering succession of so-called brushfire wars at last spurred the development of completely new kinds of tactical aircraft for use against battlefield surface targets.

There could hardly be a more complete contrast than between the Lockheed AC-130, the Fairchild A-10 Thunderbolt II, the Rockwell OV-10 Bronco and Russia's latest Stormovik, the Sukhoi Su-25. Yet all are in a way 'tactical fighters' in that they are designed to fight in a land battle.

The Lockheed AC-130 was a specially equipped version of the USAF's most widely used large turbo-prop freight transport, packed with guns, ammunition, radar, infrared, television and other sensors for finding hostile troops, trucks or armour at night and destroying them with withering fire. In a situation that completely turned the tables, it was not uncommon in the war in Vietnam for supersonic fighters, such as the F-100 Super Sabre, F-105 Thunderchief and F-4 Phantom, to spend their time finding and marking

ground targets that would then be attacked by the lumbering AC-130s!

The Fairchild A-10 Thunderbolt II is a carefully designed battlefield weapon platform with the most powerful tank-killing gun ever fitted into an aircraft. Its speed is no faster than that of World War II fighters, and it relies largely on thick armour and the ability to accept severe damage. In return it offers more first-shot lethality than has ever before been built into an aeroplane, with its deadly gun backed up by heavy loads of precision-guided missiles.

The OV-10 is an even slower turboprop machine able to dodge about over the battlefield and fire guns and rockets, guide 'smart' (laser-homing) bombs and even land and pick up casualties.

The only tactical aircraft that are even more versatile, able to operate without a purpose-built airstrip, are the various versions of the Harrier, described in the section on carrier-based aircraft on page 74 and in the Rotorcraft and V/STOL chapter on page 152.

Anti-Submarine Warfare and Maritime Aircraft

In World War I the existence of naval air arms as separate services in almost all the warring powers prompted the development of air war at sea. A further factor was the suitability of stretches of sheltered water for the take-off and landing of marine aircraft much larger than could safely use the short and often bumpy landing grounds.

To some degree military requirements over land and naval requirements at sea ran parallel; aircraft could fly reconnaissance missions, spot for the guns, drop bombs and endeavour to shoot down enemy aircraft. Anti-submarine warfare (ASW) was something quite separate which in the course of time was to lead to purpose-designed aircraft.

In Britain the RNAS (Royal Naval Air Service) constructed series of flying boats. From early 1917 the excellent F.2 series were produced as the standard RNAS boat for open-sea reconnaissance, and they proved to be tough and seaworthy. Usually powered by two Rolls-Royce Eagle engines they could reach 153km/h (95mph) and fly six-hour patrols when carrying four Lewis guns and two 104kg (230lb) flat-nosed anti-submarine bombs. The larger F.3 was a development able to carry four AS bombs and was used exclusively on ASW missions out of range of hostile aircraft.

Most of the German naval seaplanes stationed around the North Sea in World War I were Hansa Brandenburgs, designed by Ernst Heinkel. The KDW (Kampf-doppeldecker wasser, [war biplane seaplane]), W.12 and W.19 were trim biplanes which had excellent performance and up to three or four machine guns. By 1918 the extremely modern W.29 monoplane seaplane was in production, and from this Heinkel developed a long succession of outstanding reconnaissance/fighter seaplanes from his own company operating in Scandinavian 'cover' countries after the war..

In Austro-Hungary the Lohner and M-series of flying boats were used throughout the Adriatic Sea and northern Italy, and spurred the development of Italy's own Macchi flying boats which were mostly used as single-seat fighters of quite high performance, often being able to outstrip hostile landplanes. Many other types of flying boat and seaplane were produced in France, Britain, the United States, Russia and Japan. Some carried torpedoes and most could fly ASW

Top left: The Su-25 attack aircraft has extensive armour protection against ground fire and can carry a heavy warload from improvised airstrips.

Above: The Felixstowe F-2As, a big patrol aircraft used by the Royal Navy in World War I.

The Consolidated PBY Catalina was built in greater numbers than any other flying boat in history, and used in a number of roles including air/sea rescue and anti-submarine warfare.

patrols with AS bombs or depth charges, but aircraft still lacked performance, and the absence of any way of finding submarines from the air, other than by sighting them in shallow water, made kills few and far between.

Between the World Wars most countries had maritime patrol and ASW squadrons, but technical progress was modest other than the basic development of aeroplanes with all-metal stressed-skin structure and other refinements. In the mid-1930s these combined with sudden jumps in available engine powe to revolutionize the capability of maritime aircraft. The US Navy, for example, used the Naval Aircraft Factory's PH series flying boats from June 1932, with a range of 2,400km (1,490 miles). By 1936 the Consolidated PBY Catalina was being delivered – the most-produced flying boat in history, with over 4,000 of all versions built by 1945 – with two 1,200hp engines and range over 3,860 km (2,400 miles). In 1940 Martin began deliveries of the PBM-1 Mariner, with 1,600hp engines and range of 5,552km (3,450 miles). In 1942 Boeing flew the XPBB-1 Sea Ranger, and though this was not put into service it was a truly remarkable performer, able to carry 20 bombs of 454kg (1,000lb) and fly a 72-hour mission, covering a still-air distance of 10,140km (6,300 miles).

Nearly all the patrol flying boats of the 1930s had been biplanes, but these disappeared swiftly after the start of World War II, with a few notable exceptions such as the RAF's faithful Walrus amphibian, which was the chief ASR (air/sea rescue) aircraft of the RAF and also served with the Fleet Air Arm. Another ancient biplane that proved its value was the German Heinkel He 59, a big twinfloat seaplane, used as an ambulance, ASR aircraft, a minelayer and as an electronic-warfare platform.

A Short Sunderland of RAF Coastal Command returns from a sortie in the North Altantic hunting German U-Boats.

Probably the nation that suffered most from submarines (German U-boats) was Britain, and it was Britain that led in the development of ASV (air/surface vessel) radar. Radar capable of detecting surface ships was easy, but the main objective was radar that could detect the small tip of a U-boat periscope. The early ASV radars were bulky and needed large aerial arrays. These were carried by the famous Sunderland flying boats in the 1941-43 period and the Coastal Command Liberator which were the first aircraft able to fly patrols long enough to close the gap in the mid-west Atlantic where U-boats had been able to surface unmolested. By 1944 the ASV Mk V radar was in use. This was carried under the nose of Wellingtons, under both outer wings of Sunderlands and above the hull of the PBM-3D and -3S Mariner. All these could detect a U-boat at periscope depth, even in extremely stormy seas.

In the Pacific the Imperial Japanese Navy used a diversity of seaplanes and flying boats, the most popular seaplane being the trusty Aichi E13A1 and the best flying boat the exceptionally powerful and well-armed Kawanishi H8K. Many of the Japanese seaplanes were single-seat fighters, intended to sweep enemies from the sky in areas where the Japanese had no airstrips available. Although remarkable technical achievements, they were inevitably outclassed by the best Allied land- or carrier-based fighters, and the same has been true of water-based fighters ever since.

The Luftwaffe was orientated towards land battles, but nevertheless produced many maritime aircraft. Two formidable seaplanes were the cannon-armed Ar 196B and the extremely tough twin-engined He 115, extensively used for minelaying and other oceanic duties. The curious diesel-engined Bv 138 flying boat had a short hull and high tail carried on twin booms. The chief long-range oceanic aircraft of the Luftwaffe was the four-engined Fw 200C Condor, which despite structural weakness earned the title 'Scourge of the Atlantic' from Churchill and in its final sub-types carried the Hs 293 radio-guided missile for use against Allied ships. An even larger patrol aircraft was the Ju 290, and two examples were built of the six-engined Ju 390, one of the largest and heaviest landplanes of the war. The six-engined Bv 222 Wiking was used mainly as a transport flying boat.

Italy was proud of its S.M.79 Sparviero three-engined torpedo-bombers, and extensive use was also made of the Cant Z.506B three-engined seaplane and the Z.501 single-engined flying boat.

In the Soviet Union float seaplanes were few, but the Beriev MBR-2 and MDR-6 flying boats were used in large numbers for coastal reconnaissance and many other duties though, so far as is known, seldom on combat missions. Both had high-mounted stressed-skin wings, but the MBR-2 had a wooden hull and was already ten years old when war came to the Soviet Union in 1941. Since 1945 the Beriev bureau has been the only one in the world to continue to produce military water-based aircraft in large numbers. The Be-6, with two 2,400hp piston engines and, from 1954, the first complete set of oceanic and ASW

Right: First flown in May 1945 and ultimately powered by two 3,700hp Turbo-Compound engines plus two J34 booster jet pods, the Lockheed P-2 Neptune set the standard for long-range ocean-patrol aircraft.

Top: Known as the Scourge of the Atlantic, the Fw 200 Condor was the Luftwaffe's main long-range reconnaisance aircraft, helping locate Allied convoys for the lurking U-boat packs.

Above: The Beriev Be-6 was used in large numbers by the Soviet Union for coastal reconnaissance and air/sea rescue.

equipment to fly in a Russian aircraft, served with the AV-MF (naval air force) from 1950 until the mid 1960s, ending its days as a transport. First flown on 20 July 1956, the record-breaking Be-10 twinjet was an exceptional design, with a large hull and all-swept surfaces, the wings having anhedral to put the wingtip floats near the water on short fixed pylons. However, the Be-10 proved unsuitable for operations in heavy seas or strong winds and equipped just two units of the Black Sea Fleet.

The less advanced Be-12 has been in AV-MF service since 1964 for all kinds of ocean patrol and ASW missions. An amphibian, with retractable tailwheel-type landing gear, the Be-12, unofficially called the *Chaika* (seagull), carries radars, MAD (magnetic-anomaly direction gear for finding submarines by sensing their disturbance of the terrestrial magnetic field) and sonar detection equipment, as well as extensive electronic systems for communications, navigation and intelligence gathering. In 1982 Beriev began to design the Be-12's replacement, the Be-42, a new twin-jet amphibian capable of 760km/h (472mph). This unusually impressive aircraft is equipped with a multi-mode search/attack radar (which can also detect weather and determine wave height), MAD boom, weapons bays for torpedoes and other stores and a flight refuelling probe.

In contrast, almost all Western maritime aircraft since the 1950s have been landplanes. Numerically the most important has been the large twin-engined Lockheed P2V (later P-2) Neptune, which in 1946 set a world record by flying 18,083km (11,236 miles) non-stop from Australia to Ohio. Eight major versions of Neptune were used by almost all NATO and many other air forces in 1950-79, the later variants usually having two jet pods under the wings to boost the two basic 3,700hp Wright Turbo-Compound engines. A contemporary of the Neptune was the fractionally larger Shackleton developed in Britain from the Lancaster bomber. Canada used the Britannia turboprop airliner as the basis for its extremely large and capable CL-28 Argus, in service from 1958. In the 1960s several European NATO partners collaborated to build the Br.1150 Atlantic, with a cavernous weapons bay, two turboprops and an overall efficiency which exceeded that of any rival. The type is back in production as the Atlantique ATL.2 for the French Aéronavale.

Lockheed won a US Navy competition for a new off-the-shelf patrol aircraft in 1958 with the P-3 Orion, based on the Electra airliner and powered by four Allison T56 turboprops. The P-3 has been

The Lockheed P-3 Orion turboprop is the most successful maritime aircraft in history. Current versions can be armed with Harpoon air-to-surface missiles as well as various torpedoes, mines and depth charges.

The RAF's equivalent to the P-3 is the Nimrod MR.2, which remains unique as the world's only land-based, pure-jet maritime patrol aircraft.

Top left: E.H. Dunning's Sopwith Pup takes off from the raised deck platform of HMS *Furious* in 1917. He subsequently was killed after an attempted landing.

Top right: The 'obsolete' Fairey Swordfish served with distinction as a torpedo-bomber and radar-equipped anti-shipping aircraft.

Above left: Grumman's pugnacious pre-war biplane fighters had the novelty of retractable landing gear; the F3F-2 saw front-line service until June 1941.

Above right: Grumman's big Avenger torpedo-bomber was a classic carrier aircraft. The space-saving Sto-Wing enabled the wings to fold back along the fuselage.

consistently upgraded to keep pace with the latest developments in submarine detection and is still a very active programme. Export customers include Australia, Canada, Iran, Japan, The Netherlands, New Zealand, Norway, Pakistan, Portugal, South Korea and Spain. The US Customs service operates P-3 AEWs for anti-drug patrols.

The corresponding Russian aircraft is the Il-38, likewise derived from a civil airliner, in this case the Il-18 of 1957. Powered by four Ivchenko turboprops, the Il-38 has a large pressurised fuselage like the Orion but has a smaller internal weapon bay and no external pylons. About 60 Il-38s remain in AV-MF service and the sole export customer is the Indian Navy.

built on the landing gear. In principle this was very like the deck arrester system of a modern carrier.

For the early part of World War I the warring powers did little with aeroplanes at sea apart from carrying small groups of seaplanes on a tender (small craft such as converted ferries). In November 1915 a British Royal Naval Air Service pilot took off from a ship, and in August 1917 another RNAS pilot 'landed-on', in each case with the ship at speed in the open sea; but it was not until 1918 that the first aircraft carrier was commissioned. Even then the 1911 scheme of arrester wires was not followed-up. At first sailors ran out and tried to cling on to the wing tips to hold the aircraft down and bring it to a halt. Then longitu-

Right: The last of Grumman's great piston-engined fighters was the fast-climbing F8F Bearcat, which arrived just too late to see combat in World War II.

Far right: Much more at home than contemporary British fighters, the F4F Wildcat gave its pilot a good view of the deck for touch down and had sturdy landing gear.

Left: A flight of Japanese dive bombers are readied for another sortie.

Britain uses an outstanding and unique jet for ocean reconnaissance, the British Aerospace Nimrod MR.2. Originally based on the de Havilland Comet airliner, the Nimrod has a much larger fuselage with an enormous weapon bays. These bays are so large the Nimrod has seldom had to carry any weapons or other stores externally. The Nimrod AEW.3 variant was a grossly rebuilt version with giant aerial domes on the nose and tail. A series of delays caused by system integration problems led to the programme being scrapped in favour of the Boeing Sentry AEW.1.

Carrier-based Aircraft

The first man to take off in an aeroplane from a ship was Eugene Ely, of the United States, who on 14 November 1910 successfully piloted his Curtiss off a makeshift 25m (83ft) platform over the foredeck of the US cruiser *Birmingham.* Two months later, on 18 January 1911, he flew out from San Francisco and successfully landed on a platform built at the stern of another cruiser, *Pennsylvania.* Ropes had been stretched across this platform with sandbags at each end, and the Curtiss caught these ropes with hooks

dinal wires were fixed along the deck, the pilot trying to rub along them on landing. Some aircraft, such as the Fairey Campania (named for the first long-deck seaplane tender), were seaplanes which took off on deck trollies and landed in the water alongside the ship. Landplanes often dispensed with their wheels and operated on plain skids, which were unsprung and jarred the pilot. By 1918 many manufacturers had produced special ship-planes, such as the Sopwith 2F.1 Camel, the naval version of the famous fighter. The 2F.1 had several changes including steel centre-section struts instead of wood and a quickly detachable rear fuselage. The latter feature enabled more aircraft to be stored below the flight deck.

Deck take-offs using seaplanes on trollies endured into the 1920s, and some seaplanes were constructed as true amphibians with wheels built into the floats. Increasingly the carrier-based fighter diverged from its land counterpart, nearly always because the life aboard a ship made additional demands. By the mid-1920s it was almost universal for wings to be made with hinges and locking pins so that they could fold back to occupy less space. The structure had to be

strong enough to stand up to constant manhandling, manoeuvring on pitching decks and the stresses of storms at sea. As wooden construction was unsuitable the structure was almost always non-corrodible or Alclad, a special light alloy coated with pure aluminium. Many navies continued to use fabric-covered aircraft until almost the end of World War II but most welcomed stressed-skin as a good way of avoiding most superficial tears and dents. Landing gears had to be stronger to stand up to landing on a pitching or rolling deck.

By 1930 several carriers in Britain, France, the United States and Japan were in operation with two basic new installations, both initially of a hydraulic nature. In the bows was at least one catapult, to shoot aircraft into the air in a short distance. At the stern was a series of arrester wires to bring landing aircraft rapidly to a halt. Both made severe new demands on aircraft. The addition of catapult hooks or 'spools' not only demanded massive local strengthening but also called for a rethink throughout the aircraft; every single part or item of equipment had to be fixed more firmly than before. The catapult usually had a large hydraulic ram, whose travel was often multiplied by a cable and pulley system to drive a sliding shuttle or trolley on the deck. Catapults of a somewhat different type, often arranged on a large pivot to face the wind, were added to most of the world's newer or larger warships, such as battleships and heavy cruisers. These carried seaplanes which in a naval engagement could be shot off to spot for the heavy guns. Afterwards they landed alongside and were picked up by crane.

The landing system took a long time to become efficient and reasonably safe. By 1933 the universal system was to stretch about eight heavy cables transversely across the rear of the flight deck, each fastened to an energy-absorbing system. The best method was to make the arrester wire a closed loop, half over the deck and half inside the ship carried on pulleys, and fix the centre of the lower portion to a single arrester gear. To take care of landings that fail to pick up a wire and do not 'bolt' (go round again for another try) a barrier is raised across the deck, usually a flexible fence of vertical ropes.

In the 1920s it became accepted that all these severe requirements inevitably resulted in carrier-based aircraft being slower, clumsier and less manoeuvrable than land-based counterparts. The Blackburn was a typical British fleet aircraft of the 1920s, ugly and sluggish yet tough and capable of doing its job. A few fighters, such as the American Boeing F4B and British Hawker Nimrod, were naval versions of land aircraft and did their best to minimise their penalties. Of course, carrying a torpedo inevitably meant a large and heavy aeroplane which until World War II could only be fitted into carriers with difficulty.

By 1935 the strong trend towards the monoplane extended to naval aircraft, and though inferior performers the new breed of carrier-based machines had almost double the speed and greater load-carrying capability. One

The Douglas Skyraider or 'Able Dog' (AD-1) combined a heavy weapon load with long-range and endurance.

Top: Few aviators have enjoyed a better view of the flight deck than from the cockpit of a Sea Hawk, the Royal Navy's 1950s fighter-bomber.

Above: Hook down, a de Havilland Sea Vixen all-weather fighter lines up on the angled flight deck of HMS *Ark Royal* in the early 1960s.

Apart from the US Navy, Britain's Fleet Air Arm was the only F-4 customer to operate Phantoms from aircraft carriers. An F-4K of No 892 (Omega) Squadron is readied for a cat shot from HMS *Ark Royal* during her final cruise in 1977.

Right: Last of the Grumman 'cats' is the F-14 Tomcat air superiority fighter, which was designed to shoot down low-flying cruise missiles as well as aircraft.

Far right: An A-6E Intruder all-weather attack aircraft all set for a 'trap', US Navy speak for snagging the arrestor wires and coming to a stop.

Originally limited to anti-submarine warfare, the Lockheed S-3 Viking now carries underwing missiles and bombs for surface attack.

The McDonnell Douglas F/A-18 Hornet multi-role fighter can switch from surface-attack to air-combat modes on the same mission.

A Sea Harrier F/A2 multi-role V/STOL fighter hovers before touching down on the latest HMS *Ark Royal*.

exceptional biplane, the British Swordfish, proved so tough and useful that it outlasted various intended replacements and continued throughout World War II. In the US and Japanese navies great emphasis was placed on the dive bomber, and large numbers of such excellent machines as the Douglas SBD Dauntless and Aichi D3A wrought havoc because of their ability to accurately bomb warships. But the early torpedo monoplanes, such as the Douglas TBD Devastator and Nakajima B5N, were very vulnerable to fighters and anti-aircraft fire. The best Allied torpedo bomber was the Grumman TBF Avenger, which had an internal bay for a 0.56mm (22in) torpedo and a heavy machine-gun in a power-driven dorsal turret.

Britain failed to build modern naval fighters, but produced carrier-based versions of two proven land fighters, known as the Sea Hurricane and Seafire. American design teams doubled engine power to over 2,000hp in 1940, resulting in such formidable machines as the F4U Corsair and F6F Hellcat, which completely mastered the Japanese A6M 'Zero'. By 1944 the Grumman F7F Tigercat was being cleared for carrier use with two 2,000hp engines and not only devastating armament but also air-interception radar. British thinking preferred two-seat fighters, despite their poorer performance, because at sea it was judged that a professional navigator would more likely to find the way back to the carrier. The first two-seat monoplane for the Royal Navy was the Fulmar, which though slow could defeat most aircraft in the Mediterranean in 1940. The fastest of the piston-engined fighters was the 752km/h (467mph) de Havilland Sea Hornet, which at last had adequate range and in later form carried radar and an observer.

Early naval jet fighters were short on range and endurance, and also suffered from long take-off runs. By 1950 Britain was revolutionizing carrier operations with three great advances. The steam catapult was a long tube recessed into the deck with travel long enough to need no pulleys yet with dramatically greater power to match the needs of any kind of aircraft. The mirror sight helps landing pilots stay on the correct glide-path, with further assistance by the LSO (landing signals officer) or 'batsman' who instructs the pilot to make necessary corrections.

Today the US Navy's *Nimitz*-class nuclear-powered carriers are the largest warships in history, with displacements exceeding 90,000 tonnes and a complement of more than 5,000 men. These supercarriers operate a total of 90 aircraft, the most impressive being the F-14D Tomcat interceptor, armed with a mix of up to eight IR- and radar-guided missiles and capable of Mach 2.4. Another large carrier aircraft is the E-2C Hawkeye, like the F-14D a Grumman product, with two 4,910hp turboprops and carrying the largest load of surveillance radars, ECM, computers and communications ever to go to sea in the Awacs role. A transport version is the C-2A Greyhound, called a COD (carrier onboard delivery) aircraft, used to maintain liaison between ship and shore. Standard ASW aircraft is the S-3B Viking, with a crew of four, advanced radar, IR (infra-red) seeker, MAD gear, large batteries of sonobuoys, comprehensive ECM and a wide range of ASW weapons in an amazingly ingeniously packed fuselage much shorter than the F-14D. The Viking can carry Harpoon missiles and other stores on its wing pylons. The ES-3A version is a conversion of the S-3A for electronic warfare, a task it shares with the more numerous Grumman EA-6B Prowler. The Prowler is based on the Intruder, the A-6E being the ultimate version of this veteran naval bomber. The McDonnell Douglas F-18 Hornet multi-role fighter/attack aircraft is the world's most numerous carrier-borne jet with more than 1,000 delivered to the US Navy and Marine Corps.

Britain abandoned conventional carriers in favour of smaller (19,810 tonne) *Invincible*-class warships equipped with Sea Harrier F/A.2 fighter/attack aircraft and ASW and AEW helicopters. The vectored-thrust Harrier family is discussed in chapter 5. The foredeck of the ship has a curved 'ski jump' so that when a rolling take-off is made the aircraft is projected high into an upward trajectory. This improves safety in the event of take-off engine failure (the pilot can eject in good time) and allows a much heavier weapon load to be carried. Ski-jumps have also been used experimentally by shore-based USN F-18 Hornets and were incorporated into the design of small Spanish and Italian carriers for the AV-8B Harrier II. The Indian Navy is also a member of the ski-jump club, operating Sea Harrier FRS Mk 51s from the carrier *Viraat,* formerly HMS *Hermes* of Falklands fame. Other ski-jumpers include the navalized MiG-29K and Sukhoi Su-27K, both of which completed carrier trials in 1993 aboard the nuclear-powered *Admiral Kuznetsov.* Held by the ship's restrainers, the aircraft would run up to full afterburner before release, using the ski-jump to become airborne in about 100m.

Beginning in 1972, the Soviet Union gained valuable experience of naval jet-lift with the Yakovlev Yak-36M, essentially an operational training aircraft incorporating a limited warfare capability. By 1976 this V/STOL design was flying off ASW cruisers (using VTOL) and large battlecruiser-type carriers such as the *Minsk*. The subsequent Yak-38M and the more capable Yak-141 are described in the chapter 5.

France has rejected the V/STOL option, prefering instead to operate a pair of conventional carriers, the *Clemenceau* and *Foch,* with a mix of veteran F-8E (FN) Crusader fighters, Etendard IV attack aircraft, Exocet-armed Super Etendard strike fighters and Alizé anti-submarine patrol aircraft. The Rafale M01 combat prototype made its first deck landing on the *Foch* in 1993 and the first Rafale M naval fighter squadron is scheduled to form in 1998.

Trainers and Transports

Trainer and transport aircraft have important civilian roles, but in this section only military examples are considered. To some extent all the earliest aeroplanes were trainers, and often the designer was also the builder who taught himself to manage the machine. Many aspects of flight, especially the stall and spin, remained worrying enigmas, and until well into World

The docile Avro 504K trainer helped to instill the basics in fledgeling RAF pilots during the inter-war years.

The North American T-6 served for nearly 60 years and is surely the greatest trainer of them all.

Seen here in pre-war US Army Air Corps colours, the PT-17 Stearman was a large, solid aeroplane that inspired confidence.

The Silver Star was Canadair's licence-built version of the Lockheed T-33 or 'T-bird', the best-selling Western jet trainer.

De Havilland's D.H.82A Tiger Moths continued to torment tyros at RAF Elementary Flying Schools in the early 1950s.

War I there was no formal system of training at all. The pupil simply flew with a qualified pilot and watched the latter's actions. The instructor was often a front-line pilot who had been wounded or for some other reason was not on operations. To a considerable degree the training was decided by whether or not the pupil was killed. If he survived, he was sent into action. At many schools the casualty rate exceeded 30 per cent.

It was one of the wounded RFC pilots who, appaled at the way instruction was done, told the RFC leader General Hugh Trenchard. The latter replied: 'Go and do something about it'. The result was a completely systematic syllabus of instruction together with properly run schools and specially designed trainer aircraft. From 1917 until well into the 1930s the most numerous RAF trainer was the Avro 504, a trim and safe biplane made in prodigious quantities (exceeding 10,000), seating the instructor behind the pupil with a speaking tube intercom consisting of a simple pipe system with mouthpieces and earphones. Trainers were almost all biplanes until World War II. Even then, biplanes dominated the primary phase, but the mass-produced (10,346) Boeing Kaydet was exceptionally large and powerful. The Soviet Union's Po-2 biplane, dating from 1926, was built in enormous numbers and, despite having a small engine, was used for front-line tactical harassment and attack missions. The Luftwaffe soon did the same, using more than 6,000 primary trainer biplanes in action on the Eastern front. These aircraft were armed with various machine guns, light bombs and rockets, and operated on wheels, skis and floats.

There had, since World War I, been various advanced trainers which were often dual-control versions of oper-

The MiG-15UTI provided ideal preparation for the front-line jet fighters operated by Soviet, Eastern Bloc and Third World air forces, like Pakistan.

ational types. In the mid-1930s specially designed monoplanes came into the picture, and by 1945 more than 20,000 examples had been produced of the North American AT-6 (later T-6) Texan, called Harvard by the British. Powered by a 550hp engine, this all-metal stressed-skin monoplane was ideal for all forms of advanced instruction including aerobatics, gunnery, simple bombing and navigation, and the type remained in service with the South African Air Force until 1995.

After World War II Britain toyed with three-seat trainers, and for a time used Harvards as *ab initio* machines, subsequently using an all-jet sequence such as the Jet Provost followed by the nimble Gnat T.1, the latter aircraft being forever associated with Red Arrows formation aerobatic team. In common with most air forces, the USAF continues to use light-planes, namely the British-built Slingsby T-3A Firefly, to weed out at an early stage pupils lacking natural aptitude. Then instruction proceeds on the Cessna T-37 twinjet or 'Tweet', with side-by-side seating, before going on to the tandem-seat Northrop T-38 Talon, the only purpose-designed trainer with supersonic performance. Almost all modern trainers have the instructor seated behind the pupil. Such machines as the Hawk, Alpha Jet, Macchi 339, CASA C.101 Aviojet, and L-39 Albatros have sufficient power to fulfil a secondary role as light attack or reconnaissance aircraft.

By the late 1970s, the high cost of pilot training was beginning to bite into defence budgets. The US Navy was one of the first to recognize the potential of tandem-seat, single-engined, turboprop trainers, which offer jet-like handling with relatively low purchase and operating costs. Types such as the Beech T-34C Turbo Mentor and Pilatus PC-7 are modified versions of piston-engined aircraft. In contrast, the Embraer Tucano was designed as a turboprop trainer from scratch and has a raised rear seat. After initial screening on the Firefly, the RAF currently uses the Tucano-Hawk sequence. Other Hawk customers such as Saudi Arabia have chosen the latest PC-9 turboprop for the initial part of the main training syllabus, while

the US Navy uses the Turbo Mentor and its own carrier-capable Hawk, the T-45. The USAF has followed the fashion for turboprops, selecting the Beech Mk II (a modified PC-9 with a pressurized cockpit and ejection seats) to replace its T-37s, which have been in service since 1955. The Beech Mk II will also supersede the USN's Turbo Mentor as part of the Joint Primary Aircrew Training System (JPATS) programme. At the other end of the training spectrum, the USAF is making its 30-year-old T-38s more representative of current front-line fighters by installing head-up displays, multi-function head-down displays and GPS.

Until well into the 1920s there were hardly any military transport aircraft, and those that did exist were converted bombers used for opening up pioneer air routes or conveying statesmen to peace conferences. One of the earliest purpose-designed transports was the RAF's Vernon, of 1922, which led to the Victoria and Valentia, each seating about 17 equipped troops and not only flying every kind of transport mission in distant outposts of empire but on occasion even dropping bombs. As early as 1923 American Air Service pilots had managed to refuel each other in flight, but this way of extending range or endurance did not become an operational method until after World War II (except for civil flights by Imperial Airways in 1939). Few flight refuelling experiments took place outside Britain and the United States.

The most numerous transport of World War II was the C-47 Skytrain, a version of the Douglas DC-3 airliner, but in the post-war years military transport made great strides. Via the C-74 Douglas created the C-124 Globemaster with seating for up to 200 troops and with great clamshell nose doors. Douglas later built a much

The most successful British military aircraft of recent times, the Hawk trainer/attack aircraft is thought of as a 'pilot's plane'.

The Cessna T-37 was one of the world's first basic jet trainers, but its unpressurized cockpit and dated instrumentation are now a liability.

The tandem cockpit of the Short Tucano turboprop trainer is closely modelled on that of the Hawk, the next stage for RAF fast jet pilots.

The Curtiss C-46 Commando was considerably larger than the C-47, and will always be associated with the 'Hump' supply missions from India into China in 1942-45.

US paratroops march out to their C-47 Skytrain, the aircraft that created the legend of the DC-3, its civil equivalent.

The Lockheed C-130 Hercules, the leading military transport for over 40 years, is still in operation all over the world, the latest version being the C-130J with new avionics, engines and propellers.

more powerful aircraft, the C-133 Cargomaster with four 6,000hp turboprops, a pressurized interior and full-section rear doors and ramp, which in the early 1960s was kept busy carrying the new breed of intercontinental missiles. But before this aircraft appeared Lockheed had produced the C-130 Hercules, and for over 40 years this has been the leading military transport, sold to almost all major non-Communist nations and still in production. Powered by four Allison T56 engines, the C-130 has been continually improved and updated. Its design introduced all the desirable features which had never before been united in one aircraft: pressurization, high-speed turbine propulsion, unobstructed cargo hold with low level floor, soft-field landing gears, full-section rear doors and ramp for ground or air unloading, flight refuelling, all-weather equipment and size matched to 92 troops or 23,133kg (51,000lb) cargo. By 1995 more than 2,000 Hercules had been delivered. In the same year the RAF became the first customer for the latest C-130J, which features new Allison turboprops, advanced propellers and a new electronic two-crew flight deck. During the programme the same factory also delivered 285 considerably larger C-141A StarLifters, with turbofan engines, and 81 gigantic C-5A Galaxies. Powered by the first 'wide-body' turbofans, four Pratt & Whitney TF39s, the Galaxy carries up to 120 tonnes (265,000lb) of cargo including almost every kind of US Army vehicle from Jeeps to the M1 main battle tank. The USAF later took delivery of 50 C-5Bs, which have a much stronger wing and incorporate many detail improvements. At the 1985 Paris airshow Antonov revealed the even bigger An-124, which has a maximum payload of 150 tonnes (330,693lb) and a maximum take-off weight of 405 tonnes (892,872lb).

In the late 1940s the need of USAF Strategic Air Command to fly unprecedented global missions led to the development of a production system of flight refuelling, and the construction of a mighty fleet of tankers. The selected system was the Boeing Flying Boom, in which the receiver aircraft flies below and behind the tanker, at very close range, and a 'boomer' crewman in the tanker 'flies' an extensible boom (a pipe with flight controls for aiming its direction) into a receptacle on the receiver. The first tanker was the Boeing KC-97, a version of the civil Stratocruiser, of which 888 were delivered to SAC, some later being fitted with booster jet pods. In 1957 production deliveries began of the much larger and more capable KC-135, a smaller version of the civil 707, of which 792 were delivered at a very high rate. Later versions of the KC-135 family had the original J57 turbojets replaced by more powerful and more efficient TF33 turbofans, the ultimate tanker/trans-

Using its kneeling landing gear and nose vizor, this C-5B Galaxy is disgorging a UH-60A helicopter. Provided its wings were loaded separately, the C-47 taking off in the background would fit inside the C-5 with room to spare.

port version being the KC-135R with CFM56s turbofans. The USAF also operates 59 KC-10A Extender tanker/transports based on the DC-10-30CF. Flown by Air Combat Command, the Extender is equipped for both flying boom and probe and drogue refuelling.

Boeing also delivered a diverse array of other military versions of the 707, some of them configured for flight refuelling by the British probe and drogue method in which the tanker merely trails a long hose with a conical drogue on the end into which the receiver thrusts a probe connected to its fuel-system. The latest military 707 is the US Army/USAF E-8C Joint-Surveillance Target and Attack Radar System (J-STARS), a flying battlefield management centre

The Antonov An-124 is bigger than its US counterpart, the C-5, and is able to carry heavier loads from shorter airfields.

equipped with an advanced side-looking radar under the fuselage. All J-STARS aircraft are refurbished commercial 707s, of which there is a plentiful supply. Similarly, a pair of ex-American Airlines 707s have been converted into EC-18D cruise missile control aircraft. Since 1960 large numbers of the C-135 family have been rebuilt into special-purpose aircraft concerned with electronic intelligence, spaceflight, strategic command and control, and many other tasks.

Today the most powerful aircraft in any air force are the E-4B airborne command posts of the USAF, based on the 747-200B airframe, in which a crew of about 60 would form the seat of government of the United

As well as providing in-flight refuelling, this KC-10 Extender can simultaneously carry all the equipment and spares needed to support the long-range deployment of these F-16s.

States in time of crisis. Two specially-equipped 747-200Bs are stationed at Andrews Air Force Base, Washington DC, for use as Presidential transports under the designation VC-25A.

COMMERCIAL AIRCRAFT

The development of the aircraft to safely carry passengers in significant numbers has been one of the great success stories in the history of aviation – so much so that today, people take air travel for granted, a situation unimaginable just a century ago.

3

In the first decade of this century, on 16 November 1909, the world's first airline was founded. This was Deutsche Luftschiffahrts AG, generally known as Delag, with headquarters at Frankfurt-am-Main, Germany, and its purpose was to operate passenger flights with Zeppelin airships and to train Zeppelin crews. On 19 June 1910, Count Ferdinand von Zeppelin's seventh airship, the 147.97m (485ft 6in) long LZ7 *Deutschland* made its first flight. It had been ordered by Delag and, although short-lived, was the first powered aircraft to carry passengers.

Delag had plans for a system of Zeppelin-operated air services, built a number of airship stations with sheds, and even published maps of the routes, but activities were limited to voyages from and between these stations and no scheduled services were operated. By the time World War I began Delag had operated seven passenger Zeppelins, made 1,588 flights covering 172,535km (107,211 miles) and carried 33,722 passengers and crew without injury.

It was on the other side of the Atlantic, in Florida, that the only pre-World War I scheduled air services were operated. On 4 December 1913, the St Petersburg-Tampa Airboat Line was established, and at 10.00 on New Year's Day 1914 a single-engined 75hp Benoist biplane flying boat, piloted by Tony Jannus, left St Petersburg for the crossing of Tampa Bay and alighted at Tampa 23 minutes later to complete the world's first scheduled airline service. The city of St Petersburg subsidized the service, and demand made necessary the use of a second flying boat.

The next important step was taken in Britain, when the fledgling Royal Air Force set up a Communication Wing to provide fast transport, mainly between London and Paris, for members of the Government and other officials attending the Peace Conference. Using mostly D.H.4s, 4As and, later, Handley Page O/400 twin-engined bombers, regular London-Paris services began on 10 January 1919. This was the start of cross-Channel air services, and it is claimed that the modified O/400 *Silver Star* carried the first non-military cross-Channel passengers and also made the first passenger night flight across the Channel.

Great Britain

Aircraft Transport and Travel (AT and T), although founded in 1916, had to wait for the return of peace and for government permission before it could begin commercial operations. However, all was eventually ready, and a civil Customs airport was established at Hounslow, near the present London Airport at Heathrow, for the start of scheduled services on 25 August 1919. At 12.40 a de Havilland 16 took off with four passengers on the first scheduled London-Paris service. On that same morning at 09.05, an AT and T D.H.4A had left Hounslow for Paris with one passenger and some goods; this flight has often been reported incorrectly as the inaugural service.

A second British airline, Handley Page Transport, was formed on 14 June that year, and on 25 August one of the company's O/400s flew from London to Paris with journalists. Regular Paris services did not begin until 2 September, when Lt-Col W. Sholto Douglas (later Lord Douglas of Kirtleside) flew an O/7 from Cricklewood to Le Bourget. Handley Page also opened a London-Brussels service on 23 September 1919, and a London-Amsterdam service on 6 July 1920, although AT and T had already begun a London-Amsterdam service on 17 May with the Dutch KLM.

British companies soon found themselves competing with each other and with subsizied continental companies for very limited traffic. On 28 February 1921, all British air services were temporarily halted due to lack of finance. The government decided to set up a national airline – Imperial Airways – on 31 March 1924, with £1 million capital and a guaranteed subsidy of £1 million spread over ten years. Imperial took over the fleets and operations of A T and T, Handley Page Transport, the Daimler Airway and The Instone Airline for the opening of services on 26 April.

Most of the aircraft used by the pioneer British airlines were of two families: Airco and Handley Page. AT and T, having close associations with Airco, chose de Havilland designs. The RAF Communication Squadrons had used single-engined D.H.4 two-seat bombers, and some of these were converted to D.H.4As with two passenger seats over which there was a hinged cover with windows. AT and T had four of these aircraft and eight D.H.16s, which were four-passenger adaptations of the D.H.9 bomber design. Both types were of wooden construction, powered by Rolls-Royce Eagle engines, and cruised at about 160km/h (100mph).

Following the D.H.4A and D.H.16, de Havilland designed the purely civil D.H.18, with 450hp Napier Lion engine and eight seats. This type appeared in 1920 and was used by AT and T and Instone. A much improved development was the Lion-powered eight-passenger D.H.34 which first flew on 26 March 1922, and went into service with Daimler Airway on 2 April! It also served with Instone and one was exported to Russia.

The RAF Communication Squadrons had used the large Handley Page O/400 with two Eagle engines. A few had passenger cabins in place of the bomb cells, while others only had the military equipment removed and seats installed. Handley Page Transport used O/400s, with austere cabins, but developed a number of sub-types with improved accommodation. These included the O/7, O/10 and the O/11 freighter. In all of these aircraft two passengers could be carried in the open nose cockpit. The cruising speed was about 112km/h (70mph) and passenger accommodation was 14 in the O/7, 12 in the O/10 and 5 in the cargo O/11.

Based on the O/400 series, Handley Page designed and built the W.8 with reduced wing span, better passenger accommodation and a single fin and rudder in place of the O/400's box-like structure. The sole W.8, with 12 to 14 seats and Lion engines, first flew on 4 December 1919, saw limited service with Handley Page Transport and was followed in 1922 by three 12/14-seat Eagle-powered W.8bs.

On 30 April 1920, Instone took delivery of an aeroplane that was destined to become the best known of all in those pioneering days. It was the Vickers Vimy Commercial named *City of London*. This was practically the same as the modified Vimy bombers which in 1919 made the first non-stop transatlantic flight and the first England-Australia flight, but incorporated a new fuselage having seats for as many as ten fare-paying passengers.

British Marine Air Navigation, for its cross-Channel services, used three wooden Supermarine Sea Eagle amphibian flying boats. These had a Lion or Eagle engine with pusher propeller and a small six-seat cabin in the bows.

The first airline passengers flew in converted bombers until new designs became available. Using D.H.4As, S.Instone & Co. began a public London-Paris service on 18 February 1920.

France

France quickly set about the development of air services after the war, formed a number of airlines and made plans for trunk routes to South America and the Far East. On 8 February 1919, a Farman Goliath flew from Paris to Kenley, near London, with 11 military passengers. It is often claimed that this was the start of French cross-Channel services, but, although this is untrue, France did open the first regular scheduled international passenger service as early as 22 March 1919, when Farman began a weekly Paris-Brussels service.

Early in 1919 an association of French aircraft manufacturers established Compagnie des Messageries Aériennes (CMA), and this airline developed a system of air services beginning with a daily link between Paris and Lille from 1 May. Breguet 14 single-engined biplanes were used and it was this type with which CMA began Paris-London services on 16 September, later working in pool with Handley Page Transport. Compagnie des Grands Express Aériens was also founded in 1919, but did not begin operations until the following year, starting a Paris-London service with Farman Goliaths on 29 March.

The network of French air routes rapidly expanded and services were begun between France and Corsica and France and North Africa. But the great French dream was an air service to South America, and Pierre Latécoère, the aircraft manufacturer, set about its achievement. The route through Spain to West Africa was opened in stages for the carriage of mail and operated as far as Casablanca by April 1920. Services were initially worked under the title Lignes Aériennes Latécoère, but in April 1921 the name was changed to Cie Generale d'Entreprises Aéronautiques, to be succeeded by Cie Générale Aéropostale in 1927. Operating under severe climatic conditions and crossing stretches of desert where a forced landing could mean death or torture for the crew at the hands of hostile tribesmen, the line was pushed forward through Agadir, Cap Juby, Villa Cisneros, Port Étienne and St Louis to Dakar, the full route to West Africa being opened in June 1925.

French airlines were also looking towards the Orient, and the first step was the founding, on 23 April 1920, of Cie Franco-Roumaine de Navigation Aérienne. This airline opened the first sector of its eastward route, from Paris to Strasbourg, on 20 September 1920. Prague was reached in that October and Warsaw in the following summer. In May 1922 the Paris-Strasbourg-Prague-Vienna-Budapest route was opened, Bucharest was reached in September, and by 3 October the entire route was open to Constantinople (now Istanbul). This route across Europe involved flying in mountainous terrain and through some of the continent's worst weather, and therefore represented a great achievement. Up to 1923 all flights were made with single-engined aircraft and confined to daylight, but in that year three-engined Caudron C.61s were introduced and night flying was pioneered with the first such service between Strasbourg and Paris on 2 September 1923, and between Bucharest and Belgrade on 20 September. On the first day of 1925 the company's name was changed to CIDNA, and by the end of

In the 1920s, air travel was noisy, draughty and often dangerous but had an elegance all of its own. The Farman F.60 Goliath carried 12 passengers at up to 120km/h (75mph).

1927 the line was operating no less than 76 aircraft.

Night flying was also pioneered on the Paris-London route in June 1922 when Grands Express made a return night flight with a Goliath, but it was not until April 1929 that regular night services were flown over the route – by Air Union, which in 1923 had been created by the merger of CMA and Grands Express.

The numerous French pioneer airlines employed a very wide range of aircraft. Wartime Salmson 2-A.2 and Breguet 14 single-engined reconnaissance and bomber biplanes were used in large numbers, Latécoère employing well over 100 of the latter on the route to West Africa.

Franco-Roumaine used Salmsons and some single-engined Potez biplanes before acquiring a fleet of Blériot Spad cabin biplanes. The first of these was the Spad 33 of 1920, and it was developed into a whole family of similar aircraft with seats for four to six passengers and a variety of engines including, in later models, the air-cooled Jupiter. More than 100 of these attractive little biplanes were built, and some could cruise at 170km/h (106mph).

Widely used by the Farman Line, CMA, Grands Express and some non-French airlines, was the Farman Goliath. This was designed as a twin-engined bomber but converted to have two passenger cabins with seats for up to 12 passengers. The wing span was 26.5m (86ft 10in), most had two 260hp Salmson water-cooled radial engines, and the cruising speed was about 120km/h (75mph).

Germany

Germany also made an early start in establishing regular services. Numerous companies began operating, but the two most important were Deutsche Luft-Reederei (DLR) and Deutscher Aero Lloyd. DLR began Europe's first sustained regular civil daily passenger services when it opened the Berlin-Weimar route on 5 February 1919. The operation grew rapidly and employed a large fleet of ex-military single-engined biplanes, mostly the L.V.G. C VI, with room for two passengers in the open rear cockpit, but there were also considerable numbers of A.E.G. J IIs and some twin-engined A.E.G. G Vs and Friedrichshafen G IIIas.

Junkers began flying a Dessau-Weimar service in March 1919 with a modified J 10 two-seat attack aircraft. This was a low-wing cantilever monoplane of all-metal construction with corrugated metal skin, and is almost certainly the first all-metal aeroplane to have operated an air service. In 1921 Junkers set up Junkers-Luftverkehr to operate air services and promote its F 13 cabin monoplane. The F 13 was the first all-metal aeroplane designed and built as a transport, having an enclosed cabin for four passengers, making its first flight on 25 June 1919. More than 300 were built,.

In January 1926 Deutsche Luft Hansa was created by the merging of Aero Lloyd and Junkers-Luftverkehr and operations began on 6 April. Thereafter Luft Hansa (written as one word from the beginning of 1934) was the German national airline, but a number of small airlines continued to exist.

Although short-lived, there was one German airline operation which must be mentioned. This was the postwar revival of Delag, with ambitious plans for airship services within Germany and on international routes, and two new Zeppelins, the LZ 120 *Bodensee* (Lake Constance) and LZ 121 *Nordstern* (North Star) were built. The *Bodensee* flew on 20 August 1919, and, with accommodation for 21 to 27 passengers, began working a Friedrichshafen-Berlin service on 24 August, flying in opposite directions on alternate days. *Bodensee* flew until December, made 103 flights (including one from Berlin to Stockholm) and carried 2,253 revenue passengers, but the Inter-Allied Control Commission would not allow the service to restart in 1920.

Numerous other European countries began air transport operations. In Belgium SNETA did pioneering work leading to the formation of Sabena in 1923. KLM Royal Dutch Airlines was founded in October 1919. Although it did not initially operate its own services, KLM was to play a major part in developing world air transport and still operates under its original title. DDL – Danish Air Lines – was another very early European airline, beginning a Copenhagen-Warnemünde seaplane service on 7 August 1920. Today DDL is a constituent of SAS – Scandinavian Airlines System.

The Junkers F 13 was an extremely advanced aeroplane for 1921 but had no cabin heating – passengers were given blankets to keep warm.

United States Concentrates on the Mail

The first stage in opening up US nationwide airmail services was the start on 15 May 1918 of a mail service linking Washington, Philadelphia and New York, using Curtiss JN-4 biplanes flown by Army pilots.

The Post Office took over the US Aerial Mail Service on 12 August 1918. Specially built Standard JR-1B mailplanes were introduced and by the end of the year the service had achieved an average 91 per cent regularity. The Washington-New York mail service was closed down at the end of May 1921, by which time the entire transcontinental mail service was in being.

Late in 1918 the Post Office acquired a large number of war-surplus aircraft, including more than 100 US-built DH-4Bs with 400hp Liberty engines. This fleet made it possible to start establishing the coast-to-coast service and on 15 May 1919, the Chicago-Cleveland sector was opened, saving 16hr on the Chicago-New York journey. On 1 July the New York-Cleveland sector was opened, with through New York-Chicago flights from September, and the San Francisco-Sacramento section was opened on 31 July. On 15 May 1920, the mail route was opened from Chicago to Omaha via Iowa City and Des Moines, and the full route came into operation on 8 September with the opening of the Sacramento-Salt Lake City and Salt Lake City-Omaha stages. Branch lines were also opened between Chicago and St Louis and Chicago and the twin cities Minneapolis/St Paul.

To save time it was decided to make experimental flights in each direction, with night flying over some stages. On 22 February 1921, two aircraft took off from each end of the route and so began a saga that is now part of American history. One of the eastbound aircraft crashed in Nevada, killing the pilot, and only one of the west-bound aircraft managed to reach Chicago because of extremely bad weather, and at that point the flight was abandoned. The surviving eastbound mail was taken over at Salt Lake City by Frank Yeager, who flew through the night to Cheyenne and North Platte, where he handed over to Jack Knight for the flight to Omaha. Because of the termination of the westbound flight there wasn't an aircraft at Omaha, and Knight secured a place in history by flying on to Chicago. Ernest Allison flew the last stage to New York, and the total coast-to-coast time was 33hr 20min.

In 1922 a start was made on lighting the mail route. The aerodromes were equipped with beacons, boundary and obstruction lights and landing-area floodlights. At the regular stops there were revolving beacons of 500,000 candle-power, and at emergency landing grounds 50,000 candle-power beacons. Flashing gas beacons were installed every three miles along the route, and by the end of 1925 the entire 3,860km (2,400 miles) of route had been lit at a cost of some $550,000.

During 1926/27 the Post Office Department turned over its airmail services to private contractors. When the Post Office's own operations ceased it had flown more than 22 million kilometres (133 million miles) with 93 per cent regularity and carried more than 300 million letters; but there had been 4,437 forced landings due to weather and 2,095 because of mechanical trouble. Worse still, there had been 200 crashes with 32 pilots killed, 11 other fatalities and 37 seriously injured.

Aerodynamically clean and efficent, the Boeing Model 40A flew the US Mail between Chicago and San Francisco with Boeing Air Transport Inc.

Consolidation of Air Travel in Europe

In Europe the pioneer years of air transport continued through the 1920s and, according to definition, into the 1930s. For most of this time many routes were operated only in the summer, and night services were only gradually introduced. There was steady development of aircraft, particularly in Germany and the Netherlands, and the air-cooled engine largely replaced the water-cooled engine, with its attendant plumbing problems and heavy radiators. Radio came into increasing use, airport lighting was developed, and Germany, in particular, devoted attention to developing ways of navigating and landing in bad weather.

Although Imperial Airways operated a very small European route system, it did improve its fleet, at first with developments of the early Handley Pages but from 1926 with a small number of three-engined Armstrong Whitworth Argosy 18/20-seat biplanes. Unlike their British predecessors, these had metal structures although they still employed fabric covering.

A much greater improvement in standards came in 1931 when Imperial Airways began using a fleet of Handley Page H.P.42 Hannibal and H.P.45 Heracles biplanes. These were large four-engined aircraft with Jupiter engines, 38 seats on European services and 16 to 24 on the Egypt-India and Egypt-Central Africa routes. On Heracles two stewards were carried and full meals were served, and during peacetime this fleet operated with perfect safety. The only problem was their low speed of around 160km/h (100mph). The Handley Pages remained in operation until World War II although some smaller and faster aircraft had been added to the fleet by this time, including the beautiful de Havilland Albatross monoplanes, known as the Frobisher class by Imperial Airways, which cruised at 338km/h (210mph).

In 1937 a second British operator, British Airways, began using fast Lockheed Electras on European services and later added Lockheed 14s. They flew to Germany, Poland and Scandinavia as well as Paris and, in terms of speed, Imperial Airways was shown in a bad light. It was finally agreed to amalgamate the two airlines and BOAC – British Overseas Airways Corporation – resulted.

The sleek Lockheed Model 14 was state-of-the-art in the mid-1930s, with Fowler flaps, two-speed superchargers and fully-feathering propellers. It could sustain 306km/h (190mph).

France continued the expansion of its air routes and used a wide variety of indigenous aircraft, mostly biplanes, including the single-engined Breguet 280T and twin-engined Lioré et Olivier 21. But CIDNA had introduced the three-engined low-wing Wibault 280T monoplane on its Paris-Istanbul route and Air Union had at least two on the London-Paris route before Air France was formed in 1933 as the successor to these airlines and Aéropostale, Air Orient and the Farman Line. The new organization introduced a further wide range of types including the twin-engined Potez 62 and Bloch 220 and the three-engined Dewoitine series.

Sabena expanded its routes with Fokker F.VIIb-3ms, and later introduced three-engined Savoia-Marchetti monoplanes. KLM used a whole series of Fokker monoplanes for its European passenger and cargo network, including the four-engined F.XXII and F.XXXVI which appeared in 1934 and 1935 respectively. But the Fokkers, with their wooden wings and welded steel-frame fuselages and, except in one case, non-retractable undercarriages, were outmoded by the Douglas DC-2 and DC-3, and KLM became the first European operator of these advanced aeroplanes.

It was the German airline Lufthansa which dominated the air transport map of Europe. When the airline was founded it took over 162 aircraft of 19 different types. The largest batches of standard, or reasonably standard, aeroplanes were 46 Junkers F 13s, 19 Fokker-Grulich F.IIs and 13 F.IIIs. There were also numbers of Dornier Komets, and it was one of these that operated the airline's first service. Three-engined Junkers G 24s were used for the first night service on 1 May 1926, and three-engined Rohrbach Rolands pioneered trans-Alpine services from 1928.

Lufthansa expanded rapidly and in its third year had a European network of more than 33,000km (20,500 miles) over which it flew 10 million kilometres (6,214,000 miles) and carried 85,833 passengers and 1,300 tons of cargo, mail and baggage. The airline had the biggest domestic network of services in Europe, and also served most of the continent's main cities.

In 1932 Lufthansa began operation of a very famous aeroplane, the Junkers Ju 52/3m. This was a three-engined low-wing monoplane with accommodation for 17 passengers, was of all-metal construction with corrugated skin and, although not particularly fast, was extremely reliable. Lufthansa was to use about 230 with a maximum of 78 at any one time. The Ju 52/3m was widely used as a civil and military

A Handley Page H.P.42 of Imperial Airways takes on passengers at Croydon Airport. The passage to India took six and a half days.

The record-breaking Fokker F.VIIB/3m trimotor made a huge contribution to long-distance airline operations. This KLM example operated between Holland and Java.

transport; nearly 5,000 were built, and most prewar European airlines used them at some time – two on floats continued to find employment in Norway until 1956.

Lufthansa also introduced a number of limited-capacity high-speed aircraft including the four-passenger single-engined Heinkel He 70, commissioned on *Blitz* (Lightning or Express) services in Germany in June 1934, and the twin-engined ten-passenger He 111 which had a smoking cabin and began service in 1936. The four-engined 40-passenger Junkers Ju 90 and 25/26-passenger Focke-Wulf Fw 200 Condor were prevented by war from showing their full potential.

Almost every European country operated its own air services. A number of small Swiss companies were founded and at the end of 1919 one of these was renamed Ad Astra Aero. Initially it operated a number of small flying boats from the Swiss lakes, but did not begin regular scheduled operations until June 1922 when it began Geneva-Zurich-Nuremberg services with Junkers F 13s. This airline expanded its operations, mostly with Junkers aircraft, and, in 1931, amalgamated with Balair to form Swissair. Balair had begun services in 1926 and was equipped with Fokkers.

Since its inception Swissair has been one of Europe's most technically progressive airlines, has introduced a range of advanced aircraft and was among the first to adopt such types as the DC-2 and DC-3. It was Swissair's introduction of the Lockheed Orion monoplane with retractable undercarriage in May 1932 that led Germany to produce the high-performance Heinkel He 70 and Junkers Ju 60 and Ju 160.

Scandinavian air transport differed from that in other parts of Europe because of terrain and the difficulty of providing aerodromes. DDL, formed in Denmark in 1918, began operation with a seaplane, but otherwise was able to develop its routes with landplanes; Sweden and Norway, however, had to rely mainly on seaplanes.

AB Aerotransport – Swedish Air Lines – began services in June 1924 between Stockholm and Helsinki using Junkers F 13 floatplanes. As traffic grew a three-engined Junkers G 24 was added and in August 1932 a Ju 52/3m floatplane – almost certainly the first regular airline operations of the Ju 52/3m, even before Lufthansa. Lack of a land aerodrome at Stockholm forced seaplane operation to continue until May 1936, when Bromma Airport was opened. However, ABA had

established services to Denmark, Germany, Amsterdam and London from the airport at Malmo on the west coast. ABA was an early operator of DC-3s, acquiring three in 1937. Like Swissair, ABA was a technically advanced airline, as its fleet composition shows, and it also opened the first experimental night mail service in Europe when, on the night of 18/19 June 1928, an F 13 with onboard sorting facilities flew from a military aerodrome near Stockholm to London in four stages via Malmo, Hamburg and Amsterdam.

Top: Safe and robust, the Junkers Ju 52/3m was Europe's leading airliner in the 1930s. This 'Tante Ju' (Aunt Ju) served with Danish Air Lines.

Above: Danish Air Lines also operated the Focke-Wulf Fw 200 Condor, which first flew in 1937. It demonstrated its huge potential by flying from Berlin to New York non-stop in 1938.

Marine Aircraft in Europe

Much use of marine aircraft was made in Europe in the pioneer years of air transport. There was an erroneous belief that seaplanes and flying boats offered greater security on overwater crossings. Britain used flying boats on the trans-Mediterranean section of the Empire routes. France and Italy, with many Mediterranean and Adriatic routes, were Europe's biggest users of commercial seaplanes and flying boats, although Germany used such aircraft on coastal resort services and in the Baltic.

When the England-India route was opened in 1929, Imperial Airways used Short Calcutta flying boats on the trans-Mediterranean section. They were 12-passenger metal-hulled biplanes with three 540hp Bristol Jupiter engines, and the first example flew in February 1928. The Calcutta was followed by the Short Kent, of similar configuration but with four 555hp Jupiter engines and improved accommodation for 16 passengers. There were only three Kents, comprising the Scipio class, and entered service in May 1931.

In July 1936 Short Brothers launched the *Canopus*, the first of the S.23 C-class flying boats. These had been designed for the Empire Air Mail Programme and were very advanced high-wing all-metal monoplanes powered by four 920hp Bristol Pegasus engines, had accommodation for 16 to 24 passengers and a top speed of just on 320km/h (200mph). *Canopus* made the first scheduled flight of the type, from Alexandria to Brindisi on 30 October 1936. Eventually the S.23-Cs worked the entire routes between Southampton and Sydney and Southampton and Durban, and some remained in service until after World War II.

Sandringham and Solent developments of the C-class operated some of BOAC's postwar routes, and the last British flying boat services were those operated by Aquila Airways' Solents to Madeira until the end of September 1958.

Flying at about her maximum ceiling of 500m (1,640ft), the giant 12-engined Dornier Do X flying boat cruises over the Rhine en route for Amsterdam on the first stage of her ten-month journey from Lake Constance to New York in 1931.

The Do X was the largest aircraft in the world in its day and once took off with 169 people aboard – including nine stowaways. Three decks contained a bar, smoking/writing rooms, a bathroom, a lounge, sleeping quarters, and a kitchen and dining room.

The German resort services were mostly flown by small seaplanes and the Baltic services by Dornier Wals. The first Dornier Wal flew in November 1922 and, because of Allied restrictions on German aircraft production, most early Wals were built in Italy and Italian airlines employed them in considerable numbers. The Wal was an all-metal monoplane with the wing strut mounted above the hull and braced to the stabilizing sponsons, or sea wings. Two engines were mounted back to back on top of the wing, and the passengers occupied a cabin in the forward part of the hull. There were many versions of the Wal, with different engines, weights, performance and accommodation, but the early examples had seats for eight to ten passengers and were usually powered by Rolls-Royce Eagle or Hispano-Suiza engines. SANA was the biggest operator of passenger Wals, and put them into service in April 1926 on a Genoa-Rome-Naples-Palermo service.

There were three major flying boat constructors in Italy – Cant, Macchi and Savoia-Marchetti. The Cants were biplanes, mostly of wooden construction and SISA used the single-engined four-passenger Cant 10ter on its Trieste-Venice-Pavia-Turin service, which opened in April 1926, and on its Adriatic services. To supplement them SISA had a fleet of three-engined ten-passenger Cant 22s. Aero Espresso used a twin-engined eight-passenger Macchi M.24bis biplane flying boat on its Brindisi-Athens-Istanbul service.

Although the biplane served well into the 1930s, it was the Italian monoplanes that proved of most interest. In 1924 Savoia built a twin-hulled monoplane torpedo-bomber to the design of Alessandro Marchetti, and from this developed a passenger aircraft for Aero Espresso's then planned Brindisi-Istanbul service. This was the S.55C with thick-section 24m (78ft 9in) span wooden wing, accommodation for four or five passengers in each hull, triple rudders and two tandem-mounted 400/450hp Isotta-Fraschini engines. These aircraft went into service in 1926 and were followed in 1928 by the more powerful S.55P version, of which SAM had 14 or 15 on trans-Mediterranean services.

Developed from the S.55 was the S.66 of 1932 with a wingspan of 33m (108ft), three 550 or 750hp Fiat engines mounted side by side, and the twin hulls could accommodate up to 18 passengers. It is believed that 24 were built. They were operated by Aero Espresso, SAM and SANA, and some passed to Ala Littoria, working services between Italy and Tunis, Tripoli and Haifa. A number survived to be taken over for war service.

As early as 1923 L'Aéronavale started using twin-engined four-passenger Lioré et Olivier 13 wooden flying boats between Antibes and Ajaccio, and in May that year a Latécoère affiliate opened a Marseilles-Algiers service with them. More than 30 were built. Also in 1923, CAMS had begun production of a series of civil and military flying boats designed by Maurice Hurel. One of them was the wooden CAMS 53 biplane with two tandem 500hp Hispano-Suiza engines and a small cabin for four passengers. It was introduced by Aéropostale on the Marseilles-Algiers route in October 1928. The biggest French biplane flying boat to enter passenger service was the 35.06m (115ft) span Breguet 530 Saigon, with three 785hp Hispano-Suiza engines, three-class accommodation for 19 to 20 passengers and a maximum weight of 15,000kg (33,069lb).

As a replacement for its CAMS 53s, Air Union had also ordered a fleet of four-engined 10 to 15 passenger Lioré et Olivier H 242 monoplane flying boats. These had their 350hp Gnome Rhone Titan Major engines in tandem pairs above the wing, and 14 went into service with Air France at the beginning of 1934.

The last trans-Mediterranean flying boat services of Air France were those operated to Algiers immediately after the war by two Lioré et Olivier H 246 four-engined 24 to 26 passenger monoplanes.

Its outer engines running to maintain station on the mooring buoy, *Canopus* was one of the great Short C-class or 'Empire Boats' introduced by Imperial Airways in 1937.

The Dornier Wal's epic flights across the North and South Atlantic included the first east-west crossing by a flying boat in August 1930.

Mail and Passenger Services in the USA

On 1 March 1925, Ryan Airlines opened its Los Angeles-San Diego Air Line with modified Standard biplanes and a Douglas Cloudster, and this is claimed to have been the first regular passenger service wholly over the US mainland to be maintained throughout the year.

The first major legislative step in creating an airline industry was the passing of the Contract Air Mail Act (known as the Kelly Act) in February 1925. This provided for the transfer of mail carriage to private operators, and it was followed in May 1926 by the Air Commerce Act, which instructed the Secretary of Commerce to designate and establish airways for mail and passengers, organize air navigation and licence aircraft and pilots. This Act came into force at midnight on 31 December 1926.

The history of United States air transport over the next few years was extremely complex, with numerous airlines competing for mail contracts. Some were small concerns, but others were backed by large financial organizations and closely linked with the aircraft manufacturing industry. Here only the briefest details of this intricate picture can be given.

The first five mail contracts were let on 7 October 1925, and 12 airlines began operating the services between February 1926 and April 1927 as feeders to the transcontinental mail route which was still being operated by the Post Office.

The Ford Motor Company had begun private daily services for express parcels between Detroit and Chicago on 3 April 1925, using single-engined all-metal Ford 2-AT monoplanes. Ford secured Contract Air Mail Routes (CAM) 6 and 7 covering Detroit-Chicago and Detroit-Cleveland and was the first to operate, beginning on 15 February 1926. Passengers were carried from August that year.

Next to start was Varney Air Lines, on CAM 5, between Pasco, Washington State, and Elko, Nevada, via Boise, Idaho. Leon Cuddeback flew the first service on 6 April 1926, using one of the airline's fleet of Curtiss-powered Swallow biplanes, but the operation was immediately suspended until the Swallows could be re-engined with air-cooled Wright Whirlwinds.

Also in April 1926 Robertson Aircraft Corporation began flying the mail on CAM 2 between St Louis and Chicago, and this operation is claimed as the first step in the eventual creation of the present American Airlines. Western Air Express began working CAM 4 between Los Angeles and Salt Lake City with Douglas M-2 biplanes, and opened its first passenger service over the route on 23 May that year.

CAM 1, New York-Boston, was awarded to Colonial Air Transport, but the services did not start until June 1926 and passenger service, with Fokkers, began almost a year later in April 1927. PRT – Philadelphia Rapid Transit Service – obtained CAM 13 for Philadelphia-Washington and operated three flights a day from 6 July 1926. Whereas most of the mail carriers used passengers as a fill-up load or ignored them entirely, PRT, with its fleet of imported Fokker F VIIa-3ms, catered for passengers and used mail as a fill-up.

The prize routes were those covered by CAM 17, from New York to Chicago, and CAM 18, San Francisco to Chicago. National Air Transport (NAT), which was founded in May 1925, secured CAM 17 and began operating it with Curtiss Carrier Pigeons on 1 September 1927, having opened CAM 3, Chicago-Dallas, the previous year. NAT was not very interested in passenger traffic and soon acquired a fleet of 18 ex-Post Office Douglas mail-planes, but, later, did buy Ford Trimotors.

Boeing, however, secured the San Francisco-Chicago route and was very interested in passengers. The company built a fleet of 24 Model 40A bi-planes for the route. They were powered by 420hp Pratt & Whitney Wasp engines and could carry pilot, two pas-

Ford's foray into airliner construction was the dependable Trimotor, called the 'Tin Goose' because of its corrugated metal skin.

sengers and 545kg (1,200lb) of mail, and were superior in payload and performance to the aircraft operated by NAT and most other mail carriers. By midnight on 30 June 1927, the Boeing 40s were deployed along the route and service began the following day.

Western Air Express (WAE) had hoped to get the San Francisco-Chicago mail contract, but Boeing's tender was much lower. Instead WAE developed a Los Angeles-San Francisco passenger service with Fokkers and established a high reputation for reliability and safety.

In 1926 and 1927 two events took place which had a marked effect on the growth of air transport in the US. The first was the appearance of the Ford Trimotor, which first flew in June 1926. This was an all-metal high-wing monoplane powered by three 200/300hp Wright Whirlwind engines, and had accommodation for 10 or 11 passengers in its original 4-AT version. Later came the 5-AT with 400/450hp Pratt & Whitney Wasps and seats for 13 to 15. The other event, in May 1927, was Lindbergh's solo flight from New York to Paris and it created enormous interest in aviation.

In May 1928 Transcontinental Air Transport (TAT) was formed, and began planning a transcontinental route using Ford Trimotors on which meals could be carried, although the first air stewardesses appeared on Boeing's Model 80s in 1930. TAT came to an agreement with the railways for an air-rail coast-to-coast service. It began on 7 July 1929. Westbound passengers left New York's Pennsylvania Station in the Airway

Limited and travelled overnight to Port Columbus in Ohio, where a special combined air-rail terminal had been built. From there they flew to Waynoka in Okalahoma where they transferred to the Atchison, Topeka and Santa Fe Railroad for the night journey to Clovis in New Mexico. The final stage by air took them to Los Angeles, and from there they could continue free to San Francisco by train or by plane. The New York-Los Angeles journey took exactly 48 hours and the fare ranged from $337 to $403 one way.

In the east, on 1 May 1928, Pitcairn Aviation began operating CAM 19 between New York and Atlanta with Pitcairn Mailwings and, using the lighted airway, did some night flying. That December the airline took over Florida Airways' Atlanta-Miami route, and the company became Eastern Air Transport in January 1930. The route was extended to Boston and passengers were carried over part of it from August. In December 1930 Curtiss Condors were introduced, and were also used by TAT. These were large twin-engined biplanes with 600hp Curtiss Conqueror engines and 18 seats. They led in 1933 to the T-32 model, which could carry 12 passengers in sleeping berths.

In 1929 Walter Folger Brown became Postmaster General, and he had strong views on how US airways should be developed. The Post Office contract for the central transcontinental route – CAM 34 New York-Los Angeles – was up for tender, but before TAT could secure the contract Brown forced the merger of TAT

Often claimed as the prototype of the modern airliner, the Boeing 247 featured retractable landing gear (seen here locked down), and was the first transport with de-icing and enough power to climb on one engine.

with Western Air Express, thus forming Transcontinental and Western Air (TWA). The new airline began the first coast-to-coast all-air through service on 25 October 1930, using Ford Trimotors on the New York-Los Angeles route with a nightstop at Kansas City and an overall time of 36 hours.

American Airways, formed on 25 January 1930, obtained the southern route CAM 33 via Nashville and Dallas by a series of route extensions and company take-overs. Then in July 1931 United Air Lines was organized to take over officially Boeing Air Transport, NAT, PAT and Varney, which for some time had been working under the United title. Thus, by mid-1931, the Big Four had been created out of nearly 30 airlines of varying size. They were American Airways, Eastern Air Transport, TWA and United Air Lines.

Although this is but a brief summary of the early development of US air transport, mention must be made of the Ludington Line and of two more transport aircraft. Ludington was an airline which really believed in passengers, and on 1 September 1930, began a service 'every hour on the hour' from 08.00 to 17.00 over the Newark (New York)-Camden (Philadelphia)-Washington route, mainly with Stinson Trimotor monoplanes. In the two years before the company was taken over by Eastern it carried 124,000 passengers.

An event of great importance was Boeing's production of the Model 247 ten-passenger low-wing all-metal monoplane with two Pratt & Whitney Wasp engines and retractable undercarriage. This can be claimed as the prototype of the modern airliner. The Boeing 247 first flew on 8 February 1933, 60 were ordered for the United group, and they went into service with Boeing Air Transport, National Air Transport and Pacific Air Transport and became United Air Lines' standard equipment up to the end of 1936. The Boeing 247 was able to climb with one engine inoperative and cruise at 250km/h (155mph), and it made obsolete all other US airline equipment.

Boeing 247s were not available to non-United group airlines, and so TWA asked Douglas to produce a competitive aircraft. This was the DC-1, of similar layout to the Boeing. It first flew on 1 July 1933, and TWA ordered 20 of the improved production DC-2s. But before the DC-2 could enter service, in July 1934, President Roosevelt, believing that some airlines had been unduly privileged in securing contracts, cancelled all the main contracts on 9 February 1934, thus ending an important chapter in US airline history. Under White House instructions the last mail flight had to be completed on 19 February.

The US Army Air Corps was then given the task of flying the mail. The 43,450km (27,000 mile) network of mail routes was reduced to 25,750km (16,000 miles), and about 150 aircraft of various types were allocated to the operation. The weather was bad, the crews were inexperienced and ten pilots were killed before the last flight on 1 June.

The President admitted that he had been wrong, and in April 1934 the Postmaster General, James Farley, called in the airlines to find ways of salvaging what remained of the nation's airways. Temporary mail contracts were awarded, and among the conditions required to qualify for a contract was the stipulation that no contract carrier could be associated with an aircraft manufacturer.

The Big Four were reorganized as American Airlines, Eastern Air Lines, TWA Inc and United Air Lines, and of the 32 new mail contracts they were awarded 15, with TWA and United both getting mail contracts for transcontinental routes – Newark-Los Angeles and Newark-Oakland respectively. Eastern got three important routes, Newark-New Orleans, Newark-Miami and Chicago-Jacksonville, while America's routes included Newark-Chicago and Newark-Boston. By combining Newark-Fort Worth and Fort Worth-Los Angeles they gained a transcontinental route, although it was not as direct as TWA's and United's.

Australia

After completing the first flight from Britain to Australia in December 1919, Ross and Keith Smith continued across the continent to Sydney, Melbourne and Adelaide. In preparation for the flight across Australia a route was surveyed, aerodromes prepared and fuel and oil provided. Responsible for this work on the Darwin-Longreach section were W. Hudson Fysh and P. J. McGuinness, and it was these men, with others, who founded Queensland and Northern Territory Aerial Services (QANTAS) on 16 November 1920.

It was to Norman Brearley's West Australian Airways that the honour went of starting the first subsidized air service in Australia. On 4 December 1921, a Bristol Tourer took off from Geraldton, the railhead north of Perth, to inaugurate a weekly mail service to Carnarvon, Onslow, Roebourne, Port Hedland, Broome and Derby. The route was extended to Perth in January 1924, and from Derby to Wyndham in July 1930. In 1929 a weekly Perth-Adelaide Service began using de Havilland Hercules biplanes, and Vickers Viastra monoplanes were introduced in 1931, covering the journey in less than 24 hours.

On 2 November 1922, QANTAS opened its first scheduled service when P. J. McGinness flew an Armstrong Whitworth F.K.8 from Charleville to Longreach with mail, and on the next day Hudson Fysh flew on with mail and one passenger to Cloncurry.

QANTAS steadily expanded its operations in Queensland, and in 1931 took part in the first experimental England-Australia mail flights, carrying the mail from Darwin to Brisbane. QANTAS was chosen as the partner to Imperial Airways to carry passengers and mail between Singapore and Brisbane when the England-Australia service opened in December 1934. A new company, Qantas Empire Airways (referred to hereafter as Qantas), was registered in January 1934 with Imperial Airways and Qantas each holding half the share capital.

Qantas ordered a fleet of D.H.86 four-engined biplanes for the Brisbane-Singapore operation, but, when the first service left Brisbane on 10 December 1934, they had to use a single-engined D.H.61 and D.H.50 because of the late delivery, and Imperial Airways worked the Darwin-Singapore sector until February 1935. Passengers were carried over the entire England-Australia route from April.

In 1936 came an insignificant event which, years later, was to have a major influence on Australian air transport. Reginald Ansett had been refused a licence for a bus service between Hamilton and Melbourne, so, on 16 February 1936, he began an air service between these points, for which a licence was not required. After World War II Ansett was to get control of ANA and take over other companies to form Australia's largest private airline.

Canada

In Canada, during 1920, about 12,070km (7,500 miles) of landplane and seaplane routes were surveyed, the first flight to penetrate the Northwest Territories was made in the following year, and in 1923 the first air mail flight was made between Newfoundland and Labrador.

On 11 September 1924, Laurentide Air Service and Canadian Pacific Railway established an air service linking the railway at Angliers with the Quebec goldfields at Rouyn.

The biplane tail of the Vickers Viastra had a rather stuck-on appearance but its sturdy high wing ensured good ground clearance for the propellers when operating from bumpy airfields in the Australian bush. This example was delivered to QANTAS in the early 1930s.

This was the first regular air service introduced in Canada for the carriage of passengers, mail and freight.

Much of Canada's early air transport was on these lines, with air services linking remote areas with the nearest rail-head. In summer the aircraft operated as landplanes and seaplanes, but the harsh winter climate enforced a change to skis.

Many concerns were involved in these early operations, mostly using single-engined aircraft. On 26 December 1926, Western Canada Airways began operations at Sioux Lookout and regular services were begun to Rolling Portage and Red Lake mining districts, and over the next few years a fairly extensive route network was established. On 3 March 1930, the airline began the nightly *Prairie Air Mail* service over the Winnipeg-Calgary and Regina-Edmonton routes. The initial service was flown by a Fokker Universal, and these were the first scheduled night flights in Canada.

On 25 November 1930, Canadian Airways Ltd began operations, having been formed by Canadian Pacific Railway, Canadian National Railway, Western Canada Airways and a group of airlines controlled by Aviation Corporation of Canada. The new concern established services in many parts of the country and undertook a lot of mail and freight carriage. But although it linked many pairs of cities, it did not provide a transcontinental service.

However, work went ahead on preparing airports and navigational services for a transcontinental route and on 10 April 1937, Trans-Canada Air Lines (TCA) was created by a Government Act. Survey flights over the route began from Vancouver in July 1937 and on 1 September that year TCA began operation with a Vancouver-Seattle service flown by Lockheed Electras. Early in 1938 Vancouver-Winnipeg mail and cargo services began, and that October the route was extended to Toronto, Ottawa and Montreal, mail being carried from the beginning of December. On 1 March 1939, the full-scale official trans-continental mail service was inaugurated, and passengers were carried from April on this route and on the Lethbridge-Calgary-Edmonton route. TCA now operates as Air Canada.

The other major Canadian airline is CP Air, which was formed on 30 January 1942, as Canadian Pacific Air Lines. This was founded as a subsidiary of Canadian Pacific Railway, and represented the merger of Arrow Airways, Canadian Airways, Dominion Skyways, Ginger Coote Airways, Mackenzie Air Service, Prairie Airways, Quebec Airways, Starratt Airways, Wings Ltd and Yukon Southern Air Transport. The initial CPA fleet consisted of some 77 aircraft.

Africa

On 31 July 1929, Mrs F. K. Wilson founded Wilson Airways in Nairobi, and when Imperial Airways' Central Africa route was opened Wilson Airways operated connecting flights between Kisumu, on Lake Victoria, and Nairobi, using a de Havilland Puss Moth.

With the introduction of the Empire Air Mail Programme in 1937, Imperial Airways introduced flying boats via a coastal route to Durban, and Wilson Airways opened a weekly Kisumu-Nairobi-Moshi-Dodoma-Mbeya-Mpika-Broken Hill-Lusaka mail service to connect with Imperial Airways at Kisumu.

Exuding speed, Lockheed's all-metal Model 10 Electra of 1934 had flashing performance and was aimed at smaller airlines and private operators.

In 1931 two airlines were formed in Central Africa, Rhodesian Aviation and Christowitz Air Services (in Nyasaland). The former opened a weekly Bulawayo-Salisbury service, subsidized by the Government of Southern Rhodesia and the Beit Trustees. The service was only operated as required and used South African-registered Puss Moths. In 1933 Rhodesian Aviation began a weekly passenger and goods service over the Salisbury-Gatooma-Que Que-Gwelo Bulawayo-Johannesburg route with a Fox Moth, and Christowitz began a Salisbury-Blantyre service. Then in October 1933 Rhodesia and Nyasaland Airways (RANA) was formed. This acquired the assets of Rhodesian Aviation, taking over the Salisbury-Johannesburg service, which was terminated at Bulawayo, and in 1934 the Christowitz Salisbury-Blantyre service. RANA also developed new routes and operated services connecting with Imperial Airways flying boat operations.

South Africa was slow in setting up any form of air transport, and it was only in March 1925 that the South African Air Force began a weekly experimental mail service over the Cape Town-East London-Port Elizabeth-Mossel Bay-Durban route, using D.H.9s. Only 32 flights were made and it was not until over four years later that a private air service began when Union Airways opened a Cape Town-Port Elizabeth service with extensions to Durban and Johannesburg.

A change in policy came with the founding, on 1 February 1934, of South African Airways (SAA), which began operation with aircraft and staff taken over from Union Airways. SAA introduced Junkers Ju 52/3ms, and these were the first multi-engined aircraft used by a South African airline.

At the beginning of February 1935 SAA took over South-West Africa Airways. The airline steadily expanded its network and on 1 April 1936, took over the Cape Town-Johannesburg sector of the England-South Africa route. Junkers Ju 86s were added to the fleet in 1937, and by the time all civil flying was suspended in May 1940, SAA had opened routes to Lusaka, Broken Hill, Nairobi, Kisumu and Lourenço Marques.

India

The first Government air mail flight in the world took place in India when, on 18 February 1911, Henri Pequet, in a Humber biplane, flew mail from Allahabad to Naini Junction about 8km (5 miles) away. The first actual mail service in India began on 24 January 1920, when the RAF opened a weekly service between Bombay and Karachi. This was maintained for only a few weeks, and there was no Indian air service until 15 October 1932, when Tata Sons opened a

Karachi-Ahmedabad-Bombay-Bellary-Madras mail service, using a Puss Moth, to connect with Imperial Airways' England-Karachi flights.

In May and June 1933 two airlines were formed in India. The first, Indian National Airways (INA), was established to participate as a shareholder in the second, Indian Trans-Continental Airways, and to develop services in northern India. Indian Trans-Continental was set up to operate the trans-India route in association with Imperial Airways, beginning the Karachi-Calcutta service on 7 July 1933, with Armstrong Whitworth Atlanta monoplanes.

On 1 December 1933, INA started a weekly Calcutta-Rangoon service with Dragons, and on the same day opened the first daily air service in India – between Calcutta and Dacca.

New Zealand

A number of short-lived air services were operated in New Zealand during the 1920s, and in 1930-31 Dominion Airways operated a Desoutter monoplane on about 100 flights between Hastings and Gisborne before the loss of the Desoutter ended the undertaking. Air Travel (NZ) started a small service with a Fox

Favoured by 'mini' airlines in the far flung reaches of the Empire, the de Havilland D.H.85 Leopard Moth could accommodate two passengers and their baggage.

Moth on the last day of 1934, East Coast Airways began a twice daily Napier-Gisborne service with Dragons in mid-May 1935, and at the end of that December Cook Strait Airways opened a Wellington-Blenheim-Nelson service with two Dragon Rapides.

The year 1935 saw the founding of Union Airways of New Zealand as an offshoot of Union Steam Ship Co, and this airline began a daily Palmerston North-Blenheim-Christchurch-Dunedin service on 16 January 1936, with D.H.86s. The airline commissioned three Lockheed Electras in June 1937 and put them on a daily Auckland-Wellington service. Union Airways purchased East Coast Airways in July 1938, and the following March opened a Palmerston North-Napier-Gisborne-Auckland service. After the war Air Travel (NZ), Cook Strait Airways and Union Airways were all absorbed by the newly founded New Zealand National Airways Corporation.

The South Atlantic

Having opened the air route between Toulouse and Dakar, France set about establishing services between Natal in Brazil and Buenos Aires. Airports were prepared and radio equipment installed, at an estimated cost of $1.5 million. Aeropostal Brasileira and Aeroposta Argentina were established as subsidiaries of Aeropostale, and the Natal-Buenos Aires services was opened in November 1927. The dream of a service linking France and South America came true on 1 March 1928, when the route from Toulouse to Buenos Aires was opened for mail, with a transit time of eight days, but the ocean sector had to be operated by ships.

Great as were the achievements of what was known as The Line, the South America route could not be regarded as satisfactory until the entire route could be covered by air. The first attempt was made in 1930, when on 12-13 May Jean Mermoz flew the ocean crossing from St Louis, Senegal, to Natal in 21 hour in the Latécoère 28 seaplane *Comte de la Vaulx*. But a single-engined floatplane was not suitable for the ocean crossing, so the three-engined Couzinet 70 *Arc-en-Ciel* landplane and the four-engined Blériot 5190 flying boat *Santos-Dumont* were ordered.

On 16 January 1933, Mermoz flew the *Arc-en-Ciel* from St Louis to Natal in 14 hours 27 minutes. After modifications, it began regular South Atlantic mail flights at low frequency from May 1934, completing eight ocean crossings by the end of the year. Flown by Lucien Bossoutrot, the *Santos-Dumont* made its first crossing, from Dakar to Natal, on 27 November 1934, and began regular service with Air France early in 1935.

The construction of the Blériot flying boat had been delayed by financial problems, and as a result it was beaten into service by the four-engined Latécoère 300 flying boat *Croix du Sud* (Southern Cross). This boat made its first crossing on 3 January 1934, and continued as far as Rio de Janeiro. However, on 7 December 1936, radio contact was lost with the *Croix de Sud* about four hours after it left Dakar. The flying boat, its famous commander Mermoz, and his crew were never found.

Air France also employed a number of large four-engined Farman landplanes on the South Atlantic route, beginning

The performance of the long-range Armstrong Whitworth Atlanta was less than sparkling due to its fixed-pitch propellers and fixed undercarriage.

with the F.220 *Le-Centaure*, which made its first Dakar-Natal flight on 3 June 1935. In November 1937 the last of these, the F.2231 *Chef Pilote L. Guerrero*, owned by the French Government, flew from Paris to Santiago in 52hr 42min and made the Dakar-Natal crossing in 11hr 5min.

Germany used different methods in establishing its services to South America. Luftschiffbau Zeppelin decided to use the LZ 127 *Graf Zeppelin* on the route and on 18 May 1930, this airship left Friedrichshafen on a trial flight to Rio de Janeiro. This was followed by further trials in 1931. As a result the airship left Friedrichshafen on 20 March 1932, to open a regular service to Recife in Brazil, and this flight carried paying passengers – the first ever to fly on a trans-ocean air service.

Germany's second method of flying to South America was to use landplanes between Germany and Africa and in South America and flying boats over the ocean. A system was devised for catapulting the flying boats from depot ships because they could not take off under their own power with sufficient fuel and while carrying a payload. The Dornier 8-ton Wal was used initially and the first experimental crossing made on 6 June 1933. Regular mail services began in 1934; the entire route from Berlin to Buenos Aires was scheduled for four to five days. The 10-ton Wal was introduced on the route and, after trials over the North Atlantic in 1936, the much-improved Do 18s began working over the South Atlantic.

The third country to begin South Atlantic air services was Italy. Ala Littoria Linee Atlantiche was set up as the Atlantic division of Ala Littoria, and had begun taking delivery of a special fleet of Savoia-Marchetti S.M.83 three-engined monoplanes before Linee Aeree Transcontinentali Italiane (LATI) was established to operate the services. After proving flights, a regular Rome-Rio de Janeiro service was inaugurated in December 1939. Avoiding British and French territory, the route was via Seville, Villa Cisneros, the Cape Verde Islands, Natal and Recife.

Air Travel in Latin America

Most of the early airlines in South America were established by Germans, the first being SCADTA, which was founded in Colombia in 1919. This airline had a fleet of Junkers F-13 seaplanes and, after a period of experimental operation, opened a regular service in 1921 over the Magdalena River route linking the port of Barranquilla with Girardot, the railhead for Bogota. The distance was 1,046km (650 miles) and the flight took seven hours, compared with a week by steamer. New routes were added and more modern equipment acquired until finally, in 1940, the airline was merged with another small company to form today's Avianca.

The next airline to be formed, again by Germans, was Lloyd Aereo Boliviano (LAB). Equipped with F 13s, this company was founded in August 1925, and by the end of the year was running regular services between Cochabamba and Santa Cruz, taking three hours against the surface time of four days. This company was almost certainly the first to operate Junkers Ju 52/3ms, although it did so on military operations during the Gran Chaco war in 1932. LAB is still the Bolivian national airline.

In 1927 two airlines were founded in Brazil, Varig and Syndicato Condor. Condor opened a Rio de Janeiro-Pôrto Alegre-Rio Grande do Sul service in October, and during the year handed over the Pôrto Alegre-Rio Grande sector to Varig. Both companies used German aircraft, mostly Junkers, with floatplanes predominating, and built up a route system, initially in the coastal regions. In 1942 Condor was reorganized as Serviços Aéreos Cruzeiro do Sul and was taken over in 1975 by Varig, which remains the principal Brazilian airline.

In Peru Elmer Faucett founded Compania de Aviación Faucett in 1928, and by the following year had established air services extending the length of the country, from Ecuador in the north to Chile in the south. Faucett was unusual in that it built many of its own aircraft, based on Stinson single-engine monoplanes.

Sikorsky's popular S-38 flying boat was used by many airlines to open up new routes that included overflying water, particularly in South America.

In 1928 Aeroposta Argentina opened services from Bahia Blanca, south of Buenos Aires, to the oil centre of Comodoro Rivadavia 950km (590 miles) further south, and from Buenos Aires to Asuncion in Paraguay. In July 1929 the great barrier of the Andes was conquered with the opening of the Buenos Aires-Santiago service, and French air services had reached the Pacific coast. Much of the flying was done at night and the weather was frequently appalling. On the route to Comodoro Rivadavia there were very strong winds to contend with, but it was the service across the Andes which called for a very high standard of flying and a great amount of bravery.

A military air service was introduced in Chile in 1929. This ran north from Santiago to Arica near the Peruvian border. It was taken over by Linea Aerea Nacional (LAN) in 1934, at first flying mail and then passengers, and since that time a considerable route system has been developed, including transatlantic services. LAN is the only airline to serve Easter Island, which it includes on its Chile-Tahiti route.

The US airline which became deeply involved in Latin America was Pan American Airways. It began regular contract mail services between Key West and Havana on 28 October 1927, using Fokker F.VIIa-3m monoplanes, and carried passengers from January 1928. PAA developed a network of services in the Caribbean, mostly using Sikorsky amphibians, and its routes reached as far as Christobal in the Panama Canal Zone. Extension southward down the west coast of South America was blocked by the Grace shipping line, so in 1929 Panagra was formed, with Pan American and Grace each holding 50 per cent of the shares.

Although Pan American had to settle for a half share in South American west coast operations, the company would not compromise on the east coast. In March 1929 NYRBA (New York, Rio and Buenos Aires Line) was founded, and that August it began in Buenos Aires-Montevideo service. The next month a mail and passenger service was started between Buenos Aires and Santiago with Ford Trimotors.

Before the east coast route could be opened to the US it was necessary to obtain suitable aircraft. There were long overwater sectors and few landing grounds, so 14 Consolidated Commodore flying boats were ordered. These were large monoplanes powered by two Pratt & Whitney Hornet engines, could carry 20 to 32 passengers and had a range of 1,600 km (1,000 miles). On 18 February 1930, the route between Miami and Buenos Aires was opened, the 14,485km (9,000 miles) being flown in seven days.

Pan American urgently needed long-range aircraft with bigger payloads, and the need was met by three specially designed Sikorsky S-40s. These were large flying boats with four Pratt & Whitney Hornets, tail units carried on twin booms, and accommodation for 32 passengers. A more advanced and important flying boat was the Sikorsky S-42, powered by four Hornets with accommodation for 32 passengers. The S-42 cruised at 274km/h (170mph) and had a normal range of 1,930km (1,200 miles). Ten examples of three models were built, and the type was introduced on the Miami-Rio de Janeiro route on 16 August 1934.

Mexico has had a large number of airlines, its first being Cia Mexicana de Aviacion (CMA), which began work in August 1924, carrying wages to the oil fields near Tampico with Lincoln Standard biplanes. This was devised to avoid bandits. Under the title Mexicana, CMA is now a major international airline. Mexico's other major airline, Aeromexico, was created in 1934 as Aeronaves de Mexico.

Flaps down, a Sikorsky S-42 prepares to complete another Caribbean service for Pan American. Together with the Martin 130 and Boeing 314, the S-42 was one of the classic pre-war American flying boats.

> Marred by only its fixed landing gear, the Lockheed Vega was an astonishingly clean machine and as fast as contemporary fighters when it appeared in 1927.

Conquering the Pacific

The first air crossing of the Pacific was not made until 1928. In July 1931 Charles Lindbergh and his wife made a survey of a northern route in a Lockheed Sirius single-engined seaplane, flying to Japan via Alaska, Siberia and the Kuriles, but political problems prevented the establishment of such a route.

The only alternative was to use island stepping stones which were United States territory, and bases were therefore prepared on Wake Island and Guam to enable a service to operate from San Francisco to Manila via Honolulu, Wake and Guam. This gave stages of 3,853km (2,394 miles) from San Francisco to Hawaii, 3,693km (2,295 miles) to Wake, 2,414km (1,500 miles) to Guam and 2,565km (1,594 miles) to Manila.

To obtain aircraft for the operation of a regular service, Pan American issued a specification for a flying boat capable of flying 4,023 km (2,500 miles) against a 48km/h (30mph) headwind while carrying a crew of four and at least 136kg (300lb) of mail. To this specification Martin built three M-130 flying boats, each powered by four 800/950hp Pratt & Whitney Twin Wasp engines. The boats had a span of 39 62m (130ft), weighed 23,700kg (52,252lb) fully loaded and could carry 41 passengers, although only 14 seats were installed for the Pacific route. Cruising speed was 253km/h (157mph) and the range 5,150km (3,200 miles), or 6,437km (4,000 miles) if the flying boat was only carrying mail.

The M-130s were named *China Clipper, Philippine Clipper* and *Hawaii Clipper*, and the first was delivered in October 1935. The *China Clipper,* under the command of Capt Edwin Musick, inaugurated the trans-Pacific mail service when it left Alameda on 22 November 1935, and it alighted at Manila 59hr 48min later. Paying passengers were carried from 21 October 1936.

Early in 1937 the Sikorsky S-42B *Hong Kong Clipper* was delivered, and that spring it made a survey of the southern Pacific route to Auckland, New Zealand, subsequently being used to extend the trans-Pacific operation from Manila to Hong Kong, the first service being on 27-28 April. This gave Pan American a direct link to China through the China National Aviation Corporation's Hong Kong-Canton-Shanghai service. From that time the Martin M-130s were completing the San Francisco-Manila out and back flights in 14 days.

On 23 December 1937, Pan American inaugurated a San Francisco-Auckland service via Hawaii, Kingman Reef and Samoa, but the S-42B, with its commander, Edwin Musick, and crew, was lost on the second flight and the service had to be suspended. But on 12 July 1940, a fortnightly service was opened via Hawaii, Canton Island and New Caledonia using one of the new Boeing 314s, with passengers being carried from 13 September.

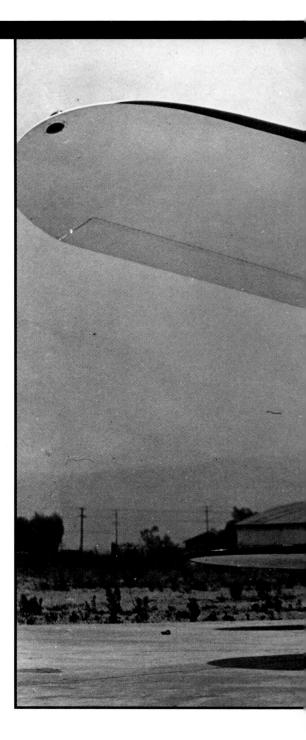

The Modern Airliner

The principal passenger aircraft in use in the United States in the late 1920s and early 1930s were Fokker F.VIIs and Ford Trimotors. They had accommodation for 8 to 15 passengers, but cruised at only a little over 160km/h (100mph), and for much of the time very few of their seats were occupied. Some people believed there was a need for smaller and faster aeroplanes, and as a result there was a period when numerous airlines were operating fleets of small single-engined monoplanes capable of cruising at more than 241km/h (150mph).

John Northrop and Gerrard Vultee designed a superb four-passenger high-wing monoplane called the Lockheed Vega. It was a wooden aeroplane, powered by a Wasp engine, and it first flew in July 1927. The Vega entered service with International Airlines on 17 September 1928, and subsequently there were several versions, including one with a metal fuselage. Cruising speed was 217-241 km/h (135-150mph), and the type was used by a number of

airlines, including Braniff and TWA. Very similar was the parasol-winged Lockheed Air Express which was produced for Western Air Express.

The last of Lockheed's single-engined high-speed transports was the six-passenger Orion, which had a low-mounted wing and retractable undercarriage. It went into service with Bowen Air Lines in May 1931 and is claimed as the first transport aircraft capable of 320km/h (200mph). American Airways, Northwest Airways and Varney Speed Lines were among the Orion users and two were exported to Swissair.

The most advanced of these single-engined mono-planes was the Vultee V-1A, which could carry eight passengers and cruise at 340km/h (211mph). The Vultee was of all-metal construction and had retractable undercarriage. American Airlines intro-duced the type in September 1934.

There were also two Boeing prototypes. These were the Model 200 and 221, both named Monomail. They were all-metal low-wing monoplanes, each powered by a 575hp Pratt & Whitney Hornet. The Model 200 was originally a single-seat mail and cargo carrier. It was followed in 1930 by the longer Model 221 with non-retractable undercarriage and a cabin for six passen-gers. It went into service with Boeing Air Transport, and like the Model 221A was later lengthened to pro-vide two extra seats.

On 19 February 1934, the Douglas DC-1 made its dramatic coast-to-coast flight, by which time TWA had already ordered 20 of the 14-passenger production DC-2s. They were powered by two Wright Cyclones, giving a maximum cruising speed of 315km/h (196mph) and a range of just over 1,600km (1,000 miles). The first DC-2 was delivered to TWA on 14 May 1934, and four days later made a proving flight from Columbus to Pittsburgh and Newark. On 1 August DC-2s began transcontinental operation on the Newark-Chicago-Kansas City-Alburquerque-Los Angeles route to an 18-hour schedule.

On 5 May 1934, American Airlines had begun transcontinental sleeper services with Curtiss Condors, and had also used them to build up fre-quency on its New York-Boston route. Condors were no match for the DC-2, and so American Airlines asked Douglas for a sleeper development of the DC-2.

Douglas enlarged the DC-2 by widening and lengthening its fuselage and added 3.04m (10ft) to its wing span. Powered by two 1,000hp Cyclone engines and having 14 sleeping berths, this new type was known as the DST – Douglas Sleeper Transport.

American Airlines had ordered ten DSTs, but after its first flight on 17 December 1935, increased the

Startlingly modern, the Douglas DC-2 incorporated an all-metal structure, radial engines and retractable landing gear in a design of unprecedented efficency. American Airlines left their aircraft unpainted.

order and changed it to cover eight DSTs and 12 dayplanes – DC-3s with 21 seats. The first DST was delivered in June 1936 and, used as a dayplane, went into ser-vice on the New York-Chicago route on 25 June. On 15 September American was able to inaugurate its *American Mercury* skysleeper transcontinental service with an eastbound schedule of 16 hours.

Thus was launched one of the world's great transport aeroplanes, the DC-3, of which by far the biggest percentage was powered by 1,200hp Pratt & Whitney Twin Wasps. It was to be built in numerous civil and military versions, with a total of 10,655 produced in the United States and others being built in Japan and, under licence, in the Soviet Union. After the war large numbers of surplus military DC-3s became available to civil operators, and in the postwar years almost every airline operated them at some period. About 200 DC-3s are still in service, some being turboprop conversions.

Lockheed also embarked on production of a series of fast twin-engined mono-planes. The first was the ten-passenger Model 10A Electra with 450hp Pratt & Whitney Wasp Junior engines and a cruising speed close to 322km/h (200mph). The Electra was introduced on 11 August 1934, by Northwest Airlines. The original British Airways had seven, and also bought nine of the more powerful 12-passen-ger Model 14s, which were about 64km/h (40mph) faster.

The major United States airlines required an aeroplane with greater capacity and range than the DC-3 and, in March 1936, the Big Four and Pan American each came to an agreement to share the cost of developing the four-engined Douglas DC-4E. It was powered by 1,450hp Pratt & Whitney Twin Hornets, and cruised at 322km/h (200mph). The DC-4E had a nosewheel undercarriage, the first on a big transport, triple fins, and production models were to be pressurized. United Air Lines ordered six 52-passenger sleeper DC-4Es in July 1939, having put the prototype into exper-imental operation in the previous month. But the aeroplane was found to be unsuit-able, the order was cancelled, and the only example was exported to Japan.

The last American transport landplane to go into service before the Japanese attack on Pearl Harbor was the Boeing 307 Stratoliner. Although only ten were built,

it has an important place in history as the first pressurized aeroplane to go into airline service. The Stratoliner was a low-wing monoplane with a wing span of 32 69m (107ft 3in), powered by four 900hp Wright Cyclones and having a maximum weight of 19,051 kg (42,000lb). It cruised at 354km/h (220mph) and had a range of 3,846km (2,390 miles). This design employed the wings, nacelles, powerplant and tail surfaces of the B-17 Flying Fortress bomber, but had a completely new circular-section fuselage with pressurized accommodation for 33 passengers and 5 crew. The first aircraft flew on the last day of 1938, but was lost before delivery to Pan American. PAA had three, TWA five, and Howard Hughes had a modified aircraft for record breaking.

TWA introduced the Stratoliner on its transcontinental route on 8 July 1940, and cut eastbound times to 13 hours 40 minutes. Pan American based its Stratoliners in Miami for Latin American operations, but at the end of 1941 these aircraft were ordered into war service with TWA's fleet being used over the North Atlantic. After the war the TWA aircraft, much modified, were put back into civil operation with 38 seats and increased take-off weight. Some Stratoliners saw service in Latin America and the Far East for several years, a few remaining in use until the mid-1960s.

United Kingdom Domestic Airlines

When sustained air services were established in the UK, those that were successful were based on routes which involved a water crossing. In the spring of 1932 British Amphibious Air Lines began irregular operation of such a route, between Blackpool and the Isle of Man, using a Saunders-Roe Cutty Sark amphibian.

Two other events of importance in 1932 were the opening of a twice-daily Bristol-Cardiff service which began on 26 September, and the first flight of the de Havilland D.H.84 Dragon on 24 November. Norman Edgar's service was to develop into a sizeable operation under the title Western Airways, and the Dragon was to make possible economic short-haul airline operations in the UK and many other parts of the world. The Dragon was a six-passenger biplane with two 130hp de Havilland Gipsy Major engines, and 115 were built in the United Kingdom and 87 in Australia.

On 8 May Highland Airways opened a regular service linking Inverness and Kirkwall in Orkney, via Wick. A Monospar S.T.4 monoplane was used and, in spite of appalling weather, set such a high standard of regularity that the airline was awarded the first domestic mail contract. The airline extended its routes to include Aberdeen and Shetland. In Glasgow, John Sword established Midland and Scottish Air Ferries (M&SAF), and on 8 May made its first recorded ambu-

With servicing platforms still in place, an American Airlines' DC-3 Flagship Sleeper is readied for the night shift.

lance flight, from Islay to Glasgow. The air ambulance is still an essential element of Scottish air transport. Regular passenger services were begun on 1 June over the Glasgow-Campbeltown-Islay route, with Dragons, and M&SAF were to develop a number of routes before closing down at the end of September 1934.

On 18 December 1933, Jersey Airways began a daily Portsmouth-Jersey service. There was no airport on Jersey until 1937, so the fleet of Dragons operated from the beach at St Aubin's Bay near St Helier. Sometimes the whole fleet was on the beach at the same time, because schedules were governed by the tides and the fleet tended to fly in a loose formation.

Having suffered as a result of increasing road competition, the four mainline railways had obtained rights to operate domestic air services. On 21 March 1934, they registered Railway Air Services, with the London Midland and Scottish Railway, London and North Eastern Railway, Great Western Railway, Southern Railway and Imperial Airways as the shareholders; Imperial Airways was responsible for undertaking flying operations. The main RAS operation was to be the *Royal Mail* trunk route linking London, Birmingham, Manchester, Belfast and Glasgow. Using D.H.86s, the opening was set for 20 August, but the weather was atrocious and only part of the route could be flown. Full working began the next day. This route, with modifications, continued throughout the years up until the war, but RAS's other routes were mainly confined to summer months, catering for holiday traffic.

On 30 September 1935, three domestic airlines, Hillman's Airways, Spartan Air Lines and United Airways, were merged to form Allied British Airways. The name was changed to British Airways on 29 October, and in the following August the company absorbed British Continental Airways. British Airways operated some domestic routes and controlled a number of United Kingdom domestic airlines, but its main effort was concentrated on developing fast and efficient services to the continent.

Although Aer Lingus is the Irish national airline, its beginning was closely involved with the United Kingdom domestic operations. The airline was founded on 22 May 1936, and a week later began a daily Dublin-Bristol service. In the same month it started working between Dublin and the Isle of Man, and in September opened a Dublin-Liverpool service and extended its Bristol service to London. All these operations were in association with Blackpool and West Coast Air Services, and they went under the title 'Irish Sea Airways'. Dragons were used on the first three routes, and D.H.86s flew to London.

A variety of aircraft served the UK routes, but the biggest contribution was made by the de Havilland biplanes – the D.H.84 Dragon, D.H.86 and D.H.89 Dragon Rapide. The Dragon Rapide had first flown in April 1934; it was a much improved Dragon with two 200hp Gipsy Six engines, there were seats for six to eight passengers, and the cruising speed was about 210km/h (130mph). Several hundred Dragon Rapides were built; they served airlines in many parts of the world and a few were still employed in the early 1970s.

Named RMA *Lord Shaftesbury*, this de Havilland Dragon Rapide was still operating BEA services to the Channel Islands in the 1960s. The wartime RAF version was the Dominie navigation trainer.

The North Atlantic

It is not surprising that from the earliest days of aviation there were dreams of North Atlantic services, but the problems of making these dreams reality were formidable. The shortest direct ocean crossing, between the present Shannon Airport, in Ireland, and Gander, in Newfoundland, is 3,177km (1,974 miles). North Atlantic weather is notoriously bad, with frequent fog in the Newfoundland area and very strong westerly prevailing winds. Pioneer west-east crossings were made in 1919. However, it was not until April 1928 that an aeroplane crossed the Atlantic Ocean from east to west, when Baron von Hünefeld, Cmdt J. Fitzmaurice and Hermann Köhl flew from Ireland to Greenly Island off Labrador in the Junkers W 33 *Bremen*.

As early as 1928 Pan American Airways began investigating North Atlantic routes. Numerous surveys were made, including one by Lindbergh, who studied a northern route via Greenland and Iceland, making his flight in a Lockheed Sirius seaplane. Aircraft range was the major problem, and only in 1937 did trial flights begin.

France began designing a large transatlantic flying boat in 1930. During the design stage it had to be considerably modified, and emerged in January 1935 as the Latécoère 521. It was a 42-tonne monoplane powered by six 800/860hp Hispano-Suiza engines. It was designed to carry 30 passengers on Atlantic routes or 70 over the Mediterranean, and its range was 4,000km (2,485 miles). Its first successful North Atlantic flight, from Biscarosse to New York via Lisbon and the Azores, was made in August 1938, and it subsequently made trial flights over various North Atlantic routes.

Germany undertook North Atlantic trial flights during 1936 using two Dornier Do 18 twin-engined flying boats. They were catapulted from the depot ship *Schwabenland* near the Azores, and from it the *Zephir* flew to New York in 22 hours 12 minutes on 11 September, arriving with 10 hours reserve fuel. By 20 October, when the trials ceased, the two Do 18s had flown 37,637km (23,386 miles) on eight flights over various North Atlantic routes. In the periods August-November 1937 and July-October 1938 a further 20 flights were made by three Blohm und Voss Ha 139 four-engined seaplanes operating from the *Sehwabenland* and the *Friesenland*.

But the honour of operating regular North Atlantic air services still went to Germany, when the Zeppelin LZ 129 *Hindenburg* began operation in 1936. Operated by Deutsche Zeppelin-Reederei, the *Hindenburg* left Friedrichshafen for New York with the first paying passengers on 6 May 1936, and on its return flight landed at Frankfurt, which became the regular European terminal. Ten return flights were

The sharp end of a Dragon Rapide reveals the simple cockpit layout (there are only a few instruments) and superb view, which was even better once the tail was raised for take-off.

made before the service was suspended for the winter; so great was the demand that the airship's accommodation had to be increased from the original 50. During the first season 1,309 passengers were carried, and the fastest flight from Lakehurst, New Jersey, to Frankfurt was made in 43 hours 53 minutes. A programme of 18 return services was announced for 1937, and on 3 May the airship left Frankfurt with 97 passengers and crew, but three days later fire broke out as the ship was landing at Lakehurst and 35 people lost their lives. German Zeppelin services came to an end.

Germany did not re-establish North Atlantic air services until 1955, but in August 1938 made a spectacular non-stop flight from Berlin to New York in 24 hours 56 minutes and back in 19 hours 55 minutes. This flight was made by a special Focke-Wulf Condor, and was the first across the ocean by a four-engined landplane.

The first regular service by heavier-than-air craft to be operated over part of the North Atlantic began on 16 June 1937, when Imperial Airways opened a Bermuda-New York service with the C-class flying boat *Cavalier*, and Pan American started working a reciprocal service with the Sikorsky S-42 *Bermuda Clipper*. Then on 5-6 July that year the two airlines made their first North Atlantic survey flights. The special long-range C-class *Caledonia* flew from Foynes on the Shannon to Botwood in Newfoundland in 15 hours 3 minutes, and the Sikorsky S-42 *Clipper III* flew in the opposite direction. *Caledonia* continued to Montreal and New York, and the Sikorsky flew on to Southampton.

Neither the C-class boats nor the S-42 were suitable for commercial operation because they could not carry sufficient fuel and a payload. Pan American ordered the large Boeing 314 for its services, and Imperial Airways undertook experiments designed to increase the range of its aircraft. One experiment involved refuelling in the air. An aircraft can carry a greater load than it can lift off the ground or water, so modified C-class boats were built which could take off with a payload and then receive their fuel supply from tanker aircraft via a flexible hose.

The other experiment involved launching a small aircraft from the back of a larger one. The Short-Mayo Composite Aircraft consisted of a modified C-class boat, on top of which was mounted a small floatplane. Take-off could be achieved with the power of all eight engines and the lift of both sets of wings, and then at a safe height the aircraft would separate, the smaller mailplane flying across the ocean and the flying boat returning to its base. The launch aircraft was the Short S.21 *Maia;* the mailplane the S.20 *Mercury*. The first separation took place successfully near Rochester on 6 February 1938, and on 20-21 July the *Mercury* made the first commercial crossing of the North Atlantic by a heavier-than-air craft when it flew from Foynes non-stop to Montreal in 20 hours 20 minutes carrying mail and newspapers. From Montreal *Mercury* flew on to Port Washington, New York, but it played no further part in North Atlantic transport.

Urged on by a combined 6,000hp from its Wright Double Cylone engines, a Boeing Model 314 of Pan American makes a magnificent sight as it departs Baltimore in 1939.

On 4 April 1939, Pan American's Boeing 314 *Yankee Clipper* arrived at Southampton on its first proving flight from New York, and on 20 May the same aircraft left New York on the inaugural mail service. Flying via the Azores, Lisbon and Marseilles it arrived at Southampton on 23 May and left on the first westbound service the next day. The northern mail route was opened on 24 June by the same aircraft, and on 28 June the *Dixie Clipper* left Port Washington on the inaugural southern-route passenger service – the first by a heavier-than-air craft. On 8 July, with 17 passengers, the *Yankee Clipper* left Port Washington on the inaugural service over the northern route, via Shediac, Botwood and Foynes. The fare was $375.

On 4 August Britain began a weekly experimental mail service between Southampton and New York via Foynes, Botwood and Montreal, using S.30 C-class flying boats which were refuelled in flight from Handley Page Harrow tankers based at Shannon and Botwood. The full programme of 16 flights was completed on 30 September in spite of war having started. Because of the war Pan American terminated its services at Foynes, and then withdrew altogether on 3 October.

BOAC, as successor to Imperial Airways, operated a C-class flying boat on four round trips between Poole, in Dorset, and New York via Botwood and Montreal during the period 3 August-23 September 1940, and one round trip during October. These flights, most of which were made while the Battle of Britain was in progress, carried mail, despatches and official passengers, but the first truly commercial British North Atlantic services did not effectively begin until 1 July 1946.

A New Generation of Transport Aircraft

World War II brought about three major changes in air transport. These were the design and construction of higher-capacity, longer-range aircraft capable of transoceanic operation, the large-scale construction of land airports, and worldwide operations by US airlines. In the first full year of peace after the war, the scheduled services of the world's airlines carried 18 million passengers, double the 1945 total, and in 1949 the total for the year was 27 million. For some time to come the passenger total was to double every five years, while cargo tonnage was to grow even faster. These enormous traffic totals were largely due to the production of a remarkable series of transport aeroplanes mostly designed and manufactured in the USA.

The DC-4 was a low-wing monoplane with a nosewheel undercarriage and four 1,450hp Pratt & Whitney R-2000 engines. Initially it had 44 seats, but high-density seating for up to 86 was later installed. American Overseas Airlines introduced the DC-4 on New York-Hurn (for London) services at the end of October 1945. There were two intermediate fuelling stops and the scheduled time was 23 hours 48 minutes. On 7 March 1946, DC-4s went into US domestic service on the New

Though Pan American replaced its flying boats with DC-4s, it continued the tradition of naming its aircraft 'Clippers'. This is *Clipper Racer*, freshly painted in PAA's new postwar livery.

York-Los Angeles route with American Airlines. DC-4s (many of them ex-military C-54 and R5D Skymasters) were used by most US carriers and by many airlines throughout the world. Douglas delivered a total of 1,242 DC-4s.

The DC-4 was a magnificent aeroplane, but it was unpressurized and its cruising speed of 352km/h (219mph) was no match for the other US wartime transport, the Lockheed Constellation. This had been designed for TWA as a long-range aircraft, but it did not fly until January 1943. TWA and Pan American had each ordered Constellations, but the small num-

ber built went to the United States Army Air Force as C-69s, and they entered service in April 1944.

After the war civil production was resumed and the military aircraft were brought up to civil standard. Pan American began a Constellation service between New York and Bermuda on 3 February 1946, and in the same month TWA introduced Constellations on its New York-Paris and New York-Los Angeles services. The original Constellation had four 2,500hp Wright Cyclone R-3350 engines and 44 seats – later increased to as many as 81 in some configurations. It had a pressurized cabin, and at 480km/h (298mph) its cruising speed was at least 127km/h (79mph) higher than the DC-4's. A total of 233 were produced.

The superior performance of the Constellation led Douglas to build the comparable DC-6, with pressurized cabins and a maximum cruising speed of just over

The DC-6 was the pressurized development of the DC-4 and gave airlines a superb transcontinental workhorse. Another 'Six' is on finals to land as this Braniff International Airways' aircraft is turned round at Dallas.

482km/h (300mph). The DC-6 had the same 35.81m (117ft 6in) span as the DC-4 but was longer, had accommodation for 50 to 86 passengers, and was powered by four 2,400hp Pratt & Whitney R-2800 engines.

American Airlines and United Air Lines were the first to operate DC-6s, introducing them on 27 April 1947, on the New York-Chicago and transcontinental routes respectively. Its eastbound transcontinental scheduled time was 10 hours. It was used by many major airlines and 170 were built.

Douglas followed the DC-6 with the longer fuselage DC-6A and DC-6B, which had increased range. The DC-6A was a cargo aircraft mainly used by the US Air Force and Navy, but the DC-6B proved to be one of the finest piston-engined passenger aircraft ever produced. It entered service on 29 April 1951 on American Airlines' transcontinental route, began service with 54 seats but, later, in high-density configuration could seat 102 passengers. The DC-6B cruised at 507km/h (315mph) and had a range of just over 4,830km (3,000 miles). It was used by a large number of airlines, a total of 288 being built. With the advent of jets, many DC-6Bs were converted into cargo aircraft and a few of these are still in use today.

Lockheed developed the Constellation into the L.1049 Super Constellation, with 5.48m (18ft) increase in fuselage length and 2,700hp Cyclone engines. It went into service as a 66-seat aircraft with Eastern Air Lines on 17 December 1951.

At about that time Curtiss-Wright's 3,250/ 3,400hp Turbo-Compound engine became available, and both Douglas and Lockheed developed their aircraft to make use of the new engine. Douglas slightly lengthened the DC-6B, but retained the same wing and produced the longer range DC-7, while Lockheed retained the basic Super Constellation airframe to produce the Turbo-Compound-powered L.1049C, D, E, G and H.

The DC-7 was the first aircraft capable of operating US transcontinental services in both directions without stops, and American Airlines introduced it on non-stop New York-Los Angeles services on 29 November 1953, scheduled to take 8 hours 45 minutes on the westbound flight, and 8 hours eastbound. Only 110 DC-7s were built, all of which were initially purchased by US airlines. Some were later converted into DC-7F freighters.

TWA had begun non-stop coast-to-coast services with L.1049C Super Constellations between Los Angeles and New York on 19 October 1953, but these had to stop at Chicago for fuel on westbound flights. However, the L.1049G, with wing tip fuel tanks, enabled TWA to match American Airlines' non-stop performance in both directions.

The DC-7 and L.1049G had made US transcontinental non-stop operation a practical undertaking, but at that time non-stop North Atlantic operation in both directions was rarely possible. In order to attain this desirable goal, Douglas added 3m (10ft) to the span of the DC-7 and increased its fuel tankage. It thus became the DC-7C Seven Seas with 7,412km (4,606 miles) range and North Atlantic non-stop capability. Pan American introduced them on the route on 1 June 1956 – many other airlines also adopted the type.

Lockheed went further than Douglas and designed

DC-7 'Mainliners' were used on United Air Lines' non-stop New York-Hawaii service until replaced by DC-8s in 1960-61. The transition to jets was extremely rapid with aircraft that were once the pride of the fleet being consigned to the scrap heap or converted to freighters.

a completely new 45.72m (150ft) span one-piece wing, containing fuel for more than 9,655km (6,000 miles), and mated this with the Super Constellation fuselage to form the L.1649A Starliner, with up to 99 seats. It entered service with TWA on the New York-London service on 1 June 1957.

These two very advanced piston-engined aircraft also made possible one-stop services between Europe and Japan over the Polar route, with a call at Anchorage in Alaska. SAS was first with the DC-7C on the Copenhagen-Tokyo route in February 1957, and Air France followed with L.1649As flying between Paris and Tokyo.

In addition to the Douglas and Lockheed types, there was one other large American four-engined airliner – the Boeing Stratocruiser. This was bigger than the other types, and had a lounge and bar on a lower deck. It had seats for up to 100 passengers, was powered by four 3,500hp Pratt & Whitney Wasp Major engines, and entered service over the North Atlantic with Pan American in 1949. Only 55 civil Stratocruisers were built, and they earned a poor reputation because of engine and propeller problems. In spite of this they were popular with crews and passengers, and maintained BOAC and Pan American first-class North Atlantic services until the introduction of jet aircraft in 1958.

In the immediate postwar years there was an urgent need for a twin-engined short-haul aeroplane to replace the DC-3, and several countries designed aircraft to meet this requirement. In the United States, Martin and Convair both produced aircraft in this category. They were low-wing monoplanes with nosewheel undercarriages and 2,500hp Pratt & Whitney R-2800 engines.

The 42-seat Martin 2-0-2 was unpressurized and entered service in autumn 1947 with Northwest Airlines in the US and LAN in Chile. The type was involved in a number of serious accidents, and one suffered a wing failure which led to the aircraft being withdrawn. After strengthening, the 2-0-2 returned to service in 1950 as the Martin 2-0-2A. It was followed by the 48 to 52-seat pressurized Martin 4-0-4, which entered service with TWA in October 1951. A total of 149 aircraft of was built.

Much greater success was enjoyed by the Convair-Liner. The CV-240, with 40 seats and a pressurized cabin, entered service in June 1948 with American Airlines. It quickly found favour, and 176 civil examples were built. The improved 44-passenger CV-340 followed in 1952, and in 1956 the 52 to 56 seat CV-440 Metropolitan made its debut. More than 1,000 civil and military Convair-Liners were built, of which more than 240 were later re-engined with propeller-turbines.

In Britain in the early postwar years BOAC was using DC-3s, Avro Lancastrians and Yorks developed from the Lancaster bomber, and Short flying boats. But plans had been made for new aircraft, and two of them flew before the end of 1945. They were the Vickers-Armstrong Viking, developed from the Wellington bomber, and the

The L-104G Super Constellation was one of the finest piston-engined airliners ever produced. With tip tanks and the 'Connie's' trademark triple-fins, this classic Lufthansa L-1049G is a sight to behold.

Bristol 170 Freighter/ Wayfarer. The Viking was a mid-wing monoplane with two Bristol Hercules engines, an unpressurized cabin, and a tailwheel undercarriage. It cruised at about 320km/h (200 mph), and on entering service with BEA on 1 September 1946, had 27 seats. For several years it was the airline's principal type. It served with many airlines, and 163 were built.

The Bristol 170 was very different. It was a high-wing monoplane with a slab-sided fuselage, non-retractable undercarriage and two Hercules engines. The Wayfarer was a passenger aircraft, but the Freighter undertook the duties which its name implied – the best known operation being Silver City Airways' cross-Channel vehicle ferries, which it and the longer-fuselage Superfreighter undertook for many years. The type also operated cargo services between North and South Island in New Zealand for over 30 years.

France's first postwar transport aircraft to enter airline service was the 33-seat Sud-Est SE.161 Languedoc which, as the Bloch 161, had made its first flight in September 1939, but could not be produced until after the war. Originally powered by four Gnome Rhone engines, most had Pratt & Whitney R-1830s. A total of 100 Languedocs was built, entering service with Air France on the Paris-Algiers route in May 1946 and serving a number of airlines in Europe and the Middle East.

Turbine Power

In Britain the Brabazon Committee was set up in December 1942 to make recommendations for the development of postwar transport aircraft. Among its recommendations was the design and production of a North Atlantic turbojet aeroplane, Brabazon Type IV, and a short-haul propeller-turbine type, Brabazon Type IIB.

The Type IV evolved through a number of designs to become the de Havilland Comet – the first turbojet airliner to enter commercial service. Two types were designed to meet the Type IIB recommendation: the Armstrong Whitworth Apollo, of which only two prototypes were-built, and the Vickers-Armstrong Viscount. Turbine power was to change the standard of airline flight by reducing vibration and interior noise levels. In the case of the turbojet, flight times were to be virtually halved.

The prototype Viscount, the V.630, made its first flight on 16 July 1948. It was a low-wing monoplane with a pressurized cabin for 32 passengers, and was powered by four 1,380hp Rolls-Royce Dart turbines driving four-blade propellers. Although the V.630 was considered too small to be economic, BEA did use it to operate the first ever services by a turbine-powered aeroplane. On 29 July 1950, it flew from Northolt, west of London, to Le Bourget, Paris, carrying 14 passengers and 12 guests. It went on to operate between London and Edinburgh.

Rolls-Royce increased the power of the Dart and enabled Vickers to stretch the Viscount to become a 47 to 60 seat aircraft as the V.700. BEA placed an order for 20 and regular Viscount services began on 18 April 1953, when RMA *Sir Ernest Shackleton* operated the London-Rome-Athens-Nicosia service. The Viscount immediately proved a success, being produced in several versions and sold in many parts of the world, including the USA and China. A total of 438 were built.

The Comet 1 was a very clean low-wing monoplane with four de Havilland Ghost turbojets buried in the wing roots. There was accommodation for 36 passengers in two cabins and pressurization enabled it to fly at levels over 12,190m (40,000ft). The first prototype flew on 27 July 1949, and soon made a number of spectacular overseas flights. BOAC took delivery of ten Comet 1s and on 2 May 1952, operated the world's first jet service over the London-Johannesburg route. With their cruising speed of 788km/h (490mph), Comets covered the 10,821km (6,724 miles) in less than 24 hours. On the London-Singapore route they cut the time from 21 days to 25 hours, and they reduced the London-Tokyo time from 86 to 33¼ hours.

Air France and UAT introduced Comets, and they were ordered by several other airlines. But exactly a year after their introduction a Comet broke up in flight near Calcutta, and in January 1954 another disintegrated and fell into the sea near Elba. After modifications the Comet was put back into service, but less than three weeks later a third Comet broke up, and the type was withdrawn from commercial service.

Pressure failure of the cabin, specifically bursting of the square windows in the original model, was said to have caused the failures, and some fuselage redesign resulted. Comet 2s, already under construction, were modified and went to the RAF. Work went ahead on the Rolls-Royce Avon-powered Comet 4 with a longer fuselage, seats for up to 81, and additional fuel tanks.

BOAC ordered 19 Comet 4s and on 4 October 1958, operated the first ever North Atlantic jet services, the London-New York flight being made in 10 hours 22 minutes with a fuel stop at Gander. The eastbound flight was made non-stop in 6 hours 11 minutes. A shorter-span, longer-fuselage Comet 4B, with seats for up to 101, was introduced by BEA on 1 April 1960, and in the same year the Comet 4C was commissioned – this combined the Comet 4 wings with the Comet 4B fuselage. A total of 74 Comet 4-series aircraft were completed.

The second European turbojet airliner to enter service was the French Sud-Aviation SE.210 Caravelle. It was a twin-engined aircraft and the first to have its turbojets mounted on either side of the rear fuselage. This layout reduced the engine noise entering the passenger cabin and was adopted by the later Douglas DC-9, BAC One-Eleven and Tupolev Tu-124, among others. To save on development costs, the design of the nose and windscreen came from the Comet.

The Caravelle was designed primarily for operation between France and North Africa. It first flew on 27 May 1955, was powered by two Rolls-Royce Avons and, as the Caravelle I, had seats for up to 80 passengers. The Caravelle I entered service with Air France in May 1959 on the Paris-Rome-Istanbul route, and with SAS between Copenhagen and Cairo.

Numerous versions of the Caravelle were produced, up to the 128-passenger Caravelle 12B, and they were operated in many parts of the world, including the United States, where United Air Lines had 20. The 10R was the first version of the Caravelle not to be powered by Avons, being fitted with Pratt & Whitney JT8D-1 turbofans as developed for the Boeing 727. The Super Caravelle was the last in a series of exceptionally fine aeroplanes, having a maximum cruising speed of 835 km/h (518mph), a range of 2,655km (1,650miles) and seating for 105 passengers. A total of 280 Caravelles were built and a few survivors remained in service as late as 1991.

In early 1947, BOAC issued a specification for a Medium Range Empire (MRE) transport, and Bristol's response was the Type 175 with four Centaurus piston engines. Subsequently it was agreed that Bristol Proteus propeller-turbines would be used and in this form, as the Britannia, the prototype flew on 16 August 1952. The Britannia was a large low-wing monoplane with seats for up to 90 passengers and a take-off weight of 70,305kg (155,000lb).

BOAC introduced the Britannia 102 on the London-Johannesburg route on 1 February 1957 and

Named *Canopus* after
an Imperial Airways'
C-class flying
boat, BOAC's brand
new stratocruiser
arrives at Heathrow
after its inaugural
transatlantic flight
in October 1949.

British Midland was one of many enthusiastic operators of second-hand Viscounts, especially when oil prices quadrupled in 1973. The last UK Viscount passenger flight was operated by British World Airways in March 1996.

the longer-range Britannia 312 on London-New York services on 19 December 1957. The latter were the first North Atlantic service by turbine-powered aircraft. The Britannia was an extremely good aircraft, but it appeared much too late and only 85 were built.

Canadair produced a number of Britannia variants, one of which, the CL-44, went into airline service. These aircraft generally resembled the Britannia, but had Rolls-Royce Tyne propeller-turbines and lengthened fuselages. Known as the CL-44D, and provided with swing-tail fuselage for cargo loading, the type entered service with the US cargo carrier Seaboard World Airlines in July 1961. Then came the CL-44J, with even longer fuselage and accommodation for up to 214 passengers, for the cheap-fare North Atlantic services of the Icelandic airline Loftleidir.

The large propeller-turbine aircraft built for BEA was the Vickers-Armstrong Vanguard, also powered by Tynes. It could carry 139 passengers and had considerable underfloor cargo capacity. The Vanguard first flew on 20 January 1959, and began operations with BEA on 17 December 1960. In early 1961 it entered service with Trans-Canada Air Lines, the only other customer for new Vanguards. Despite its low fuel burn and logical layout, the Vanguard sold poorly – airline passengers preferred jets. Only 43 were built, and, like the Britannia, most ended their days with small ad hoc cargo operators.

Only one type of large civil propeller-turbine aeroplane, the Lockheed L.188 Electra, was built in the United States. Smaller than the Vanguard, it had accommodation for up to 99 passengers, and was powered by four Allison 501 engines. The Electra first flew on 6 December 1957, and entered service with American Airlines and Eastern Air Lines in January 1959. As a civil airliner the Electra failed to make money for Lockheed, but redesigned as the P-3 maritime patrol aircraft for the US Navy it has been a huge success.

The most successful of all the western propeller-turbine transports has been the Fokker F.27 Friendship. This is a high-wing monoplane powered by two Rolls-Royce Darts and normally accommodating about 48 passengers. The first prototype flew on 24 November 1955, and the aircraft went into production at Amsterdam in the Netherlands and also in the US as the F-27, built by Fairchild. The type first entered service in the US, with West Coast Airlines, on 28 September 1958. In Europe, Aer Lingus began operating the aircraft on Dublin-Glasgow services on 15 December 1958. Numerous versions were built, including the 56-passenger FH-227, before production switched to the updated and re-engined Fokker 50 in the late 1980s. The majority of the 786 F.27s built are still in service.

Britain's attempts to break into this market have been less successful. Handley Page made the mistake of designing the Herald with four Alvis Leonides piston engines; the delay in producing the twin-Dart Herald, which was very similar to the F.27, cost the company dearly and only 48 were completed. More successful was the low-wing Avro (later Hawker Siddeley/BAe) 748, also Dart-powered, which entered service in 1962. More than 400 civil and military examples were built, about 50 of these being assembled or constructed by Hindustan Aeronautics in India. After delivering its last 748, BAe's Woodford plant near Manchester announced its successor, the ATP (Advanced Turbo Prop). Later relaunched as the Avro Jetstream 61,

Together with Mexicana, Aerolineas Argentinas was one of only two South American customers for the Comet 4, taking delivery of its first aircraft in March 1959.

the aircraft shares a high degree of structural commonality with the 748 but has been re-engined with PW127D turboprops driving advanced lightweight Hamilton Standard propellers. Faced with stiff competition from the new generation of turboprop airliners, especially the Fokker 50, ATR42/52/72, Saab 340B and 2000, Embraer Brazilia and Dornier Do 328, barely 50 were sold before production was abandoned in 1995 as part of a joint marketing agreement between BAe and AIR of France and Italy for the Jetstream J31/41 series (a completely different aircraft) and the ATR family with 42, 52 and 72 seats.

There has also been one Japanese turbine-powered transport, the NAMC YS-11. This is a 46 to 60 passenger low-wing monoplane powered by two Dart engines. It first flew on 30 August 1962, and entered service in Japan in April 1965. More than 180 were delivered, but most of these had been replaced by the early 1990s.

The First 'Big Jets'

Not until the Comet 1 had been withdrawn from service did the first US turbojet transport make its maiden flight. At Seattle, in Washington State, on 15 July 1954, a large brown and yellow swept-wing monoplane with four pod-mounted engines took to the air and began a new era in air transport. It was the Boeing 367-80, known affectionately as the Dash 80,

and was in fact the prototype Boeing 707. This was a much more advanced aeroplane than the Comet: its wings were swept back 35°, and it embodied the experience gained with Boeing B-47 and B-52 jet bombers.

Pan American placed the first order, and the type went into production as the Model 707-100 with the customer designation 707-121. The production aeroplane had a span of 40.18m (131ft 10in), a length of 44.04m (144ft 6in), accommodation for up to 179 passengers, and a maximum weight of 116,818kg (257,000lb). It was powered by four 5,670kg (12,500lb) thrust Pratt & Whitney JT3C turbojets, cruised at 917km/h (570mph) and had a maximum range of 4,949km (3,075 miles) with full payload. The 707-121 entered revenue service with Pan American on the North Atlantic on 26 October 1958, just 22 days after the Comet 4.

This original Boeing 707 was followed by a whole family of 707 passenger and cargo variants, with different lengths and weights, and turbofan power. The passenger-carrying 707-320B and passenger cargo 707-320C were the main production models. Also developed was the short-to-medium-range version known as the Boeing 720 or, with turbofans, 720B. By the end of October 1976, 917 Boeing 707s and 720s of all models had flown more than 30 million hours and carried just under 522 million passengers.

Excluding the related KC-135, Boeing built a further 92 military versions of the 707. A large number of ex-airline 707s have been converted into freighters with strengthened floors, cargo doors and, more recently, engine hush-kits to extend their service lives in the face of more severe noise regulations. As the platform for the military E-3 AWACS, production of the 707-320 airframe continued until 1992.

The second US jet transport was the Douglas DC-8. It closely resembles the Boeing 707, and has likewise been produced in several versions. The first DC-8 flew on 30 May 1958, and the JT3C powered DC-8-10 entered service with Delta Air Lines and United Air Lines on 18 September 1959. Then followed the 20 with more powerful JT4A engines, the -30 long-range aeroplane, the -40 with Rolls-Royce Conway engines and the -50 with JT3D turbofans. There were also freight, convertible, and mixed passenger/cargo versions. All had a span of 43.41 m (142ft 5in) and a length of 45.87m (150ft 6in) and maximum seating of 177.

In 1966 the Series 60 DC-8 appeared. This was built in three main versions, the -61 with the same span as earlier models but a length of 57.09m (187ft 4in) and seating for up to 257; the -62 with 45.23m (148ft 5in) span, 47.98m (157ft 5in) length and seats for 201; and the -63, combining the wing of the -62 with the fuselage of the -61. This was the largest jet airliner in service until the arrival of the Boeing 747, withseats for up to 259.

The DC-8-61 was put into service between Los Angeles and Honolulu by United Air Lines on 25 February 1967; the DC-8-62 entered service on the Copenhagen-Los Angeles route with SAS on 22 May 1967; and the DC-8-63 was introduced by KLM on the Amsterdam-New York route in July 1967. There were cargo and convertible versions of the Series 60 aircraft, and a total of 556 DC-8s of all models was built before production ceased in favour in 1972.

The 'Super DC-8' remains popular as a long distance cargo aircraft, especially when re-engined with CFM-56 turbofans, which vastly improve overall performance. Thus modified, Series 61 and 63 aircraft become the DC-8-71 and DC-8-73 respectively.

The third US constructor of large commercial jet transports was the Convair Division of General Dynamics, which produced two types. The first was the CV-880. It was smaller than the Boeing and Douglas types, its narrower fuselage having a maximum seating capacity of 130. It was powered by four

General Electric CJ-805 engines, had a maximum weight of 87,770kg (193,500lb) and cruised at up to 989km/h (615mph). It was designed for TWA, but first went into service with Delta on 15 May 1960, over the Houston-New York, New York-New Orleans and New York-Atlanta routes. Only 65 were built.

The second Convair was the CV-990 (named Coronado by Swissair). It was designed for American Airlines and closely resembled the CV-880, but had General Electric CJ-805-23C turbofans and a maximum cruising speed of 1,005km/h (625mph), making it the world's fastest airliner until the supersonic Concorde. However, flight tests revealed unexpected drag over the trailing edge of the wing at typical cruising speeds. The problem was solved by adding four canoe-like shock bodies or 'speed pods' which extended aft of the wing, but these in turn caused wing flutter when the outer pods were full of fuel. The only cure – engine re-alignment to redistribute the wing loading – delayed the programme even more. Meanwhile sales of the 707 and DC-8 surged ahead. The CV-990 finally entered service with American Airlines and Swissair in March 1962. Although Convair built a mere 37, the type gave excellent service for many years.

Britain's clear world lead in the design and operation of jet airliners had ended with the grounding of the Comet and a valiant attempt to break into the so-called 'big jet' market met with little success. The aircraft was the Vickers-Armstrongs VC10, which was in the same category as the Boeing 707 but had its four

The elegant Sud Aviation Caravelle was a twinjet trend-setter and remained in service for more than 30 years. Delivered on 22 July 1964, this is OH-LSA *Helsinki*, Finnair's first Super Caravelle.

Bristol's 'Whispering Giant', the much-delayed Britannia 102, was soon completely outclassed by the new jets but had the consolation of operating the first turbine-powered North Atlantic passenger service with BOAC in 1957.

The Lockheed Electra entered service in 1959 and continues to be used as a cargo carrier by a number of specialist operators. This Air Bridge L-188 was photographed at Birmingham International Airport in the early 1990s.

Rolls-Royce Conway bypass engines mounted in pairs on each side of the rear fuselage, and a high-mounted tailplane and elevators.

An outstanding technical achievement, the VC10's large swept wing incorporated highly effective leading edge slats and flaps and was the largest built in Europe until the Airbus A330/340. This gave the aircraft excellent take-off and landing performance from hot and high runways in East Africa (as demanded by BOAC), enabling it to undertake some operations which would have been impossible for the early Boeings. But at the vast majority of major airports this capability was unnecessary. The extra weight of the wing structure and its high-lift devices made the VC10 less competitive than its rivals, both of which were lighter and already well established in airline service. Predictably, sales were hugely disappointing and only 54 VC10s were produced. BOAC's order for Conway-powered 707-320s did not help, though interestingly the Super VC10s on the North Atlantic run were its most profitable aircraft betweem 1968 and 1972.

The Standard VC10 could carry up to 139 passengers and had a maximum cruising speed of 933km/h (580mph). The VC10 went into service on the London-Lagos route on 29 April 1964, and was followed by the Super VC10 which was 3.96m (13ft) longer, had more powerful Conways and seating for up to 163. Super VC10s were introduced on the London-New York route on 1 April 1965. The RAF has become the biggest VC10 operator, with ten Model 1109 long-range transports (delivered new in 1965-66) and 20 tankers converted from a mix of Standards and Supers formerly owned by British Airways (BOAC), Gulf Air and East African Airways.

Medium- and Short-Range Jets

In the summer of 1956 BEA issued a specification for a 965km/h (600mph) aircraft to meet its short-to medium-range route requirements. The de Havilland 121 Trident was selected, and the Aircraft Manufacturing Co, comprising de Havilland, Fairey and Hunting, set up to build the aircraft, but de Havilland then became part of the Hawker Siddeley Group. The design was changed to meet differing BEA demands before the first aircraft made its initial flight on 9 January 1962.

The Trident had a swept wing, high T-tail and three rear-mounted Rolls-Royce Spey bypass engines. BEA ordered 24 Trident 1s with 88 seats, a cruising speed of 941km/h (585mph) and typical full-payload range of 1,448km (900

miles) with full fuel reserves. The first revenue flight by a Trident was made on 11 March 1964, and full scheduled services with Tridents began on 1 April 1964.

The Trident gave good service and played a major role in the development of automatic landing, using a triplex system to provide a very high standard of reliability and safety. The first automatic landing by an aircraft on a passenger service was made on 10 June 1965, by a Trident landing at Heathrow on arrival from Paris.

The Trident 1E with uprated engines, leading-edge slats and seating for up to 139 passengers in high-density layout, flew in November 1964. Fifteen were built, and customers included Air Ceylon, Iraqi Airways, Kuwait Airways and PIA. Then came the Trident 2E which had Rolls-Royce

The Fokker F.27 is the world's most successful turboprop airliner and in Fokker 50 form it was still being offered to customers when the Dutch company collapsed in March 1996.

Speys, increased span, seats for 97 in BEA service and increased range. This version entered service on 18 April 1968.

The last major version of the series was the Trident 3B. This had a tail-mounted Rolls-Royce RB.162 booster engine to improve take-off performance, was 5.0m (16ft 5in) longer than the earlier Tridents, and had accommodation for up to 180 passengers. BEA ordered 26, and began using them in March 1971. Finally came the Super Trident 3B with a maximum-payload range of 3,380km (2,100 miles) and seats for 152 passengers. Two Super Tridents were ordered by CAAC in China, bringing the Trident total to 117. After the discovery of wing cracks, British Airways' grounded its 3Bs (inherited from BEA) in the mid-1970s.

In the same category as the Trident, and of very similar layout, is the Boeing 727. Design began in June 1959, but Boeing regarded the decision to go into production as a major gamble. In the event, the 727 outsold every other Western jet transport by a very large margin. A grand total of 1,831 was built, the vast majority being versions of the 727-200.

From the floor up, the Model 727 has the same fuselage cross-section as the Boeing 707, namely 3.75m (148in). The wing has 32 degrees

The Avro 748 prototype takes the scenic route around its Woodford, Manchester, birthplace in 1960. Best known as the Hawker Siddeley HS.748, it became Britain's second-best selling turboprop after the Viscount.

of sweep and is fitted with triple-slotted flaps and leading-edge slats, giving the 727 much better take-off and landing performance than the original Tridents. The 727-100, powered by three Pratt & Whitney JT8D-1 turbofans and having accommodation for a maximum of 131 passengers, made its first flight on 9 February 1963, and entered service with Eastern Air Lines and United Air Lines at the beginning of February 1964. Eastern's 727 fleet gave the carrier faithful service until it went out of business in 1989. In 1991, one of United's first 727s was donated to the Museum of Flight Foundation at Everett, Washington.

Numerous versions of the Boeing 727 were produced, the last being the Advanced 727-200. Powered by JT8Ds, it can carry up to 189 passengers. Maximum take-off weight is now 94,318kg (207,500lb) compared with 72,570kg (160,000lb) for the original aeroplane.

Some of the final 'three holers', delivered in 1984, were 727-252F freighters purpose-built for Federal Express, the US overnight door-to-door freight and small package carrier. These aircraft have no cabin windows and are fitted with a large cargo door on the left-hand side of the forward fuselage. Many ex-airline 727s, some of them 30-year-old veterans, also serve with FedEx, having been retrofitted with cargo doors so as to enable the loading of palletized packets and parcels.

With the latest cockpit avionics, hushkits or quieter, more fuel-efficent engines, the 727 is a tempting, low-cost alternative to more modern airliners such as the Airbus A321. The potential market for these upgrades is very large, as plenty of 727s are less than halfway through their expected service lives. The Texas-based Dee Howard company has sold Rolls-Royce Tay 650 turbofan conversions to United Parcel Service and other customers are expected to follow the alternative is the compulsory grounding of noisy unmodified aircraft. United Air Lines' prefers to hushkit its 80-plus fleet of 727 to meet 1999 noise regulations. In early 1996, one of its 727s became the first commercial airliner to demonstrate the infra-red Enhanced Viewing System (EVS), which, when used in conjunction with a head-up display, enables the pilot the see a clear picture of the runway when landing in thick fog.

Lufthansa was one of a number of airlines (including BOAC) to specify Rolls-Royce Conway turbofans for some of its intercontinental Boeing 707s.

In addition to the big jets, there was considered to be a need for about 1,000 smaller twinjet aircraft. The first designed to meet this requirement was the British Aircraft Corporation's BAC One-Eleven, powered by two rear-mounted Speys and having accommodation for up to 89 passengers. The first announcement about the BAC One-Eleven was made in May 1961, when it was stated that British United Airways had ordered ten. The first aircraft flew on 20 August 1963, but was lost in a deep stall, and it was not until April 1965 that the production Series 200 entered service with BUA and Braniff. The Series 200 was followed first by the increased-range Series 300 and then by the similar Series 400, which was specially adapted to meet US conditions and entered service with American Airlines on 6 March 1966.

Then came the Series 500, with more powerful Speys, 1.52m (5ft) increase in span, 4.21m (13ft 10in) increase in length, strengthened landing gear, seating for up to 109 passengers and a take-off weight of 44,450kg (98,000lb) compared with 35,605kg (78,500lb) for the Series 200. BEA ordered 18 of this 'stretched' version and introduced the type on 17 November 1968. The short-field Series 475 featured modified landing gear and used the standard fuselage and accommodation of the Series 400 with the wings and engines of the Series 500. The Series 475 could be fitted with a large forward freight door if required, but only a small number were sold, bringing the total sales to more than 220. By the late 1970s, most One-Elevens had been hushkitted in order to comply with more stringent noise legislation. After being retired from airline service, many One-Elevens were converted into long-range corporate jets; some have subsequently been re-engined by Dee Howard with quieter and more fuel-efficient R-R Tay turbofans. Similarly, in 1994 Romero of Romania announced plans to use Tays for its licence-built version of the Series 500.

Douglas also produced an aircraft in this class and of similar appearance. This was the DC-9, which first flew on 25 February 1965, and entered service with Delta Air Lines on 8 December the same year. As the DC-9-10, powered by twoPratt & Whitney JT8D-1 turbofans, the aircraft had a span of 27.25m (89ft 5 in), a length of 31.82m (104ft 4 3/4in) and accommodation for 80 passengers).

As with most previous Douglas types, success was assured by producing a family of aeroplanes to suit varying requirements, and the DC-9 was soon stretched by nearly 4.57m (15ft) to produce the 105-seat 28.47m (93ft 5in) span DC-9-30. This larger type flew on 8 August 1966, and entered service on 1 February 1967, with Eastern Air Lines on its shuttle operations. About 600 DC-9-30s were delivered, including DC-9-30F or CF freighters and passenger/cargo aircraft.

The DC-9-50 first flew on 17 December 1974, and entered service with Swissair on 24 August 1975. This has a length of 40.7m (133ft 7in), accommodation for up to 139 passengers, and a maximum take-off weight of 54,884kg (121,000lb). Douglas kept on stretching

The 707's only serious rival was the Douglas DC-8, which entered service with Delta in 1959. This Air Canada DC-8-54, inbound from Montreal with engines thrust reversers still deployed, taxies past a Finnair Super Caravelle at Heathrow in the early 1970s.

the DC-9, the Super 80 version being instantly recognizable by the considerably lengthened fuselage section ahead of the wing. First delivered in 1980, the Super 80 soon became the MD-80 to reflect the company's identity within the McDonnell Douglas Corporation (MDC). DC-9 deliveries reached 976, including 43 military C-9s. All five versions of the MD-80 family have the same wing design and use the P&W JT8D-200 series of engines, but the MD-87 is shorter, offering the same passenger load (still five-abreast) as its DC-9-50 forebear but with increased thrust, better economy and higher take-off weights.

In June 1993, MDC was chosen to supply China's new 150-seat Trunkliner in a 40-aircraft MD-80/MD-90 co-production deal. Shanghai Aviation Industrial (SAIC) has been making MD-80 components (initially nose landing gear doors) since 1983 and in 1987 completed its first MD-82 from kits supplied by MDC's Long Beach plant. SAIC remains the only company assembling US-designed commercial aircraft

Resplendent in BOAC livery, this is the VC10 prototype which first flew on 29 June 1962. The Standard version was soon followed by the stretched Super.

outside the USA. It has also sent MD-80s back to Long Beach to be sold as Douglas aircraft, the five MD-83s completed in 1992 being the first Chinese-built jetliners to be exported. The MD-90 series is re-engined and incorporates the latest 'glass cockpit' technology, but retains the same wing/fuselage combination as the MD-80. With total deliveries of about 1,500 aircraft by 1995, the MD-80/90 family looks set to beat the 727 into third place in the jetliner sales league, though it has little chance of catching the 737, its principal competitor (see below).

In February 1965, Boeing took another big risk in deciding to build the 737 on the strength of a Lufthansa order for 21 aircraft. No one knew that the company was launching the most successful jetliner in history. By early 1996, some 2,783 aircraft, mostly variants of the Model 200, had carried 4.24 billion passengers and flown 64.5 million hours. The type first flew on 9 April 1967 at Boeing Field, Seattle, and the initial Model 737-100 entered service early in 1968 with Lufthansa and United Air Lines.

Because the Model 737 retains the fuselage and cross-section of the 707 and 727, most versions appear to be quite stubby, the 737-200 having a length of only 30.48m (100ft). It also differs in having its engines attached close beneath the wings. The 737 has been developed into an extended family which includes Model 300, 400, 500, 600, 700 and 800 versions, all of which are powered by CFM-56 turbofans. These Models are tailored to the passenger capacity (100-189 seats) and range requirements of customer airlines. No longer in production but the backbone of more than 100 carriers is the classic 737-200. This is powered by JT8D-17 engines, weighs up to 53,070kg (117,000lb) and can accommodate a maximum of 135 passengers.

One of Iberia's big fleet of 727-200s displays the complex slats and flaps which give its swept-wing the high-lift and drag required for approach and landing.

A McDonnell Douglas MD-83 of the German charter operator Aero Lloyd at Birmingham Airport. With 155 seats, the MD-83 is a more powerful, heavier version of the DC-9 Super 80.

With production of the Model 300, 400 and 500 continuing against a order backlog of more than 500 aircraft, Boeing announced in late 1995 a third generation of 737s. The 737-600, -700 and -800 look little different to earlier variants but feature a completely new wing of considerably increased span, offering higher lift, lower drag and increased fuel capacity. Together with the latest CFM-56-7B turbofans, the wing provides the improvements in take-off, cruise altitude and payload/range performance to keep the 737 competitive in the 150-seat jetliner market.

The new generation 737s also feature many detailed improvements, but the most striking changes are on the flight deck. The displays can emulate the electronic flight instrumentation system (EFIS) type instruments of second generation 737s (which thousands of airline pilots are familiar with) or, after inserting a disk loaded code, switch to the primary flight display and navigation display arrangement common to the 747-400 and 777. Boeing expects to deliver 2,000 new generation models over the next 20 years, which will bring total 737 sales to an astounding 5,000-plus.

In the Netherlands, Fokker designed a jet successor to the F.27 Friendship. This was the F.28 Fellowship, which flew on 9 May 1967, entering service with the Norwegian airline Braathens SAFE on 28 March 1969. The F.28 is a low-wing monoplane powered by two rear-mounted Speys. It was designed to operate from short 1,220m (4,000ft) runways and, to achieve good low-speed handling, the wing sweep was restricted to 16 degrees. The ultimate version was the Mk 6000, which was stretched to have accommodation for up 85 seats (20 more than the Mk 1000) and had a greater wing span and uprated engines. Fokker delivered its 241st and last F.28 in 1987.

Wide-Bodied Fleets

In 1960 the world's airlines, excluding those of China and the Soviet Union, carried 106 million passengers, and by 1966 this figure had nearly doubled. This rapid increase in traffic called for larger fleets of aircraft, and these added to airport and airway congestion. One way of absorbing the growth without increasing aircraft movements was to build bigger aircraft. At the same time these aircraft would reduce seat-mile costs and ease noise problems, an important aspect of air transport which was reaching intolerable levels.

The first of this new generation was made known in April 1966, when Boeing announced the Model 747 with Pan American placing an order for 25 costing $21million each. In one step the Boeing 747 was doubling the capacity, power and weight of the transport aeroplane. Building the 747 'Jumbo Jet' broke new ground, quite literally. With its existing plants working to full capacity, Boeing had to erect a giant new production complex at Everett, north of Seattle. By June 1967 the world's largest passenger jet was being built in the world's largest building.

In general appearance the 747 was similar to the 707, but was scaled up to have a wing span of 59.63m (195ft 8in), a length of 70.51m (231ft 4in) and a height from the ground to the top of the fin of 19.32m (63ft 5in). The maximum interior width is just over 6m (20ft), and the ceiling height 2.43m (8ft). Seating on the main deck can be nine- or ten-abreast (in tourist class) with two fore and aft aisles, and this feature introduced the term 'widebody'. The flight deck is on an upper level, and behind this is a passenger cabin which served as a first-class lounge in early versions. This upper deck was later extended to provide additional seating. A spiral stairway connected the upper level to the main passenger cabin. In the vast majority of 747s, the first class accommodation is now in the nose. The three cargo and baggage holds have a volume about equal to the entire volume of a cargo Boeing 707.

THY Turkish Airlines' 737-300, the most popular of the CFM-56/V.2500-powered versions. The most successful twinjet in history with nearly 3,000 delivered, the 737 just keeps on selling.

British Midland was one of the last operators of the DC-9-30, which operated its fast and friendly London-Birmingham shuttle service until the early 1990s.

The original engines in the Boeing 747 were four 18,597kg (41,000lb) thrust Pratt & Whitney JT9D-1 turbofans. The first Boeing 747 flew on 9 February 1969, the type entering service with Pan American on the New York-London route on 22 January 1970.

Pan American's 747-100s had 58 first-class and 304 economy-class seats and a maximum cruising altitude 13,715m (45,000ft). In spite of its size the aircraft was orthodox in appearance, except that it had four four-wheel main undercarriage units to spread the load on runways, taxiways and airport aprons. Maximum seating was originally quoted as 490, but 350 proved more typical. Similarly, today's 747-400 can carry up to 450 passengers, but most carriers opt for a mixed-class arrangement with 370 seats.

The 747 underwent rapid development, with increased power and consequently higher permissible weights, and the -200B with Rolls-Royce RB.211s, Pratt & Whitney JT9D-70s or General Electric CF6-50Es has a brake-release weight of up to 371,943kg (820,000lb) and has taken off at about ten tons above this weight. The final 747-200, the last of 73 freighters, was delivered in November 1991.

Boeing has the largest family of cargo aircraft in the world. The 747F features an upward-swinging nose for front-end loading of pallets or outsize loads and incorporates a mechanized cargo handling system. Cargo is loaded and unloaded along rollers which run the length of the main deck. Additional freight can be carried in the underfloor holds, just like passenger versions. The first 747-200F was delivered to Lufthansa on 9 March 1972. The 747-200C also has the upward-swinging nose, and can be operated in all-passenger configuration, as a pure freighter, or a combination of both hence the C for 'Combi' designation. Lacking the stretched upper deck or winglets of the passenger version, the -400F looks little different from the -200F, but is capable of hauling a 113,000kg (249,000lb) payload a distance of 8,100km (4,400 miles). A number of -100 and -200 passenger models have been converted into Special Freighters by Boeing with side cargo doors, strengthened main decks and more powerful engines.

In September 1973 Boeing flew the 747SR with structural reinforcement to allow high-frequency operation (flight duration of one hour or less) over short routes, which imposes greater stress on the structure – particularly the wings and landing gear. This model can carry 516 passengers. The SR (Short Range) version is unique to Japan, where it is operated on domestic services by both Japan Air Lines and All Nippon Airways. In 1994 JAL had the world's largest

747 fleet (94 aircraft) and flew every 747 variant with the exception of the SP, including two stretched upper deck 747-300SRs with seating for 563 passengers.

On Independence Day, 1975, Boeing flew the first Model 747SP (Special Performance). This has a shortened fuselage, measuring 14.73m (48ft 4in) less in length than the other 747s, but its fin is 1.52m (5ft) higher. Designed for very long-range operation over routes where traffic volume does not require the larger-capacity 747s, the SP can carry up to 321 passengers in mixed-class configuration (32 on the upper deck), and can fly 11,105km (6,900 miles) with full passenger payload.

Pan American took delivery of its first 747SP on 5 March 1976, and at the end of April introduced the type on its non-stop Los Angeles-Tokyo route. This was the longest scheduled non-stop service until Pan American began a non-stop San Francisco-Sydney service in December 1976, a distance of 11,582km (7,197 miles). Production of the SP ended in August 1982 after a run of only 44 aircraft. Most of these are still in service, some as VIP transports with the governments of Iraq, Oman, Saudi Arabia and the UAE.

Having previously offered the stretched upper deck (SUD) as a option on the final -200Bs, Boeing incorporated this modification as standard on its next 747 variant, the Model 300. Extended by 7m (23ft), the SUD contributes up to 69 seats to the all-economy total of 538 and also gives the 747 a more streamlined fuselage, though the increase in weight actually reduces maximum range. The famous spiral staircase fell victim to the revised upper deck layout, which also required separate emergency exits to meet evacuation requirements. Perhaps the best known 747-300s are the 14 'BIG TOPS' operated by Singapore Airlines, the last of which (one of three Combis) was delivered in March 1987. Lacking the range of the -200B, the 747-300 attracted relatively few customers and only 80 were built.

Boeing revitalized sales of the 747 with the Model 400, the only variant currently available. The 747-400 is significantly different to previous models, though outwardly the appearance of the aircraft is unchanged apart from the addition of winglets. The wing itself is lighter due to the extensive use of aluminium-lithium alloy skin panels. Another new feature is the optional 12,490litre (2,747gal) tailplane fuel tank, which increases maximum fuel capacity to 216,841litres (60,000gal). Up on the flight deck analogue instruments have given way to multi-screen electronic displays, enabling two pilots to safely operate the 747 for the first time. The space vacated by the redundant

Mostly acquired from Singapore Airlines, the Boeing 747-200 propelled Virgin Atlantic Airways' into the competitive North Atlantic market. It was not unknown for owner Richard Branson to help man a drinks trolley on the Gatwick-New York service.

flight engineer is now a flight crew rest area, as two additional pilots are needed on ultra long haul flights such as Qantas' 14¾ hour service between Los Angeles and Sydney, a distance of 12,050km (6,500 miles). Orders for 454 Model 400s had been taken by 1992, and deliveries should exceed those of the -200 (393 built) by 1997.

Built in 15 different variants, the 747 has been the world's largest, heaviest and most powerful airliner for more than a quarter of a century. By 1995 sales had tailed off in the face of competition from the Airbus A330/340 and the arrival of the 777, but the 747 is obviously one of the greatest industrial achievements in history. Over 1,070 Boeing 747s had been delivered and the company has an order backlog of at least 100 aircraft, enough to keep the production line running into the next century. Boeing has studied an even bigger version, the 'double-decker' 747X, to challenge the proposed 600-seat Airbus A3XX.

The Boeing 747 was too big for some airline routes, especially those flown by US domestic airlines. What they wanted was a large-capacity aircraft with transcontinental range, and McDonnell Douglas and Lockheed both built very similar three-engined aircraft to meet this need. In layout both were wide-bodied aircraft with two wing-mounted engines and one tail-mounted, although the two companies adopted different methods of mounting the rear engine. In the Douglas DC-10 the rear engine is built into the fin structure, but in the Lockheed L-1011 TriStar it is within the fuselage with the air intake above the fuselage forward of the fin.

The first DC-10 flew on 29 August 1970. This was the Series 10 version with General Electric CF6-6D turbofans, seating for 270 passengers in basic mixed-class configuration or a maximum of 345 in economy class, a maximum brake-release weight of 195,043kg (430,000lb) and a range of 6,727km (4,180 miles). Span of the -10 is 47.34m (155ft 4in), and length of 55.55m (182ft 3in). This version entered service on 5 August 1971, on American Airlines' Los Angeles-Chicago route, and on 14 August on United Air Lines' San Francisco-Washington route.

On 28 February 1972, the DC-10-20 made its first flight. This version, later redesignated -40, has a 3m (9ft 10in) increase in span, Pratt & Whitney JT9D-59 turbofans, and a still-air range of 9,060km (5,630 miles). The DC-10-20 was built for Northwest Airlines, and entered service on 16 December 1972. Fitted with more powerful engines, the first true DC-10-40 first flew on 25 July 1975, and this version remained exclusive to Japan Air Lines. Rarest of all was the DC-10-15, designed for Mexicana to operate from Mexico City, the world's highest major airport. This version combined a series -10 airframe with -30 engines for more spritely performance in hot and high conditions. Mexicana ordered seven DC-10-15s, taking delivery of its first aircraft in June 1981.

The most used DC-10 is the -30 model which first flew on 21 June 1972. This has the increased span of the -20/40, is powered by CF6-50C turbofans, has the same weight as the -20/40 but a range of 9,768km (6,070 miles). The DC-10-30 first went into service with Swissair on North Atlantic services on 15 December 1972. Installing extra tankage and more powerful engines produced the extended-range DC-10-30ER for Swissair and Finnair, the latter carrier operating a direct flight over the North Pole from Helsinki to Tokyo, a distance of 11,056km (5,966 miles). There are also convertible and pure freighter versions, the DC-10-30CF and -30F respectively, both of which can carry palletized loads. The first of nine DC-10-30Fs for FedEx was delivered on 24 January 1986.

Although it did considerably better than the TriStar, the DC-10 was never in the same sales league as the 747. The biggest operator of the DC-10 is not an airline but the USAF, who rejected the 747 in favour of a modified version of the DC-10-30CF to meet its requirement for an advanced tanker/cargo aircraft.

The KC-10 Extender is fitted with a 'flying boom' and a hose-drum unit for flight refuelling and has additional fuel cells in the lower fuselage. Including the 60 USAF KC-10s, a total of 446 DC-10s was built. Many older versions are now in desert storage, but the DC-10-30 continues to offer a profitable combination of passenger/cargo capacity and long-range for both scheduled airlines and charter operators.

The Lockheed L-1011 TriStar, which first flew on 16 November 1970, has exactly the same span as the DC-10-10 but is slightly shorter at 54.43m (178ft 7½in). It was the first aircraft to be powered by the Rolls-Royce RB.211 'big fan' engine. The original L-1011-1 TriStar could carry 272 passengers in mixed-class configuration, 330 in coach class or up to 400 in economy class. The range with 272 passengers and full fuel reserves was 6,275km (3,900 miles).

The Lockheed TriStar entered service on 26 April 1972, with Eastern Air Lines, which had placed orders and options for 50 aircraft. The other big launch customer was TWA, with a requirement for 44. A further five versions of the TriStar were introduced, including the L-1011-200 with RB.211-524 engines and a reduced payload for longer range; the -250 which combined a heavier all-up weight with more range; and the extended-range L-1011-500 with RB.211-524B engines, a shortened fuselage 50.05m (164ft 2in) in length and increased wing span 50.6m (164ft 4in) for additional fuel and less drag. Cruise efficiency was ultimately enhanced by 'active' ailerons to smooth out drag-inducing gusts, a pioneering civil application of fly by wire. Launched by British Airways in August 1976, the -500 was also bought by Delta, Pan Am, Air Canada, Air Lanka, Alia, Royal Jordanian, BWIA, LTU and TAP. The Dash 500

The first Boeing 747-400 pictured soon after its maiden flight on 29 April 1988. The Dash 400 introduced the stretched upper deck and winglets as standard, but the most dramatic change was a two-man electronic 'glass' cockpit. Boeing claims that its latest 'Jumbo' burns up to 25 per cent less fuel than older 747s.

has a range of 9,748km (5,260 miles) with a full load of 246 passengers.

In 1983, after building exactly 250 TriStars, Lockheed ended production of its one and only jetliner in order to cap mounting losses on the programme. Though not a commercial success, the TriStar was impressively engineered and still does a tremendous job carrying passengers (increasingly with charter airlines) or cargo. In 1995, Delta remained the largest TriStar operator with a fleet of 56, some 17 being Dash 500s for transatlantic services to Frankfurt and London Gatwick.

Two years after the TriStar bowed out, McDonnell Douglas announced the MD-11 as a successor to the DC-10. Existing DC-10 operators were wooed by the promise of substantial improvements in range and seat-mile costs made possible by the use of composites in the airframe and various aerodynamic refinements, including winglets. As with all but the earliest Airbuses and the Boeing 757/767, the MD-11 came with a new EFIS cockpit designed for two pilots, no flight engineer being required. In December 1986 the MD-11 was launched on the strength of an order for three aircraft plus six options from British Caledonian, though these were later cancelled when the carrier was taken over by British Airways. The first MD-11 entered service with Finnair in November 1990, by which time the company had accumulated 340 orders and options.

Unfortunately, drag proved to be higher than predicted and consequently the MD-11 was unable to meet its advertized payload/range performance. McDonnell

A loyal Douglas customer for over 50 years, Swissair operates the definitive DC-10-30ER (Extended Range) version, seen here overflying the Alps.

Douglas did all it could to rectify the situation, modifying those MD-11s already delivered at no extra cost, but many airlines decided to cancel in favour of the more advanced Airbus A340 and Boeing 777, slashing the order book to about 160 aircraft. By 1996 most of these had been delivered, the largest operator being Fedex, with a fleet of 13 MD-11F freighters plus 19 MD-11s. The standard MD-11 can accommodate 408 all-economy passengersand travel up to 12,569km (6778 miles).

In 1970 a new airliner manufacturer, Airbus Industrie, launched the world's first wide-bodied twinjet. Only slightly smaller than the DC-10 and TriStar, with a span of 44.84m (147ft 1in) and a length of 53.62m (175ft 11in), the A300 is powered by two wing-mounted General Electric CF6-50C turbofans. Maximum cabin width is 5.35m (17ft 7in) and seating ranges from 251 in mixed class to 336 in high-density nine-abreast layout. The A300 first flew on 28 October 1972, and the B2 version entered service on the Paris-London route with Air France on 23 May 1974. It

Feeling for the ground, a long-range Lockheed L-1011-500 TriStar of British West Indian Airways arrives in Caribbean climes.

has a cruising speed of 870km/h (541mph) and a range of up to 3,860km (2,400 miles). With the world jetliner market dominated by the Americans, Airbus sales were embarrassingly slow at first. But by 1980 the bulging order book for this technically outstanding aircraft was beginning to niggle the competition across the Atlantic. The success of the A300 allowed Airbus to invest in a new family of jetliners designed to compete with arch-rival Boeing.

Russian Air Transport

In 1932 Aeroflot was created when all Soviet air ser-vices came under the Chief Administration of the Civil Air Fleet. Until the German invasion of the Soviet Union in June 1941, Aeroflot gradually built up its network, and by 1940 had a route system measuring 146,300km (90,906 miles). During the war Aeroflot was engaged on essential tasks; when peace returned, faced the job of re-establishing and expanding its nationwide oper-ations and building up an international route system. Until the collapse of the Soviet Union in 1991, Aeroflot served some 3,500 destinations, operated to 65 other countries and, from 1975, carried more than 100 million passengers.

In World War II the Soviet Union had received considerable numbers of military DC-3s from the United States, and in 1939 had already begun licence production under the designation PS-84, changed in 1942 to Lisunov Li-2. In the early postwar years these Li-2s and ex-military DC-3s formed the backbone of the Aeroflot fleet. But even while the war was being fought, Sergei Ilyushin's design bureau began work on the USSR's first post-war transport aeroplane - the Il-12. This was a low-wing 21/32-seat monoplane powered by two Shvetsov ASh-82FN engines. It had a nose-wheel undercarriage, but was unpressurized. The type was introduced by Aeroflot

Boeing's first twin-engined airliner (the Model 247) and its latest (the Model 777) represent more than 60 years of progress in commercial aviation.

The A300B was the world's first wide-bodied twinjet and established the European manufac-turer Airbus as a major player in the world airliner market.

on 22 August 1947, large numbers were built, and on the last day of November 1954 the Il-12s were joined by the improved but very similar Il-14.

In the mid-1950s, the Il-12/14s were taking 33 hours to fly from Moscow to Vladivostok, with nine intermediate stops, and on the Moscow-Sverdlovsk-Novosibirsk-Irkutsk route they took 17 hours 50 minutes with 14 hours 35 min-utes flying time. These aeroplanes were obviously not acceptable for the distances which had to be covered and Stalin approved the design of the first Soviet jet transport as part of a major modernization plan. This was the Tupolev Tu-104, which made its maiden flight on 17 June 1955, and went into service on the Moscow-Omsk-Irkutsk route on 15 September 1956, more than halving the previous journey time with a schedule of under seven hours.

The Tu-104 was simply a re-fuselaged derivative of the Tu-88 bomber, having a low-mounted swept-back wing, swept tail surfaces and two Mikulin RD-3 or AM-3 turbojets close in to the fuselage. The pressurized cabins seated 50

passengers. The Tu-104 had a span of 34.54m (113ft 4in), a cruising speed of 800km/h (497mph).

The Tu-104 transformed Soviet long-distance air services, but it was not economic. It was therefore followed by the improved 70-passenger Tu-104A and 100-passenger Tu-104B, the latter entering service on the Moscow-Leningrad route on 15 April 1959. About 200 of all variants were completed and the type carried 90 million passengers before being withdrawn from service in 1981. The Tu-104 set safety and reliability records unequalled by any other Soviet aircraft.

The Ilyushin Il-18 was to prove of major importance to Aeroflot, 444 being put into service. It was powered by four Ivchenko AI-20 engines, and had accommodation for 80 passengers. The Il-18 made its first flight on 4 July 1957, when it bore the name *Moskva* (Moscow), and it went into service on the Moscow-Alma Ata and Moscow-Adler/ Sochi routes on 20 April 1959. Several versions of Il-18 were built, including the Il-18V which can seat 110 passengers, has a cruising speed of 650km/h (404mph) and a maximum payload range of 2,500km (1,552 miles).

One long-range aeroplane was unlike any other to be used in airline service. The Tupolev Tu-114, developed from the Tu-95 bomber. The 51.1 m (167ft 7¾in) wing was low-mounted and carried four massive Kuznetsov NK-12M turbines driving 5.6m (18ft 4½in) diameter eight-blade contra-rotating propellers. Fully loaded, the Tu-114 had a take-off weight of 175,000kg (385,809lb); for nearly a decade it was the biggest aeroplane in airline service, finally surpassed by the Boeing 747. It was also the fastest propeller-driven airliner ever in service, with a maximum speed of 870km/h (541mph). It entered service on the Moscow-Khabarovsk route on 24 April 1961, went onto the Moscow-Delhi route in March 1963, opened the first Soviet transatlantic service, to Havana, on 7 January 1963 and the first to North America when it began operating to Montreal on 4 November 1966. The special ultra-long-range Tu-114D had reduced seating for 120 passengers to carry the fuel needed for the Moscow-Havana service, refuelling at Murmansk, but making the 10,900km (6,450 mile) return trip non-stop. This magnificent aircraft could carry 220 passengers, but standard seating was for 170. The last of only 31 built was delivered in 1965. Before being replaced by the Il-62, the Tupolev had carried more than six million passengers.

Having re-equipped with medium- and long-range turbine-powered aircraft, Aeroflot set about the task of modernizing its short-haul fleet and introduced two new types in 1962. One was the Tu-124, which was virtually a three-quarter-scale Tu-104, and the other was the Antonov An-24, which resembled the Fokker F.27.

Indicative of the deep penetration achieved by Airbus in the US market is this 186-seat A321 of America West Airlines. When the 150-seat A320 entered service in 1988 its fly-by-wire control system was unique among airliners.

The A340 is the Airbus' ultra long-range four-engined aircraft. Austrian Airlines operates the A340-200 on international routes from Vienna.

The Tu-124, with two Soloviev D-20P turbofans, had accommodation for 44 to 56 passengers and entered service on the Moscow-Tallinn route. There was much criticism of the Tu-124, and it was replaced by the similar, but rear-engined, 64-80-seat Tu-134 and Tu-134A, which are now used in quite large numbers, some having been exported to East European airlines.

As Aeroflot began developing its long-haul international and intercontinental routes, it required a jet transport to replace the Tu-114. To meet this requirement Ilyushin designed the Il-62, which closely resembles the British VC10. The Il-62 has four rear-mounted Kuznetsov or, in the Il-62M, Soloviev turbofans, and normal seating for 186. The Il-62 first flew in January 1963, but its development was prolonged by a redesign and it did not enter service until March 1967, on domestic routes.

Aeroflot has a vast number of local services, and a modern aeroplane was required to replace the Li-2s,

Il-14s and An-2 biplanes on these operations. The type chosen was the Yakovlev Yak-40, a neat trijet with the ability to operate from small, rough fields and carry up to 32 passengers. The Yak-40 flew in October 1966, went into service in September 1968 and was exported to several countries outside the Eastern Bloc. The engines are Ivchenko AI-25 turbofans and maximum speed is 600km/h (373mph). The last Yak-40 was built in 1976, production totalling 1,011 aircraft.

On 4 October 1968, a new Soviet airliner in the shape of the Tu-154 (also a trijet) made its first flight. Though similar in performance to the Boeing 727-200, it is larger and has more powerful engines, operation from relatively short unpaved runways in remote areas being of prime importance. The prototype took to the air on 3 October 1968, development aircraft later carrying out extensive cargo and passenger proving flights before scheduled services (Moscow-Mineralnye Vody) began on 9 February 1972. The Tu-154A had more fuel and more powerful Nuznetsov NK-8-2 turbofans, but it was the Tu-154B, introduced in 1977, which represented a big jump in capability. For the first time in a Soviet jetliner, the flight control system and ILS was fully electronic, although the technology was French. The cabin was extended aft to accommodate 180 passengers and had improved pressurization.

Successor to the Tu-154 is the Tu-204. It looks as though it could have been built by Boeing or Airbus, such is the overall competence of its design. Flight control is

Part of British Aerospace's restyled Regional Jetliner family since 1992, the 146 can operate from small airports and is claimed to offer four-engined capability at twin-engined costs.

digital fly-by-wire and the wing is supercritical, both it and the tail having carbon-fibre control surfaces. Despite its high specification, low production costs mean that the Tu-204 is up to a third cheaper than its nearest rival, the Boeing 757. The Tu-204 first flew on 2 January 1989 and since then several versions have been announced with various engine/avionics options. Powered by the Rolls-Royce RB.211-535E5, the Tu-204-220 has a range of 6,330km (3,933miles) with 184 tourist class and 12 business class passengers. The standard Tu-204-100 with PS-90A turbofans has been in service with CIS (former Aeroflot) airlines since 1993 and is produced by Aviastar at Ulyanovsk in the Ukraine.

Today's Airliners

Two new Boeing twins entered service in 1982: the narrow-bodied, single-aisle 757 and the twin-aisle, wide-bodied 767. The 757 was essentially a replacement for the 727-200, whereas the 767 was designed to compete with the TriStar and DC-10 on US transcontinental routes. Both aircraft were planned with maximum flight-deck commonality to reduce development costs and incorporated fully integrated flight management systems for two-pilot operation. With its RB.211-535C turbofans, the 757 immediately established a reputation for fuel efficiency, reliability, and low noise. PW2037-powered 757s entered service with launch customer Delta in 1984, sparking a straight fight between Rolls-Royce and Pratt & Whitney. The 757-200 seats 239 passengers six-abreast and has a wing span of 37.95m (124ft 6in) and a length of 47.32m (155ft 3in). Its bigger sister, the 767, was given a big, thick wing which maximized fuel volume and allowed the aircraft to be developed and into a superb long-hauler. A 767-300ER (Extended Range) carrying 326 passengers burns almost the same amount of fuel as the older 727 burns carrying 187 passengers at the same speed.

When it entered service in 1988 the 150-seat Airbus A320 was the most technically advanced airliner in the world. Externally the first A320 looked like a normal medium-sized twinjet, but the aircraft was flown entirely via digital computers (fly by wire). Passengers also benefited from the comfortable cabin, the widest of any single-aisle airliner. The fleet passed one million flight hours in July 1992, by which

A SAAB 2000 of launch customer Crossair (left) in close company with a 340B of American Eagle; the 50-58 seat 2000 and 20-39 seat 340 are two of the world's leading turboprop regional airliners.

Above: The Franco-Italian ATR 52 sits between the 42-seat ATR 42 and 72-seat ATR 72 in the range of the AIR regional aircraft consortium.

Left: The Tupolev Tu-104A was the first Soviet turbojet transport aircraft and for a time operated the world's only scheduled jet passenger flights.

time Airbus had taken orders for nearly 700 A320s. In June of that year the stretched 186-seat A321 went into production at Deutsche Airbus, the first large civil aircraft to be built in Germany since World War II. The latest development of the A320 is the scaled-down 128-seater A319, enabling Airbus to market alternatives to the relaunched Boeing 737.

The twin-engined Airbus A330 and four-engined A340 were launched as a joint programme in 1987. Apart from the number of engines both aircraft are virtually identical. Like the A320, the flight and engine controls are fly by wire and the two pilots use sidesticks. The ultra-long-range A340 was the first to fly (October 1991) and is powered by CFM56 turbofans. In appearance the 375-

The Ilyushin Il-18 four-engined turboprop was built in far greater numbers than equivalent Western designs. The Vietnamese airline Hang Khong was one of many Communist Bloc customers.

seat A340 is very reminiscent of the 707, but is capable of flying 15,725km (9,828 miles), allowing non-stop services between Europe, Japan and Western Australia. The optional lower-deck crew rest area equipped with six beds has proved popular with several A340 customers. The medium/long-range 440-seat A330 made its maiden flight in November 1992. By early 1996, the A330 had attracted 121 orders from 15 customers. Together with the 757 and 767, the A330 is one of the types approved for ETOPS (Extended Twin Operations) across the North Atlantic and other long overwater routes.

Boeing's new generation wide-bodied twin is the 777, its first fly by wire airliner and the first 'paperless' aircraft in history, having been designed entirely on computers. Designed for ETOPS from the start and seating up to 419 passengers, the 777 combines long-haul range with twinjet economy. Spanning 60.9m (199ft 11in) the 'Triple Seven' has a bigger wing than the 747. The stan-

dard aircraft has a range of 7,010km (4,350 miles and is powered by PW4084 engines; the 777 entered service with United Airlines in June 1995.

The first Soviet wide-bodied transport, the Ilyushin Il-86, flew in December 1976 but its performance proved disappointing. Its old-technology engines made this 350-seater noisy and inefficient, so the decision to halt production in 1991 was not unexpected. Its successor is the Il-96, an almost total redesign with fly by wire controls, a new wing (with winglets), new tail surfaces, new engines, and a shorter fuselage with a completely revised structure. The most impressive version is the PW2037-powered Il-96M, which flew on 6 April 1993. This can carry 311 mixed class or 386 tourist class passengers 9,500km (5,900 miles) at a cruising speed of 850-870km/h (528-541mph). Although packed with the latest US avionics, it is completely outclassed by the 777.

Above: The mighty Tupolev Tu-114 long-range turboprop was the world's largest airliner until the introduction of the 747. This example dominated the static park at the 1965 Paris Airshow.

Operated by Air
France and British
Airways since January
1976, Concorde
remains the only
supersonic transport
in commercial
service.

Supersonic Transport

In Britain and France the decision was taken to jointly produce an airliner capable of cruising at more than Mach 2, about 2,143km/h (1,332mph). This was the enormously costly Concorde project, with Aérospatiale and the British Aircraft Corporation being responsible for the airframe and Rolls-Royce and SNECMA for the engines. The Concorde is a slim delta-winged aircraft with four Olympus 593 turbojets, a span of 25.37m(83ft 10in), a length of 61.94m(203ft 9in) and a maximum take-off weight of 181,436kg (400,000lb).

The first Concorde flew on 2 March 1969, and on 21 January 1976, the first supersonic passenger services were inaugurated – Air France flying the Paris-Dakar-Rio de Janeiro route and British Airways the London-Bahrein route. Air France also put Concordes on the Paris-Caracas route, and on 24 May 1976, Concordes of Air France and British Airways made simultaneous arrivals at Dulles Airport, Washington, inaugurating services from Paris and London respectively. On 9 December in the following year services began to run to New York. Only nine Concordes were ordered for airline service, five for British Airways and four for Air France. However, the transatlantic services (for which Concorde was designed) have proved indispensable with top business people and celebrities, enabling them to travel between London-and New York in under three and a half hours. Concorde has been very profitable for BA, the aircraft consistently carrying 80-85 per cent of their

seat capacity. By 1996 more than two million people had travelled at Mach 2, many of them tourists, all of whom have taken advantage of the relatively cheap travel deals offered by specialist companies (the aircraft are rented as required) to fly supersonically on the way to exotic destinations like Egypt or to special events like the Monaco Grand Prix.

The Soviet Union was actually first to fly a supersonic transport, its Tupolev Tu-144 making its first flight on the last day of 1968. Superficially the Tu-144 resembles the Concorde, but its career never equalled its rival, even after an extensive redesign. One of the early production aircraft broke up at the 1973 Paris Air Show, and, although the type began operating a Moscow-Alma Ata cargo service on 26 December 1975, passenger services did not begin until November 1977. After just 102 revenue flights the Moscow-Alma Ata service ended in June 1978 following a fatal accident. All of the early Tu-144s have been scrapped or used for ground instruction, while the later Tu-144Ds serve in various research roles.

The United States held a design competition for a supersonic airliner, and selected the 298-passenger variable-geometry Boeing 2707 with four General Electric engines. This aircraft would have been 96.92m (318ft) long, spanning 53.08m (174ft 2in) with the wing swept forward and 32.23m (105ft 9in) with the wing swept back 72 degrees for supersonic flight. This design was then replaced by a pure-delta type, but finally the whole supersonic project was considered to be uneconomic and, after a long series of design hold-ups, it was cancelled.

Left: A close-up of
the high-capacity
Ilyushin Il-96, a
substantially
improved fly-by-wire
version of the former
Soviet Union's first
wide-bodied airliner,
the four-engined
Il-86.

BUSINESS and LIGHT AVIATION

4

Business jets
provide the
ultimate in fast,
flexible and secure
executive transport,
while a tremendous
variety of light aircraft,
ranging from tiny home-
builts to sophisticated
designs with retractable landing gear, large passenger cabins
and airways avionics, give millions
of ordinary pilots the chance to fly
for the sheer fun of it.

Business Aircraft

The specialized business aircraft is a relatively modern phenomenon. Before World War II, the market for this class of machine was largely untapped and limited almost exclusively to the United States. Big American corporations such as the Ford were quick to recognize that aircraft saved time compared to more traditional forms of long-distance transport. Ford's fleet included its own Trimotor airliner. The Stinsons and Aeroncas of the 1930s (in common with most light aircraft of the inter-war period) were noisy, uncomfortable and unheated. They were also slow, short-range machines which lacked the capacity to carry a full complement of company executives.

Both before and after World War II, a small number of Boeing 247 and Douglas DC-2/DC-3 airliners were operated by America's leading companies, mainly those in the oil, steel, chemical and automobile industries. The trend of adapting existing designs continued in the late 1940s, when surplus military aircraft such as the P-51D Mustang fighter and the B-26 Invader twin-engined bomber were bought at knock-down prices and then converted into high-speed, long-range business aircraft. Trans-Florida's Cavalier Mustang was easily distinguishable from the standard P-51, having huge tiptanks and a passenger seat. The On Mark Marksman, a rebuild of the B-26, was virtually a new aircraft and came with a luxurious interior. Although none of them would have known at the time, these and other conversion specialists were responsible for saving a few hundred World War II combat aircraft: many of today's warbirds are yesterday's executive transports.

The twin-engined, twin-finned Beech 18 of 1937 remained the most successful executive aircraft for more than 20 years and some second-generation versions continue to operate today. The 1960s saw numerous conversions of the Beech 18/C-45 series, the most radical being PacAir's Turbo-Tradewind which replaced the elegant twin-fins with a swept single unit. Volpar were the first to give the Beech 18 a tricycle landing gear and replacing its standard Pratt & Whitney Wasp-Junior radials with more powerful Garrett-AiResearch TPE-331 turboprops saved about 363kg (800lb) and gave the aircraft a cruising speed of 407km/h (253mph) at 3,048m (10,000ft). Of course, turboprops also greatly improved the Beech 18's take-off, climb rate and single-engine performance.

The advent of the jet airliner meant that it was often quicker for executives to catch a commercial flight rather than use a company aircraft, but this was only practical for travel between major cities. Business jets were the obvious solution and by the mid-1960s

Above: A classic business jet, the LearJet 35 featured turbofan engines and had class-leading speed and altitude performance.

Below: The Raytheon Hawker 1000 offers stand-up cabin room and unsurpassed build quality.

several designs had been put into production. These included the four-jet Lockheed JetStar, North American Sabreliner, Hawker Siddeley (de Havilland-designed) HS.125, Dassault Mystere 20 and the forward-swept-wing German HFB-320 Hansa Jet.

In about 1960 Bill Lear Snr saw the potential for a cheaper high-performance twin-jet light transport. He had earlier been responsible for the executive Learstar conversion of the Lockheed 18 and made his first fortune in avionics and electronics. After selling out his interest in Lear Siegler, Bill Lear used some of the proceeds to set up the Swiss-American Aircraft Corporation (SAAC) in Geneva. It was here, in March 1961, that he finalized the design of the SAAC-23 (LearJet) with Dr Hans L. Studer, the engineer responsible for the cancelled P.16 ground attack fighter.

Bill Lear deliberately gave the LearJet the smallest cabin of any business jet on the market, having reasoned correctly that executives – already accustomed to sitting in cars for hours on end – would hardly want to stand upright or move around in an aircraft cruising at 834km/h (518mph). This minimized the fuselage cross-section (and drag) and meant that the gross weight could be kept within 5,670kg (12,500lb), giving the aircraft a much higher thrust/weight ratio than many of its rivals with the same General Electric CJ610-1 turbojets of 1,293kg (2,850lb) thrust. The cabin was provided with six seats and offered easy access to the cockpit, where the pilot and co-pilot looked through a distinctive wraparound windscreen.

SAAC planned to build the first batch of 25 aircraft in Switzerland, importing the engines, avionics, landing gear, brakes and other items from the US. The rear fuselage and tail assembly came from Heinkel in Germany, while the wings and tip-tanks were Swiss, built by Flug-und-Fahrzeugwerke at Altenrhein. But delays due to customs and supply problems persuaded Bill Lear to transfer the entire project (including production jigs, tooling and many completed components) to a new site in Wichita, Kansas.

The first LearJet flew on 7 October 1963 and early testing confirmed that it was a 'hot ship', with a better initial rate of climb than the F-100 supersonic fighter. After the first customer delivery was made in October 1964, the LearJet soon established itself as the world's best-selling business jet. Apart from the Mystere 20 (which cost nearly twice as much) it was also the fastest.

By the late 1970s the new turbofan-powered line up included the bigger, long-range 55 series. The main threat to the smaller Lears came from the Cessna Citation I and II, which remain the only commercial jets approved for single-pilot operation. Britain's HS.125 series led the European competition. Today's LearJets compete with the latest Citations, Falcons, Hawkers and Gulfstreams to offer the ultimate in personal transportation.

The Beech Super King Air 350 business turboprop is able to operate from shorter runways than most jets and is much cheaper to operate.

The long-range Gulfstream IV is in the big league of business jets and offers superb comfort over transatlantic distances.

Cessna has been making business jets since 1968. The Citation V's straight wing makes it less demanding to fly than faster competitors.

The two-seat D.H. Gipsy Moth was practical and reliable – a winning combination. Airborne from Old Warden airfield in Bedfordshire, three Gipsy Moths recall the golden age of British light aviation in the 1930s.

Launched in 1958, the Model 150 and its successor the 152 were the world's best-selling trainers for many years. The braced high wing and spring leaf landing gear are typical Cessna.

Mooney has been building high-performance four-seaters since 1955, all fitted with trademark swept-forward fins. Pictured in 1965, this is an early all-metal M.20.

Above: The PA-28 Piper Cherokee has appeared under several names since 1961, but all offer a roomy cabin for training or touring.

Light aircraft

In the 1920s and '30s one name became synonymous with light aviation – de Havilland. Located in the Edgware district of north London, de Havilland produced the D.H.60 Moth two-seat biplane. This was a safe, robust design aimed at the private owner and flying clubs. Of wooden construction with a plywood-covered fuselage and fabric-covered single-bay wings (which could be folded to minimize hangar space and allow the aircraft to be towed by a motorcar), the prototype Moth made its maiden flight on 22 February 1925 with Sir Geoffrey de Havilland at the controls. Early Moths were powered by the 60hp Cirrus, but the vast majority were fitted with the brilliant Gipsy I four-cylinder inline engine of 80-100hp designed in-house by Major Frank Halford.

The home of the post-war light aircraft is America, and until the early 1980s – when US product liability laws decimated the industry – Cessna, Piper, Beech, Mooney and Grumman dominated the market. Other manufacturers, Stinson, Taylorcraft and Aeronca among them, failed to invest in more modern designs after World War II and faded away. Today the USA has an aircraft population exceeding 180,000, overwhelmingly consisting of light aircraft. The majority of these are two or four-seat touring types, now steadily wearing out. In the peak year of 1978, US manufacturers deliv-

A early postwar Piper publicity shot of the ubiquitous J-3 Cub working down on the farm. The short-field performance of this two-seat tail-dragger remains difficult to beat after 60 years.

ered 17,000 new machines, but by 1990 the total of piston-powered aircraft had fallen to a dismal 613. Some of this decline can be attributed to a rise in fuel costs and the economic recession, but America's love affair with litigation is largely to blame.

Since World War II, Cessna has been the most successful of America's light aircraft manufacturers. Founded in 1916 by Clyde V. Cessna, by the late 1970s the company offered a range of 48 models (including business jets and crop dusters) and was producing more than 6,000 aircraft every year from its factories in Wichita, Kansas.

In addition to building aircraft for the private owner, Cessna also produced an extensive range of rugged, single-engined, utility aircraft capable of operating from dirt strips: the 185 Skywagon, 206 Stationair (both available as floatplanes) and the seven-seat Super Skywagon. Cessna's most famous twin is the 310, primarily a business aircraft designed to compete with the Piper Apache, Beech Twin Bonanza and Aero Commander. Introduced in 1953, the 310 was sleek and exuded style. Powered by two 240hp Continental engines, the 310 had a top speed of 354km/h (220mph).

Cessna's best-seller is the Model 172 Skyhawk, more than 30,000 of which were built between 1955 and 1982. This embodies the design philosophy common to the company's single-engined designs since the Model A of the 1920s, the first Cessna to be built in series. The 172 is simple, reliable, and relatively cheap to buy and operate. Like the Model A, the 172 can accommodate four people and their baggage. Unlike the Model A, the 172 is of all-metal construction

and has a tricycle undercarriage, the slim, spring leaf main gears being a Cessna trademark. Cessna singles are invariably of high-wing cantilever design, those built since the early 1960s having a swept-back fin and rudder. Compared to more exotic European designs, Cessna singles can seem dull, but pricewise no other light aircraft offers the same combination of comfort, payload, range, speed, ease of operation and short-field performance.

The 150 is Cessna's other big seller, a cosy two-seater that has trained more private pilots than any other aircraft in history. Introduced in 1959, more than 25,000 examples had been produced when production was halted in 1982. Most 150s are powered by 100 or 130hp engines and, like other models (especially the 172), the type was also built by Reims Aviation of France for the European market.

Only one other aircraft manufacturer has matched Cessna's output: the Piper Aircraft Corporation. Its story begins in 1930 at the start of the Depression when William Piper, a businessman from Bradford, Pennsylvania, bought the locally-based Taylor Brothers Aircraft Corp. Piper instigated the design of a simple high-wing monoplane built of wood and fabric over a steel tube frame. The prototype E-2 Cub first flew on 12 September 1930, powered by a two-cylinder engine. Virtually identical Cubs were still being built 40 years later. The success of the Cub (and the bigger Tri-Pacer) established Piper as America's best-selling light aircraft manufacturer. Between 1939 and 1941, Piper delivered

One of several innovative speedy canards designed for home construction by Burt Rutan, the Quickie is a superbly efficient two-seater.

The retractable nosewheel of the striking Rutan VariEZe reduces drag and simplifies parking when the aircraft is tied down after landing.

The upmarket Beech Bonanza has been in production since 1945, but in recent years the classic V-tail versions have been superseded by the conventional B36 series.

8,020 machines, satisfying roughly half of the US private aircraft market. By the time sales began to tail off in the early 1970s, more than 27,000 Cubs had been made.

Production of the four-seat PA-22 Tri-Pacer began in 1951 and by 1960 Piper had built 7,634 examples. The Tri-Pacer followed the company's low-cost high-wing formula, but in 1961 it was replaced by the low-wing all-metal Cherokee. This was developed into the six-seat PA-32 Cherokee Six, renamed as the Saratoga. The latest incarnation of the Cherokee is the Archer III, which may yet help re-establish Piper as a major force in light aircraft manufacturing

Piper's most impressive single is the Malibu, a six seater with a pressurized cabin, extensive de-icing protection and comprehensive avionics. Launched in 1984, the Malibu has suffered from niggling reliability problems with the Continental engine, but for a time this landmark design was the only Piper aircraft in production.

Training for a private pilot's licence (PPL) varies around the world but almost invariably consists of ground instruction in such subjects as principles of flight, navigation, aviation law, flight planning and basic airframe, engine and instrument construction, all usually proceeding in parallel with airborne instruction. At least half of the flying is 'dual', i.e. with a qualified instructor. Solo flying begins at the instructor's discretion, usually after 12 to 15 hours of dual flying, though often less.

The basic pilot's licence generally qualifies the holder to fly single-engined aircraft in good weather and to carry non-paying passengers; further training and tests are required to fly multi-engined aircraft, or floatplanes, or in cloud or at night using only instruments, or to give flying instruction. For the heavier piston-engined and all the turbine-powered types, a 'rating' on the licence is required as well. But the majority of amateur pilots never proceed beyond the first licence. One reason for this is the high cost of additional training, especially in Europe where fuel prices are far higher than in the US.

To learn to fly in Europe, one ordinarily begins by joining a flying club, an institution offering the social amenities of a club and a bar/restaurant as well as providing flying training and aircraft hire. In North America one would go to a Fixed-Base Operator (FBO), likely to be a larger business offering aircraft sales and maintenance as well as tuition and rentals, but without the friendly club bar .

Aerobatics

Aerobatics is the most exhilarating form of flying, whether for the pilot or for the spectator. When early aviation pioneers found themselves flying upside-down by mischance they had to find out for themselves exactly how to rectify their dilemma. A Russian pilot is generally credited with flying the first loop in public during an appearance at Kiev in 1913, but it was the years of the Great War that taught pilots to use manoeuvres to gain a tactical advantage over their opponents. Perhaps the best remembered of the wartime manoeuvres was the Immelman turn. Airforces have always set great store by aerobatic training, airline schools less so. Before the age of the missile made aerial combat possible without even seeing the target, it was the skill and determination of the pilot in flying his aircraft to the limit that usually won the day. So the military trainee would spend many hours of his training learning to fly a loop, a level roll or a stall turn that sliced accurately through 180 degrees.

Tricky to land but an utterly exhilarating aerobatic mount, the Pitts Special biplane remained a world class performer until the 1980s.

The German Extra 230 is typical of the purpose-built, ultra-aerobatic monoplanes which appeared in the late 1970s.

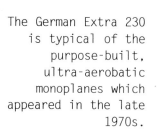

Few aeroplanes are designed just to perform aerobatics but since the setting up in 1960 of world aerobatic championships, Russia, Germany, Czechoslovakia, France, and the United States have all put a lot of design effort into producing aircraft which are competitive.

America's Pitts Special long epitomized the ideal aerobatic aircraft. It is a biplane which allows the mass to be concentrated and the span to be reduced. Less span – the Pitts measures only 6m (20ft) across – means less resistance to rolling, and when this is coupled with the ability of a biplane to offer four ailerons it is not difficult to imagine the fingertip lightness of control available to the pilot; it is easier to perform two 360-degree rolls rather than one! The major drawback with the Pitts is its small size, which makes it more difficult for competition judges to mark complex manoeuvres.

Competition aerobatics has developed a unique character which tends to make it more angular than the flowing sequences which delight a display audience. The Sukhoi Su-26M has been the king of aerobatic aircraft since it dominated the 1986 World Championsips. Powered by a 395hp radial, this awe-inspiring machine has a symmetrical wing profile and lightweight +10/-10G structure.

Better known for its combat aircraft, Sukhoi also builds brilliant competition aerobatic machines. A ride in the two-seat Su-29 is not for the faint-hearted.

The <u>most</u> <u>versatile</u> <u>of</u> <u>all</u> <u>pow-</u>
<u>ered</u> <u>aircraft,</u> the helicopter and
V/STOL jet are a relatively
recent phenomenon in the world
of aviation. Despite possessing
similar flying characteristics,
they achieve flight through
vastly different means.

ROTORCRAFT and V/STOL

5

Paul Cornu's tandem-rotor helicopter
was the first to achieve unrestrained
free flight – albeit very briefly
before breaking up on landing.

The development of rotorcraft – the term includes both helicopters and autogiros – has always been in a world of its own. Apart from ballooning, it was mainly with moving wings, designed to emulate the flapping of bird flight, that man made his first attempts to fly. From the experiments of Icarus to the contributions of Sir George Cayley in the 19th century, most of the proposed flying machines had some means of flapping or rotating their wings to produce lift.

Initially, the practical problems of mechanical complexity were quite insuperable, and it is only in the last 100 years that any significant attempts have been made to depart from the moving-wing concept. But there were still some adherents of rotating wings who were not deterred in their search for vertical take-off and landing. Although they were habitually ridiculed, there was a great deal of evidence to support their contentions. Most of the frequent aeroplane crashes of the early 20th century occurred during take-off and landing. During the first 20 years of this century a handful of designers did meet with some limited success. Among the helicopters to fly successfully in that period, the Breguet-Richet No. 1 was credited, on 29 September 1907, with being the world's first man-carrying helicopter to become airborne, albeit under restraint from tethering ropes. This machine was lifted by four biplane rotors of 8m (26ft 3in) diameter each and driven by an Antoinette engine. It remained airborne for only about one minute outside the Breguet at Douai, France, and reached a hight of just 0.6m (2ft).

On 13 November of the same year and also in France, at Lisieux, the Cornu tandem-rotor helicopter became the world's first rotating-wing aircraft to achieve unrestrained free flight, with the designer himself at the controls. This maiden flight deserves its place in history even though, at less than 30 seconds, it was of even shorter duration than Breguet's. It was powered by a 24hp Antoinette engine which drove the two twin-bladed 'paddle-wheel' rotors through a belt-and-pulley transmission system. To outward appearances, it gave the impression of having been built from bicycle parts and its short flight ended in the collapse of its frail tububular framework. Still, it was a world first.

World War I brought a temporary halt to experiments but in the period that followed there were other limited successes. In France, the quadruple-rotor Oemichen helicopter, which was additionally fitted with five small variable-pitch propellers for control purposes, actually achieved a world helicopter distance record with a flight of just over 500m (1,640ft) in 1924. Another quadruple-rotor machine, the de Bothezat helicopter, was also being flight-tested in the USA by the US Army Air Force and achieved a maximum duration of 1 minute 40 seconds. Both were incredibly complicated mechanical contraptions. Hardly less complicated was the Pescara helicopter which was lifted by twin co-axial, contrarotating biplane rotors. Built in France by a Spanish designer, it proved itself by increasing the world helicopter distance record to just about 800m (2,640ft). It was no wonder that the helicopter proponents were ridiculed by fixed-wing aeroplane pioneers. The Atlantic had already been flown non-stop by Alcock and Brown in a Vickers Vimy bomber.

The Cierva Autogiro

The breakthrough in rotating-wing design came with the invention by the Spaniard Juan de la Cierva of the autogiro. By 1925, he had proved the validity of his concept beyond all doubt and was invited to England to continue his research and development work. During the next ten years, the English company he formed produced a succession of autogiro prototypes which established all the design theory and data on which the helicopter industries of the world were founded. Tragically, Cierva himself was killed at Croydon in 1936, at the age of 41. Ironically, he was a passenger in a fixed-wing airliner when he lost his life. He had geared the greater part of his working life toward eliminating the possibility of such an accident. Nevertheless, his ideas were a vital contribution to air safety.

Cierva's invention was based on a novel design philosophy which emerged from the mathematical analysis he made of contemporary helicopter designers' problems. They were then all using their various forms of rotor system with the blades set at a high positive pitch angle, rotated by the application of power to the drive shafts on which they were mounted. In effect, they were large propellers which screwed themselves upward against the resistance of the air. There were two principal problems. On the one hand, the application of engine power to turn the rotor drive shaft produced an equal and opposite reaction which would turn the fuselage in the opposite direction when airborne. Known as torque reaction, this is a phenomenon familiar to all engineers. In order to avoid it, rotors on early helicopters were designed so that they could be used in pairs, turning in opposite directions to counteract the torque.

Following from this need to use pairs of rotors came the requirement for complex mechanical transmission systems to transmit the engine power and then elaborate structures to support the systems. Cierva's discovery was that none of this was necessary. His calculations of the aerodynamic forces at work in a simple rotor system satisfied him that, if the blades were to be set at a low positive pitch angle and started in rotational motion, the rotating system could be towed through the air in such a way that the blades would maintain a constant rotational speed in a state of equilibrium, without any application of power.

Autorotation

He termed this phenomenon autorotation and applied it in practice by building a single rotor and mounting it on a pylon above a conventional aeroplane fuselage. Instead of a complex transmission system there was simply one bear-

Cierva's Autogiros were the first truly successful rotorcraft. His C-6 Autogiro utilized the fuselage, tail and engine of the Avro 504K trainer.

The highly effective Cierva C-30 two-seater took off vertically after a short forward run and cruised at 129km/h (80mph).

ing at the head of the pylon which allowed the rotor to turn freely. There were a few teething troubles initially but he soon developed an arrangement that worked. Take-off in the early machines was achieved by hand-starting the rotation of the blades and then accelerating across the aerodrome, pulled by a conventional engine-driven propeller. As forward speed increased on the take-off run, rotor rpm also increased until the state of equilibrium was reached. At this stage, which was normally after a run of a few hundred metres, sufficient lift was being generated by the spinning blades for the machine to become airborne.

It was an elegant solution to the problem of flight with rotating wings. The extended flight-test and development work which the first practical autogiro made possible yielded, in due course, a vast accumulation of technical data on which future improved designs could be based. Subsequent refinements to the system included mechanical means to start the rotor before take-off and means of precise control of its tip-path plane in order to ensure a safe landing.

The autogiro was never able to hover but it could fly more slowly than a fixed-wing aircraft, down to less than 40km/h (25mph) without losing height, and could land with virtually no forward speed. If forward speed were reduced below this, the machine would begin to sink gently towards the ground. Rotor speed remained constant during the gliding descent. Since the control system governed the rotor's angle of tilt, and not that of the fuselage, the pilot could retain precise control right to the point of touchdown.

Cierva C-30

The most effective of the many autogiros developed during the 1930s was the Cierva C-30, of which several hundred were produced by manufacturing licensees of the Cierva Autogiro Company in the UK and Europe. Modified versions of the type were also produced in the USA. The C-30 was a two-seat machine powered by a 140bhp Armstrong Siddeley Genet Major radial engine. A power take-off from the rear of the engine crankshaft was used as a mechanical starting system for the three-bladed rotor. The two seats were arranged in tandem as open cockpits, with the pilot at the rear. The forward cockpit was located immediately below the rotorhead with its supporting pylon straddling the cockpit coaming. In this way, the weight of the passenger was exactly on the centre of gravity so that flying trim did not alter when the machine was flown solo.

The fuselage was a fabric-covered, tubular-steel structure, substantially the same as that of the Avro Cadet biplane, a successor to the famous 504K. The C-30 was, in fact, designed around this fuselage as Avro was one of Cierva's UK licensed manufacturers. From a production viewpoint it was advantageous to use an existing fuselage, although it was of course the rotor system rather than the fuselage which led to the C-30's success.

Design modifications to the standard fuselage included the fitting of a long-travel, soft-oleo landing gear, to accommodate the unique autogiro landing characteristics, and a steerable tailwheel operated by the pilot's rudder pedals. The tailplane was also of unique design. Fitted with upswept tips, the aerofoil camber was positive on the

Old Dad, a Sikorsky H-5 of the
US Navy, is given the thumbs up to
land during the Korean War.

starboard side and negative on the port side to provide a movement about the longitudinal axis (anticlockwise when viewed from the rear) and thus counteract propeller torque in forward flight.

Design maximum speed was over 160km/h (100mph). It was not always possible to achieve this, particularly at full load, but the type had a useful cruising speed in the order of 130km/h (80mph) and carried fuel for just over two hours' endurance. The Cierva C-30 was sold widely for private and club flying and a number were also bought by the military agencies of several countries, mainly for army reconnaissance evaluation. Another military role, for which their slow-flying capabilities were found to be singularly well suited during World War II, was the calibration of ground radar stations.

If the war had not erupted when it did, it is more than likely that the pattern of progress might have been very different. In the years immediately preceding the outbreak of war, however, there was a small handful of designers who, having derived benefit from the accumulated knowledge of autogiro rotor design, were beginning to show promising results with new helicopter projects. Prominent among them were Heinrich Focke in Germany, James Weir in Scotland and Igor Sikorsky in the USA.

Pioneer Helicopters

Three projects – the Focke F61, the Weir W-5 and W-6, and the Sikorsky VS-300 – began to attract the interest of their respective military authorities in the late 1930s. They were all more complex than the autogiros, which by then were flying in quite large numbers, but the ability to sustain hovering flight was of special value in a variety of military roles. Even the vertical-jump take-off facility of the latest autogiros then flying was not considered to be a suitable substitute for a hovering capability. So it was that the helicopter, when it finally began to emerge as a practical flying machine, was initially developed largely under military sponsorship and specifically as a military vehicle. This factor has influenced all its subsequent progress.

The demands made by the military upon the pioneer constructors were unbridled. There was a war to be won and the fledgling helicopter was seen to have enormous potential as a reconnaissance vehicle for swiftly moving ground forces. Initially, the interest came mainly from the US Army and the Royal Navy. Government money was poured into development contracts with the result that by 1945 Sikorsky's main and tail rotor (MTR) design had become established as the classic configuration. Following the VS-300 prototype, three new designs were developed and put into limited production by the same company to meet military orders. These were the Sikorsky R-4, R-5 and R-6. The first and last were two-seaters, supplied to special units for pilot training and operational evaluation, while the R-5 was a larger helicopter with a lifting capacity of about 508kg (1,120lb). It was the world's first helicopter designed for a specific military role, having been ordered off the drawing board by the US Navy to operate from the decks of independently routed merchant vessels on anti-submarine patrol duties.

Other US companies had also been engaged in experimental work. Notable among them was Bell Aircraft, which was developing its own design of MTR helicopter. Its principal unique feature was a giro-stabilized two-bladed rotor having one common flapping hinge for the two blades. Bell termed it a teetering or see-saw rotor, and it has become well known throughout the world as a feature of most Bell helicopters.

Post-War Developments

After World War II, the established helicopter constructors turned their attention towards a commercial market. Bell was first to be awarded a commercial helicopter certificate of airworthiness, in 1946. This was for the Model 47, which remained in production for 27 years in many two- and three-seat variants. Sikorsky was not far behind, with a four-seat civil version of the R-5, designated S-51. It quickly became apparent, though, that the helicopter was anything but a motor car for the man in the street. Such was the cost structure established by the initial pressure of

military procurement that manufacturers found the civil versions they were producing could be operated economically only in a limited number of highly specialized roles. Commercial sales were thus few and, with military interest becoming less intense, the crucial question of the hour was: 'Is the helicopter here to stay?'

In agricultural roles such as crop-spraying, for example, the high cost of the helicopter put it at a considerable disadvantage compared with fixed-wing aircraft. The same applied in other aerial-work roles, particularly in survey and construction engineering support. In some applications, however, mainly with operations in remote areas or mountainous terrain, the helicopter was able to perform timesaving miracles. In such uses its high cost was immaterial since to do the job any other way would have cost even more.

Unfortunately, the opportunities to engage in such specialized work were few, and progress in developing commercial uses for the helicopter was painfully slow for the first few years. There was, nevertheless, still something of a helicopter euphoria during this period, with new projects making their appearance all over the world. In Europe, the pre-war French and British pioneers sought to make up for the time lost during the war years.

In France, three groups in the nationalized aircraft industry were engaged in rival helicopter projects. SNCA du Nord began in 1947 but its interest survived only a few years. SNCA du Sud Ouest had acquired as part of German war reparations the services of members of a wartime Austrian design team. They had successfully built and flown the world's first jet-rotor helicopter, designed by Friedrich von Doblhoff in 1943. The Sud Ouest projects were thus all in the single jet-driven rotor (SJR) category and led to the development of the So-1221 Djinn helicopter, the only jet-rotor helicopter to go beyond the prototype stage into quantity production.

Other members of von Doblhoff's team went to Fairey Aviation in Britain, which led to the development of a Gyrodyne derivative with a jet-driven rotor and, from this, to the Rotodyne. Von Doblhoff himself went to the USA and joined McDonnell Aircraft Corporation to develop a ramjet helicopter. No jet-rotor helicopter, however, has ever achieved any marked degree of commercial operating success. Even the So-1221 Djinn helicopter was not a great success commercially. Production was discontinued after just over 100 had been built. A lightweight two-seater, the type was used mainly for pilot training and crop spraying.

The third French company, SNCA du Sud Est, followed more conventional lines in the development of MTR designs, and produced the series of helicopters which have dominated French involvement in the field. The SNCA du Sud Est and Sud Ouest were later amalgamated in Sud Aviation, which itself was subsequently regrouped under what is now the single French nationalized aircraft constructor, Aérospatiale. Among the wide

First flown in July 1959, the Bell 47G was built in huge numbers for civil and military customers. The doors for the familiar 'goldfish bowl' moulded Plexiglas canopy were often removed to improve ventilation.

range of helicopters Aerospatiale produce, three, the Puma, Gazelle and Lynx, are manufactured jointly with Westland Aircraft.

In Britain after World War II, the original Cierva Autogiro Company reformed with many of its former key engineering staff and began the development of two new designs. The first to fly, the Cierva W-9, was a two-seat single-rotor helicopter but, instead of following exactly the classic MTR configuration, it used a laterally deflected jet at the tail in place of the tail rotor for torque compensation. Concurrently, the company was also building a much larger machine, the triple-rotor Cierva W-11 Air Horse.

This, in its day, was the largest helicopter in the world, with a cargo compartment 5.79m (19ft) in length capable of carrying wheeled vehicles. Entry was by means of a ramp through clam-shell doors at the tail. The Air Horse was powered by a single water-cooled Rolls-Royce Merlin engine of 1,620bhp, the same engine that powered the famous Spitfire fighter. That the Air Horse did not mature to a successful conclusion was due mainly to lack of appreciation by the British government of the need for a much higher level of funding to support so sophisticated a design.

Three other British aircraft constructors also entered the rotating wing field at the end of the war: Westland Aircraft negotiated a manufacturing licence with Sikorsky to build the S-51 in Britain; Bristol Aeroplane Company began the development of a new MTR design with a cabin for five passengers; and Fairey Aviation Company developed a novel compound helicopter (CMP) project, also able to carry five passengers, named the Gyrodyne. All three were powered by the same type of engine, the Alvis Leonides nine-cylinder radial of 525bhp. The Fairey Gyrodyne, with its novel design for superior cruising speed, was the first rotorcraft to take the world helicopter speed record above the 200km/h (124mph) mark.

American initiative

In spite of inevitable setbacks in the comparatively early stages, helicopter projects grew both in number and variety, and nowhere was the profusion of new ideas so great as in the United States. At one time, just before 1950, there were more than 70 different active helicopter projects. Many were being built by small engineering companies or by individuals in private garages. Of these, only a few ever left the ground; many never progressed beyond the stage of being a gleam in their hopeful inventors' eyes.

One notable exception was the project of a young Californian graduate, Stanley Hiller Jr, who built his own back-yard co-axial, contra-rotating rotor (CXR) helicopter in 1944. He was fortunate in having links with a major industrial corporation which helped him to surmount the initial hurdles. He was later to develop his own servo-paddle rotor control system. Hiller Helicopters Inc, which he formed, produced more than 1,000 helicopters based on that design feature during the ensuing two decades.

Among other American companies, the two which had been predominant in pre-war autogiro development were also involved with new helicopter projects. Pitcairn Autogiro Company produced a conventional MTR helicopter, but with a novel rotorspeed governor, while Kellett Aircraft Corporation concentrated its studies on what was then the unusual twin inter-meshing-rotor (TIR) configuration. The same design was also favoured by Kaman Aircraft Corporation, which developed it to build helicopters for the USAF.

Powered by a single Rolls-Royce Merlin, the British Cierva Air Horse was the world's largest helicopter in its day.

The tandem-rotor helicopter was introduced because it was thought that limitations in feasible rotor diameters necessitated multiple rotors to lift heavier payloads. Piasecki Helicopter Corporation was the first to produce a practical twin tandem-rotor (TTR) design, and derivatives of its first tandem-rotor machine, the XHRP-1 (jocularly known as the 'Flying Banana'), were still in production by Boeing Vertol in the mid-1970s.

By 1950, most of the weaker brethren had disappeared, leaving about 10 or 12 companies to form the nucleus of what was then a Cinderella industry struggling for recognition in a highly competitive aviation market.

Korean War

It was the outbreak of war in Korea, in the mid-summer of 1950, that provided the next major impetus to transform this small group of manufacturers into the thriving helicopter industry which now exists. The US Air Force and US Navy units, equipped with the few hundred helicopters which had been delivered for evaluation, were despatched to Korea for trials under active service conditions. Their performance was far beyond the wildest expectations of the most optimistic military strategists.

Using Sikorsky S-55s, Los Angeles Airways was one of the pioneers of civil passenger helicopter operations.

The helicopter types principally involved were, initially, the Sikorsky H-5, derived from the S-51, Bell H-13 and Hiller H-23. Later, these were supplemented by the Sikorsky H-19 series, a larger machine capable of lifting ten men or a load of almost a ton, and the Piasecki HUP-1, a TTR design based aboard US Navy aircraft carriers and used for ship-to-shore work. These helicopters, in their performance of otherwise impossible rescue missions, confirmed beyond any doubt that rotating-wing aircraft were here to stay. With their unique versatility and independence of prepared landing strips, they were able to save the lives of thousands of soldiers, wounded or stranded behind enemy positions. This in itself was enough to ensure their unreserved acceptance as a new ancillary to fighting armies. Perhaps even more significant was the potential that the success of such rescue operations revealed.

Military tacticians were quick to realize that if the helicopter could quite easily infiltrate behind enemy lines to rescue wounded soldiers, it could equally penetrate with offensive personnel, weapons and supplies to mount attacks from almost any unexpected quarter. By the time the Korean war had ended, American military strategy had been completely re-orientated in line with this new philosophy. The new US Army was to be composed largely of highly mobile task forces mounted, supplied and supported entirely from the air by fleets of helicopters designed specifically for the operational tasks involved. At the same time, the helicopter's potential in marine warfare, as an anti-submarine weapon and to support marine commando raids ashore, was realized.

The new philosophy was pioneered by the American armed forces and quickly taken up by those of other nations throughout the world, including the Soviet Union where the history of rotating-wing development had had early origins but not the same degree of practical development as elsewhere.

With military procurement pressure once again calling the tune, the helicopter industry made rapid strides in the decade following the Korean war.

Military agencies were then in a much better position to write operational specifications for helicopters to fulfil special duties for which active-service experience had shown the need. Thus, with specific targets to achieve and the money to spend in terms of development contracts, helicopter construction was suddenly transformed into a boom industry and new designs began to roll off the production lines in their hundreds.

The Turbine Engine

Another significant factor, which had a particularly important influence on the rapid rate of development from the mid-1950s, was the advent of the turbine engine and its application to helicopters. In fixed-wing aircraft, the shaft turbine as a power-plant to drive a conventional propeller – known as the turboprop – was not the sweeping success for which its designers had hoped. This was largely because it was so quickly superseded by the turbojet, which could produce much higher speeds and thereby justify its much higher costs.

For helicopters, though, the shaft turbine proved ideal. It had a much lower installed weight than the piston engine, which more than offset the greater fuel loads which at first had to be carried. Consequently, helicopter designers found for the first time that they had abundant power available. Moreover, the normal operating characteristics of the turbine, which permitted extended running without fear of damage at up to about 85 per cent power, was particularly well suited to a helicopter's requirement for long periods of continuous hovering in certain military roles. The high initial cost and high fuel consumption were no drawbacks to the military, while the much shorter warm-up period before take-off and smoother operation in flight were considerable advantages.

So, with the power available, much bigger helicopters were soon found to be practicable. Earlier fears of limitations to the size of rotor systems proved groundless in practice, and the helicopter grew up. Before 1950, apart from the Cierva W-11 Air Horse prototype, the biggest production helicopters powered by piston engines were in the region of 2,500kg (5,510lb)

gross weight, with a lifting capability of some 680kg (1,500lb). Ten years later, at the outset of the Vietnam conflict in the early 1960s, transport helicopters like the Boeing Vertol CH-47A Chinook were in the air at gross weights of some 15,000kg (33,070lb). The Chinook, with twin Lycoming turbines, had a useful load capability of more than 7 tons.

Speeds too had risen. Before 1950, the world helicopter speed record stood at 201 km/h (124.9mph). By 1963, a French MTR helicopter, the Sud Aviation Super Frelon, had taken it to 341km/h (211.9mph).

In addition to the technological progress, production quantities were also increasing substantially. Four major American constructors, Bell, Boeing Vertol, Hiller and Sikorsky, were all in the big league, each with more than 1,000 helicopters produced. Bell, in fact, was well in the lead with more than 3,000. Large numbers were also being built in Europe and the Soviet Union. Some indication of the

Backbone of the air/sea rescue service, the Westland Wessex (licence-built Sikorsky S-58) has been with the RAF for more than 30 years.

extent to which the USA had by then developed the new strategic philosophy of helicopter mobility is that in the US Army alone there were some 5,000 qualified helicopter pilots. Their largest training school was equipped with more than 200 light helicopters, mainly of Bell and Hiller manufacture, and staffed by nearly 150 flying instructors.

Looking to the future at that time, the US Army sponsored a Light Observation Helicopter (LOH) design competition among the already extended industry, the prize for which was to be a production

cations and a few constructors did set up small sales organizations to supply civil adaptations of the military helicopters which comprised their main production. Their selling price was high, but for specialized tasks they could be operated on a cost-effective basis. After some 15 years of consistent, if slow, growth, there were by 1960 about 1,000 helicopters operated commercially by some 300 companies throughout the world. More than half the companies, though, may well have been operating only one, two or possibly even three small helicopters.

The Russian-built Kamov Ka 50 single-seat combat helicopter has a co-axial rotor design for high-speed and agility and is heavily armed (and armoured) with comprehensive attack and defensive systems.

contract for 3,000 turbine-powered helicopters. With military contracts of such proportions in progress and in prospect, it was not surprising that helicopter constructors could spare but scant effort to meet the admittedly small needs of commercial operators. Progress was nevertheless made in commercial appli-

Specialized Tasks

The multiplicity of tasks undertaken by these civil operators impinged upon almost every sphere of industrial and commercial activity. The thousands of kilometres flown on such tasks as overhead power-line construction and patrol, or the innumerable hours flown on crop-spraying and other agricultural work, would rarely be noticed except by those directly concerned. Similarly, the constant aerial support work done for off-shore oil prospectors became commonplace.

By its very nature, the greatest proportion of all such operations was performed in remote areas and received little publicity. Only when a helicopter was used for spectacular work in a populous area did its unique attributes become more widely known. Typical of such a single feat was the placing of the cross on the summit of the rebuilt Coventry Cathedral by an RAF Belvedere. Following this remarkable demonstration of precision lifting, aerial crane work became more widely accepted.

The growth of this particular application, combined with military needs for heavy-lift helicopters, led to the development of aircraft designed specifically for aerial crane work. In the Sikorsky S-60 and S-64 crane helicopters, provision is made in the aft of the cabin for a third set of pilot's controls, with the seat facing rearwards. When the actual lifting is to be done, the helicopter is flown with the normal controls into the hover approximately above the load. The captain then leaves his usual seat and takes over the hover with the third, aft-facing, set of controls. In this position he is looking directly downward on to the load for the precision manoeuvre and can instruct the second pilot, over the intercom, to take over and resume normal flight as soon as the load has been secured or released, as the case may be.

Mainly because of their high cost, these specialized helicopters have been slow to enter service with commercial operators, whose fleets are made up mostly of small and medium-sized machines. A recent development is the Kaman K-MAX, which is unique in being the first single pilot helicopter to be designed specifically for external load-lifting. Kaman's trademark intermeshing rotor system is much simpler than it looks and eliminates the need for a tail rotor to counteract torque effects. The lack of a tail rotor also makes the K-MAX relatively quiet – a big plus in built-up areas. The transmission system for the 1,500shp Lycoming T53-17A turboshaft is specially adapted to deal with the stresses involved in repetitive load lifting.

Passenger Transport

The one area in which the civil helicopter had not made any significant headway up till the early 1960s was the carrying of passengers. There were a few meritorious attempts, mainly in the USA, to set up helicopter airline services and these met with qualified success. The routes flown provided direct links between the principal airports of the area served – Los Angeles, San Francisco, Chicago and New York – and the outlying suburbs. Their success was qualified in that, although the adapted military transport

Kaman's K-1200 K-MAX load-lifter demonstrates the Bambi bucket forest fire-fighting system. From this angle it may appear to have a single four-blade main-rotor but actually has a unique intermeshing twin-rotor system.

The most ubiquitous commercial helicopter in production, Bell's JetRanger models dominate the light turbine helicopter market.

helicopters themselves were technically capable of providing the services, their operating economics were such that the companies needed some measure of government subsidy. There have been a few isolated exceptions, but most were forced eventually to close down for this reason. In Europe, a helicopter service centred on Brussels, operated by the Belgian airline SABENA, was discontinued; small fixed-wing turboprop airliners, which can operate from short runways, have proved far more attractive due to their lower costs, higher speeds and greater payloads. But passenger helicopters, such as the Sikorsky S-61 and Eurocopter AS 332 Super Puma, have proved to be indispensable in the offshore support role.

In its smaller sizes, too, the helicopter was as far from becoming an effective means of personal transport for the man in the street as it had ever been. In fact, by 1960 the dream of a back-garden flying machine for the masses had been completely abandoned. It was still hoped, though, that the unique vertical take-off and landing ability would enable executive transport and aerial taxi work to become an important addition to the helicopter's extensive range of applications.

One of the first helicopters to be developed specifically for this latter role was the Bell Model 47J, named the Ranger. This was not a new design but an adaptation of the earlier Model 47G, of which it used all the dynamic components. In other words, it was a 47G in all its rotating mechanisms but had a newly styled four-seat cabin in place of the transparent plastic bubble which enclosed a bench seat for three, including pilot, sitting side-by-side. The bench was retained in the 47J for the three passengers, but the cabin was extended forward to provide space for a fourth, separate, seat for the pilot. The fuselage was more streamlined, with a stressed-skin monocoque structure instead of the open tubular-steel framework of the 47G.

With these improvements, the 47J Ranger was able to attain slightly higher speeds, up to a maximum of some 169km/h (105mph), and the type was used widely for passenger transport. In contrast, however, contemporary light fixed-wing aircraft of equivalent size and power could offer something like twice the speed at about one-third of the cost, so the helicopter was again operating in a limited field. At that time, few more than 100 helicopters of this kind were in regular operation for company transport use and, in most cases, they were for a specialized requirement which precluded the use of fixed-wing aeroplanes.

The position changed dramatically with the introduction of the small turbine engine, a by-product of the American LOH design competition previously mentioned. The turbine engines first used as helicopter power-plants produced some 1,000shp. Two types were used initially, the General Electric T58, with a power range between 900shp and 1,800shp and the Lycoming T53 of some 770shp to 1,450shp. These two power units gave rise to the development of helicopters such as the Bell UH-1A Iroquois series, a ten-seat MTR helicopter; the Kaman H-43L, a TIR aircraft

Developed from the OH-6A Cayuse LOH for the US Army training requirements, the Hughes 500D was ultimately built by McDonnell Douglas.

of similar size; and, with a twin turbine installation, the 25-seat Vertol 107TTR transport helicopter and the 28-seat Sikorsky S-61 series, the latter still in service in 1996. All these types were flying by 1960.

Although the 1,000shp turbines were regarded as small by fixed-wing standards, they were far too large for use in the four- or five-seat aircraft. The French company Turbomeca was developing a range of smaller fixed-shaft turbines producing some 400shp, but it was the Allison T63 free-shaft unit, designed specifically for the US Army LOH project, which provided the breakthrough. It had a power-turbine spool no bigger than a two-litre oil can but produced 250shp (now 650shp) at its best operating speed.

All three finalists in the LOH competition, the Bell OH-4A, Hiller OH-5A and Hughes OH-6A, used this Allison T63 turbine. The declared winner was the Hughes OH-6A, a four-seater with a maximum speed of some 241 km/h (150mph), and mass-production of the type was set in motion. Of the other two, Bell developed its OH-4A prototype, which had been built to full civil airworthiness standards as one element of the competition conditions, into what was to become the Model 206A JetRanger. A refined version of this type now constitutes the mainstay of light executive helicopter fleets. The additional speed conferred by the turbine engine was enough to make helicopter transport worthwhile to a much wider field of users. Against a stiff headwind, the earlier 160km/h (100mph) helicopters were often no faster than a motor car for conventional journeys. The extra 80km/h (50mph) of the turbine helicopter placed it well ahead in any conditions. Later, Hughes was also to produce a civil version, known as the Hughes 500, of the company's own competition winner.

Vietnam and its Aftermath

When the Vietnam War began, the American armed forces were fully reorientated to the new military strategy of helicopter mobility. They were also partially equipped with a variety of light, medium and heavy transport helicopters, all turbine-powered, to put the new tactics into effect. The strategy met with virtually instant success, to the extent that some historians have dubbed the war in Vietnam 'The Helicopter War'. That the final outcome did not bring with it a conventional military victory for the new tactics was no fault of the helicopters.

The effect on the American helicopter industry of the initial successes in active service was extremely rapid expansion. Helicopters of all types were ordered in thousands; at one stage, Bell had one of the Beechcraft aeroplane factories almost exclusively engaged in producing fuselage and other components under sub-contract to meet the military demands. Experience in Vietnam also had a corresponding effect in other countries as military strategists began to follow the American lead. The idea of an army going into action without helicopter support became totally redundant.

The advances made during the ensuing decade and into the 1970s were largely a matter of degree. For example, the UH-1A Iroquois, designed by Bell as the Model 204, originally entered service just before 1960 as a ten-seat utility helicopter powered by a 1,000shp Lycoming T54-L-11 turbine. Through the years, about 20 variants of the design have been produced, amounting to some 10,000 helicopters of this one series. By early 1995, the US Army's vast fleet of Hueys had been reduced to 550 UH-1H models. The latest derivative, Bell's Model 412HP, is still instantly recognizable as a Huey despite its twin engines and quieter, more efficient, four-blade main rotor. A skid undercarriage is standard but some customers prefer the optional fixed tricycle landing gear, which avoids the need to hover-taxi. The 412 can carry up to 15 passengers and is widely used in both civilian (eg, oil rig support) and military roles. Powerplant is a 900shp PW PT6-3D Twinpack which has a substantial power reserve in the unlikely event of one engine failing or for high-altitude operation. Like most current medium-sized helicopters, the 412HP comes with a fully digital automatic flight control system (AFCS), upgradeable to autopilot modes for demanding SAR missions.

An indication of the extent of these advances can be gauged from the fact that the Lycoming T55 turbine in the Bell Model 214 (the civil version of the UH-1H) is the same basic power unit used in a twin installation to power the 15-ton Boeing Vertol CH-47 Chinook helicopter. The Chinook itself is another typical example of the

In a scene repeated countless times during the Vietnam War, Bell UH-1 Hueys touch down at a hot LZ.

Nose pitched down, an RAF Chinook heavy-lifter displays its tandem rotors to advantage. The Chinook is in service with most of today's modern armies, providing essential heavy lift capabilities to supply front line troops.

The Sikorsky S-61N has been in operation since the early 1960s, particularly in support of off-shore operations.

degree of advance made during the decade of the Vietnam War. The first prototype made its debut in 1961 as a TTR military transport helicopter. Powered by twin Lycoming T55-L-7 turbines of 2,650shp each, it was the first big helicopter in which the rear loading door opened downwards to form a drive-on ramp for loading wheeled or tracked vehicles into the cabin, which was 9.14m (30ft) long.

The later CH-47C Model 234 is capable of carrying 44 troops or a 9,400kg (21,000) payload. The rotor diameter has remained substantially the same but the systems and transmission have all been modified and strengthened to take the considerably greater power output from the twin Lycoming T55-L-11C turbines. These are rated at a maximum of 3,750shp each, with emergency reserve up to 4,500shp each. Altogether, Boeing Vertol and the Piasecki Helicopter Corporation (which it absorbed) have produced more than 2,500 tandem-rotor helicopters, production of the CH-47D continuing in 1996.

Sikorsky Aircraft, which has also graduated mainly into the construction of large helicopters, has produced even more, though not of tandem-rotor design. This company pioneered the boat-hulled helicopter with its S-61 series, which first flew on 7 August 1962. The S-61N variant has been in regular passenger service for about 30 years and continues to fly in support of offshore operations. Passenger comfort is remarkably good for such an old design, but the S-61N betrays its age with the fuel consumption of its two General Electric CT58-140-1 engines, and the fact that it has to be flown continuously hands on (the autopilot has no height or heading holds). Its replacement, the S-92 Helibus, will not be ready until the turn of the century.

The most famous relative of the S-61 (itself derived from the H-3 military transport helicopter) is the SH-3D Sea King. Although largely superseded by the SH-60 Seahawk in the US Navy, the Sea King is still used by many other navies for anti-submarine and air-sea rescue operations. One of their much publicized applications was the retrieval of American astronauts on their splash-down return from space missions. The Sea King was built under licence in England by Westland Aircraft, which also produced military transport and AEW versions. The

The 12-seat Sikorsky S-76 represents the ultimate in corporate helicopters.

latest Royal Navy Sea King HAS.5s is powered by twin Rolls-Royce Gnome H.1400-1 turbines, rated at 1,630shp each, which are derived from the General Electric T58 turbines which power the American-built version. In addition to all-weather navigation systems, the Sea King's equipment can include sonar detection apparatus plus four torpedoes and four depth charges. It is operated by a crew of four.

At the other end of the size range, the helicopter war in Vietnam brought out the light observation helicopters in their thousands. First the Hughes OH-6A Cayuse and, later, the Bell OH-58A Kiowa, derived from the original OH-4A which was itself the forerunner of the five-seat civil Bell 206 JetRanger. First flown on 10 January 1966, the JetRanger has since dominated the light turbine helicopter market. By 1995 more than 6,000 had been delivered, logging more than 32 million flight hours with the best safety record of any single-engined aircraft. The 206B-3 has a cruising speed of 224km/h (120mph) and a range of 1,288km (690miles). The LongRanger has a passenger longer cabin

than that of the JetRanger to provide space for two extra seats.

A recent development of the Cayuse is the McDonnell Douglas MD 520N NOTAR, the first production single main rotor, no tail rotor helicopter. First flight of the prototype (a converted OH-6A) took place on 17 December 1981. Thrust for anti-torque and roll control is provided by the NOTAR (NO TAil Rotor) system. This uses a variable-pitch axial fan inside the large diameter tail boom, which pressurizes it. As well as being much quieter, with NOTAR there is no danger to people approaching the tail of the helicopter. The MD 520N NOTAR utilizes much of the airframe, engine and drive shaft configuration of the MD 500 formerly built by Hughes, which sold its helicopter division to McDonnell Douglas in 1990. Deliveries began in 1991 and by early 1994 orders and options for the type topped the 200 mark. The company's twin-engined Explorer, a completely new eight-seater, was created with NOTAR from the start. The latest military Cayuse is the US Army MH-6J for special operations duty. A total of 36 MD 500s

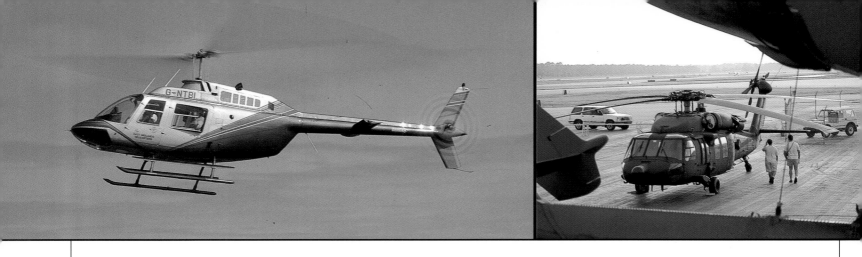

were converted into MH-6Js with folding NOTAR tail booms (for ease of loading into transport aircraft), M134 7.62mm Miniguns, BEI Hydra 70mm rocket pods and Hughes AN/AAQ-16 FLIR (forward-looking infrared).

One more significant concept emerged from the implementation of the new military strategy in Vietnam. This concerned a much faster, heavily armed helicopter which could give close support and protection to troop-transport and supply armadas moving into forward battle zones. US Army commanders in the field found that aerial support available from conventional fixed-wing fighter squadrons was sometimes too remote and inflexible to be sufficiently effective for their specialized requirements. So the idea of the helicopter gunship was born.

The best known example is probably the Bell AH-1 Cobra. This design utilized all the dynamic components of the Bell UH-1 utility helicopter in a slender, streamlined fuselage to give it a speed of up to 354km/h (220mph). It carries a crew of two, pilot and air gunner/observer, and can be armed with a range of missiles, rockets, rapid-firing machine-guns and other weapons. The type was in quantity production before the end of the Vietnam war and is still being built, many earlier versions upgraded with the more powerful engines, new weapons, fire control and air-defence jamming systems fitted to the AH-1S. Improvements such as the M65 TOW missile sight in the nose turret were also incorporated into the twin-engined AH-1T Seacobra for the US Marines. Widely exported, the Cobra is much cheaper to buy and operate than the later McDonnell Douglas AH-64 Apache attack helicopter. Since Vietnam, Cobras have seen active service in the Middle East (with Israel, a major customer) Grenada, Panama, the Gulf, Somalia and the former Yugoslavia.

The success of the Cobra undoubtedly influenced the Soviet Union, where the Mil design bureau designed the formidable Mi-24 attack helicopter. Much bigger and more powerful the AH-1, the Mi-24 adopted its tandem-seat layout for the pilot and gunner but is unique in being able to carry a squad of eight troops or cargo in the main cabin. The Mi-24 (called 'Hind' by NATO) entered production in early 1973 and, like the Cobra, it has been progressively upgraded with more effective weapons

and sophisticated anti-aircraft defence systems. Nicknamed Gorbach ('Hunchback') by its Russian crews, the Mi-24 is very heavily armed with gun packs and up to 12 anti-tank missiles or bombs, mine dispensers, grenade launchers and missiles in various combinations. During the war between Iraq and Iran in the 1980s, an Iraqi air force Mi-24 is thought to have downed an Iranian F-4 Phantom with a well aimed burst from its turret-mounted gun.

After Vietnam, attention was once more turned towards civil applications, the most significant trend being the design of light and medium-sized twin-turbine helicopters able to operate in full Instrument Flight Rules (IFR) conditions. This has entailed the development of special instrumentation, autostabilizers and a wide range of navigation aids, including Doppler radar, moving map displays and GPS. Today there are at least 30 different types of civil helicopters on the market, many of which are also suitable for military roles. Some are sophisticated executive transport helicopters such as the Italian eight-seat Agusta A109, the American 12-seat Sikorsky S-76C or the 13-seat French Eurocopter AS 365N Dauphin 2. The twin-engine reliability common to all three is essential to meet the requirements of IFR operation in air traffic control zones and also to fly into heliports located at the centre of populous areas. All three follow the classic MTR configuration and all are capable of speeds of about 240km/h (150mph) or better.

The five-seat Bell 206 series can fairly claim to be the most succcessful helicopter family in history and have logged more than 32 million flight hours in 30 years.

The Sikorsky UH-60A Blackhawk tactical transport is the US Army's prime mover on the battle-field. Less well known is the MH-60G used by the 1st Special Operations Wing.

McDonnell Douglas produces the world's only NOTAR (no tail rotor) helicopters: the Explorer (top); the MD 520M (centre); and the MD 630N (bottom).

Other twin-turboshaft, single or twin-pilot IFR helicopters include the seven-seat Eurocopter AS 355N and 11-seat BK 117, the latter proving a popular choice for air ambulance duties. In common with the smaller BO 105, rear clam shell doors allow easy access for casualties or cargo. The increasingly international nature of aerospace has also spread to the helicopter industry. Developed jointly by MBB (since combined with Aérospatiale to form Eurocopter) in Germany and Kawasaki in Japan, the BK 117 is also built under licence by IPTN in Indonesia and by Hyundai Precision Industry in South Korea.

Originally designed and built by Aérospatiale in southern France, the AS 355N is a good example of the operational flexibility offered by helicopters. Fast comfortable, and with excellent vertical (sustained hover) performance, the AS 355N's repertoire includes law enforcement, air taxi, camera platform and the inspection of high-tension overhead power lines in France and the UK, suspending 'live lines men' from an underslung basket. Like the single-engined AS 350 Ecureuil (Squirrel), or AStar in America, the AS 355N is of advanced design. The hingeless rotorhead is impressively simple and extensive use is made of composites, both in the rotor system and primary structure. Digital engine control (DEC) reduces pilot workload and allows rapid start-up and lift-off without the risk of engine damage.

The world's biggest helicopters have invariably been Russian, designed by the Siberian-born Mikhail Mil. First flown in 1957, the Mi-6 was a brilliant achievement, pioneering the use of large turbines and fixed lifting wings on rotary wing aircraft. It was then easily the world's largest helicopter, more than twice as heavy as its nearest rival, and went on set a number of world records, including speed over 100km closed circuit of 340.15km/h (211.35mph) in 1961. Loaded weight (including a 9,016 payload) was 44 tonnes (97,002lb), the limit for a vertical take-off (VTO) being an impressive 42.5 tonnes (93,695lb). Maximum fuel capacity was 17,250litres (3,794gal), giving a range of 1,450km (900 miles). The Mi-6 was a conventional MTR helicopter powered by twin TB-2BM turbines producing 5,500shp each.

The mighty Mil V-12 was twice this size again, and combined two Mi-6 rotors, each with its twin-turbine power supply, in a giant twin side-by-side rotor (TSR) configuration. The rotors with their power units were mounted at the ends of two

The business end of US Marine Corps' AH-1W SuperCobra, revealing a mixed load of rocket launchers, missiles and the multi-gun chin turret. The forward cockpit is used by the second pilot who is also gunner/ observer.

inversely tapered outrigger booms, through which transmission shafts coupled the two pairs of turbines through a common gearbox in the upper fuselage. Power could thus be transferred from either side in the event of partial failure. The capacious cargo compartment had the same dimensions as the Antonov An-22 cargo transport aircraft so as to carry the same loads. There were tip-up seats for up to 120 passengers and lifting capacity exceeded 40,624kg (89,560lb). Complex and ungainly, the V-12 crashed during its first hover in 1967, but the second machine performed impressively before being sent to the Monino museum outside Moscow. Although abandoned in favour of the far superior Mi-26, the V-12 has the consolation of being the largest helicopter ever built, a record it is likely to hold for the foreseeable future.

Mil died on 31 January 1970, but his talented team went on to produce the outstanding Mi-26. This conventional MTR design can lift the sort of loads usually associated with fixed-wing transports like the C-130 Hercules, though over shorter distances, typically 800km (497miles) with a 20-tonne payload. With a length (rotors turning) of 40.025m (131ft 3.75in) and a height (to the top of the rotor head) of 8.145m (26ft 8¾in), the Mi-26 is longer than the V-12 but slightly shorter than the Mi-6 (and its flying crane version, the Mi-10). It is, however, vastly more capable as well as being much bigger than the largest American and European helicopters. The prime requirement was the ability to transport heavy drilling equipment and pipes to remote oil and natural gas fields in Siberia, which has some of the worst weather in the world.

Test flown as the V-26 from December 1977, deliveries of production aircraft (Mi-26) for the Soviet air force and navy began in 1983, although Aeroflot demands were also given high priority. Powered by Soloviev D-135 turboshafts, the Mi-26 is available in several versions for airline (up to 96 passengers), medevac (up to 70 patients), surgical hospital, fire-fighting and flying crane requirements. The design of the main rotor is particularly impressive, and consists of eight blades with extruded high-tensile-steel spars carrying 26 glass-reinforced plastic (GRP) trailing edge sections; diameter is 32m (104ft 11.78in). The main rotor hub is machined from a titanium forging, easily the largest on any helicopter.

Compared to the Cobra, the AH-64 Apache can carry a much heavier missile load (up to 16 Hellfires) and is extensively armoured against heavy calibre weapons.

Right at the other end of the size range is the Robinson R22 Beta. Remarkably compact and beautfilly simple, this piston-engined two-seater was originally intended as an affordable alternative to the car for frustrated Californian commuters. But once again, despite driving down acquisition and operating costs to the absolute minimum, the idea of a truly personal helicopter remained exactly that – an idea. Instead the R22 Beta has become enormously successful as a basic training helicopter. Since production began in 1979 more than 2,500 have been sold worldwide. Power comes from the trusty Lycoming O-320-B2C, which is downrated to 131shp in deference to the belt-driven transmission. Peformance is quite spritely – especially when being flown pilot-only – 165km/h (90mph) being a comfortable cruising speed. The R44 Astro is a roomier four-seat development of the R22 aimed at budget-conscious customers, or those corporate clients for whom an IFR-equipped turbine helicopter would be an unnecessary extravagance. Fitted with a more powerful Lycoming O-540-F1B engine rated at 225shp, the R44 cruises at 222km/h (115mph). The R44 also makes an excellent trainer or, thanks to the extra room in the back, an ideal perch for a camera crew.

The helicopter has also benefited from the introduction of digital avionics and displays and the use of composite materials, refinements which have greatly increased controllability, reliability, component life and comfort. The electronic cockpit of the Eurocopter AS 365N2 Dauphin features a fully integrated four-axis autopilot, electronic flight information system (EFIS), and flight management system (FMS). This allows a fully automatic approach to the hover at a designated point – ideal when landing on the helideck of an oil rig at night or in bad weather. In the early days, rotor blades were manufactured on a tubular spar with wooden ribs and stringers, and covered in fabric.

Today, extruded alloy spars are used, with stainless steel and GRP also embodied. By the late 1970s, titanium began to replace steel for certain rotorhead components. Hingeless and bearingless rotor systems, together with composite rotorheads and main rotor blades, are increasingly becoming the norm for turbine-engined helicopters. Other advances include the special blade tips fitted to the European Helicopter Industries EH 101 developed by Westland and Agusta. A product of the British Experimental Rotor Programme (BERP), the advanced profile of these tips reduce drag and enabled the Lynx to establish a world helicopter speed record. Advanced rotor suspension and anti-resonance isolation systems (ARIS) are expected to produce vibration levels comparable to those of fixed-wing turboprops.

With its present-day sophisticated systems, and especially with its requirement for an extremely high degree of precision engineering, the helicopter is probably one of the most expensive means of transport yet devised by man. Its great saving grace is that, in its unique sphere, it is also, without doubt, one of the most effective.

V/STOL

The introduction of the turbojet engine, towards the end of World War II, came at a time when every available effort was being made by both sides to channel this new invention into a fighter aircraft. As events transpired, neither side was able to bring the first jet fighters into service until the war was virtually over.

Like the Apache, the Russian Mi-24 bristles with sensors and weapons. This example serves with the Slovakian air force.

A BO 105 of Trinity House comes to the hover during a lighthouse support mission. Should the worst happen, the pop-out floats mounted on the skids will keep the helicopter afloat, though not necessarily upright, in a severe sea.

After hostilities ceased, engine designers had more time to think of other future possibilities and vertical take-off, for both military and civil aircraft, was one obvious application. Even the early jet engines could develop a thrust of higher value than their own weight. By the time the Rolls-Royce Nene turbojet came into service, in the early 1950s, its maximum thrust of some 1,814kg (4,000lb) was roughly twice its own weight. There was thus ample margin for the additional weight of a supporting framework.

To evaluate the feasibility of controlling such a concept, Rolls-Royce mounted two Nenes horizontally in a tubular-steel engine test-bed and modified the engine tailpipes to direct the jet efflux vertically downwards. When it first flew, in 1953, the four-legged framework created a worldwide sensation and was promptly dubbed the 'Flying Bedstead'.

Gross take-off weight of the machine was 3,264kg (7,196lb). Maximum vertical thrust from the two Nenes was about 3,629kg (8,000lb) so there was no doubt about its vertical take-off capacity. The main experimental purpose of the test rig was to evaluate the system devised for attitude control in hovering flight. Compressed air was bled from the two engine compressors into a common collector box and then ducted into four downward-facing nozzles, one positioned forward, one aft and one at either side. After a few inevitable teething troubles had been overcome, the system worked reasonably well. About 380 tethered flights and 120 free flights were made during the comprehensive tests that followed.

The success of the 'Flying Bedstead' conjured up futuristic visions of Vertical Take-Off and Landing (VTOL) airliners operating between the centres of the world's capital cities, without the need for aerodromes and all the travelling delays associated with them. It was the fixed-wing aircraft designers' answer to the helicopter. The vision spurred Rolls-Royce into the development of a special series of lightweight turbojet engines with a remarkably high power to weight ratio. The RB.108 was designed specifically for a vertical-lift application with provision for deflecting the angle of the jet efflux by a few degrees to aid control when hovering in flight.

Pictured before the break up of the Warsaw Pact, Polish air force officers consult the map before commencing a training flight in their Mi-6 transport helicopters. The big secondary fixed-wing improved payload and range.

The first use made of this power unit was by Short Brothers & Harland in the SC-1 delta-wing research aircraft. Powered by five RB.108s, four mounted vertically in two pairs for lift and one mounted horizontally for propulsive thrust, the SC-1 became the world's first fixed-wing jet-powered VTOL aircraft to achieve vertical take-off, in 1958. The first full transition – from the hover to fully wingborne forward flight and then back to the hover sustained only by the lift jets – was made in 1960.

Provision was made in the SC-1 for the two pairs of lift engines to be swivelled fore and aft. After take-off, they were swivelled aft a few degrees so that their thrust supplemented that of the propulsive engine in the transition to forward flight. On the approach to land, the lift engines could be swivelled forward a few degrees to provide a braking effect in the transition back to hovering flight. Like the Flying Bedstead, all five engines were fitted with a compressor bleed from which high-pressure air was fed into a common duct for hovering control. The duct system terminated in four small ejector nozzles, one at each wing tip, one at the nose and one at the tail

The SC-1 was intended as the forerunner of a single-seat VTOL fighter which would use a more powerful version of the RB.108 engine for propulsive thrust. It was also intended as the scaled-down prototype of a much larger VTOL airliner. There was, however, another jet-lift system under concurrent development by Hawker and this, known as the vectored-thrust system, eventually proved superior.

Based on the Bristol Siddeley BS.53 Pegasus turbofan engine, the vectored-thrust system was first tried in the Hawker P.1127. A developed version of this prototype was later named the Kestrel when it joined a tri-national evaluation squadron of British, American and West German composition. Whereas in the Short SC-1 the greater part of thrust available was shut down during wing-borne flight, in the vectored-thrust system of the Kestrel it could all be used to attain much higher forward speeds. The efflux from the turbofan engine was ejected through four swivelling nozzles, two forward and two aft on either side of the fuselage under the wing. For vertical take-off and landing, the nozzles were swivelled to direct the jets vertically downward, while forforward flight the nozzles were swivelled to the rear to give horizontal thrust.

First hovering trials of the P.1127 began in 1960 and the first full transition from vertical take-off to conventional forward flight and then back to vertical landing was achieved in the following year. By 1964, the aircraft had attained supersonic speed in a shal-low dive and more powerful, truly supersonic, versions were under development.

Meanwhile, in Europe, the French company Marcel Dassault was developing a VTOL adaptation of one of its Mirage fighters. By replacing the SNECMA Atar turbojet with a smaller Bristol Siddeley Orpheus turbojet, space was made in the fuselage for installing eight Rolls-Royce RB.108 lift jets, mounted vertically in four pairs. This aircraft, called the *Balzac,* began flight trials in 1962 and was the forerunner of the Mirage III-V prototypes, which in turn were designed to lead on to a Mach 2 VTOL fighter-bomber. The production version of the Mirage III-V was planned to have a SNECMA-developed after-burning TF-306 (based on the Pratt & Whitney TF30) as its much more powerful main propulsion unit, and eight Rolls-Royce RB.162 jets for vertical lift. The RB.162 was a developed version of the RB.108 and produced just over twice the thrust. Development of the Mirage III-V was, however, discontinued after an unfortunate series of accidents, despite the prototypes having made successful transitions from hovering to forward flight and vice versa, as well as achieving super-sonic speeds.

The more powerful Rolls-Royce lift jets were also chosen by the German company Dornier, which produced an ambitious prototype for a VTOL transport aircraft. It was designed as a high-wing monoplane with a cruising speed of 750km/h (466mph). The prototype, designated Do 31E, had two banks each of four RB.162s to provide a total lift thrust of some 16,000kg (35,274lb),

The mightiest Mil of them all is the Mi-26, easily the world's largest helicopter.

The twin-turbine Eurocopter Twin Squirrel has power in reserve for a variety roles including law enforcement, air ambulance and corporate transport.

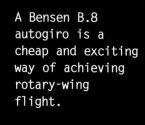

A Bensen B.8 autogiro is a cheap and exciting way of achieving rotary-wing flight.

The 360-degree radar and BERP blade tips stand out in this view of the Royal Navy's latest helicopter, the anti-submarine EH 101 Merlin.

mounted in wing-tip pods. This was supplemented at take-off by the vectored thrust of twin Bristol Siddeley Pegasus 5 turbofans which combined to add some 10,433kg (23,000lb) to the static lift thrust. The production version was planned to have still higher take-off thrust, with ten RB.162 lift jets.

Control in hovering flight was by a combination of differential thrust on the lift jets, for lateral control, and small 'puffer' nozzles at the tail for fore-and-aft control. Two of the tail nozzles were directed downwards and two upwards, all four being fed by ducted high-pressure air bled from the lift engines.

To test this proposed control system, Dornier built an open-framework hovering rig powered by four Rolls-Royce RB.108 lift jets. This test rig had much longer arms than the original 'Flying Bedstead'. Its overall dimensions were similar to the wing span and length of the actual Do 31E prototype so that control movements would be comparable with those to be expected in the actual aircraft when it flew, which was in 1967. The hovering rig flew in 1964 but the main project was later discontinued. A similar hovering rig was built by Fiat, in Italy, but was abandoned in 1966 before free flight was attempted.

Another German project, developed by the Entwicklungsring Sud research group formed by Bolkow, Heinkel and Messerschmitt in 1960, adopted yet another design configuration. Designated VJ-101C, it was a small high-wing monoplane which had six Rolls-Royce RB.108 lift jets installed in three pairs. One pair was mounted vertically in the fuselage, immediately abaft the pilot's cockpit, while the second and third pairs were in swivelling wing tip pods. For vertical take-off, all six lift jets were used, with the wing tip pods swivelled into the vertical position. To make the transition into forward flight, the wing tip

pods were swivelled forwards through a 90-degree arc until their efflux provided horizontal thrust. As forward speed increased, with the wing taking over the lift function, the forward pair of lift engines was shut down. The prototype started flight trials in 1963 but the project was abandoned in the following year.

Concurrently, a variety of different projects was in the course of development in the USA. In 1963, Lockheed produced and flew its XV-4A jet-lift VTOL fighter prototype, powered by twin Pratt & Whitney JT12A-3 turbojets rated at 1,497kg (3,300lb) static thrust each. Named *Hummingbird*, the XV-4A was a mid-wing monoplane. The two engines, mounted horizontally in nacelles alongside the centre fuselage, were arranged to provide either horizontal or vertical thrust. Design maximum speed was 837km/h (520mph). The system functioned reasonably well, but performance was not sufficient to warrant continuation of the project.

Ryan Aeronautical conceived a different way of achieving vertical take-off. Using what was known as the fan-in-wing system, the SV-5A prototype obtained its vertical thrust from two 1.59m (5ft 2½in) diameter, 36-blade lift fans mounted horizontally in the wings. A third, smaller, lift fan was mounted in the nose for control purposes. Around the periphery of each fan were fitted small turbine blades, or scoops, on to which the efflux from the twin General Electric J85-5 turbojets impinged to produce a fan speed of 2,640rpm at the full rated power of 1,206kg (2.658lb) static thrust on each engine.

Hinged semi-circular doors in the upper and lower wing surfaces above and below the fans were opened during the take-off. Below each fan there was also a series of transverse louvres, adjustable under pilot control. A thumb-wheel on the control column was used to rotate these louvres and so deflect the fan thrust rearwards to gain forward speed from the hovering position. Conventional wing-borne flight was established in this aircraft at approximately 225km/h (140mph), whereupon the turbojet efflux was transferred from the peripheral scoops on the fans to normal tail-pipe ejection and the fan doors were closed.

Flight trials of the Ryan XV-5A began in 1964 but, although the concept proved practicable, it too was later abandoned. Ryan was also involved in the experimental development of a 'tail-sitter' jet aircraft, the X-13, which was designed to take off

Light and small with a snug two-seat cockpit, the piston-engined Robinson R22 Beta is a remarkably successful basic trainer.

vertically from a gantry. This, however, proved impracticable for a number of reasons. More successful was the company's contribution, with Hiller Helicopters, to the Ling-Temco-Vought XC-142A tilt-wing research military transport. Powered by four 2,850shp General Electric T64-1 shaft turbines, driving 4.72m (15ft 6in) diameter variable-pitch propellers, the XC-142A was designed to carry wheeled vehicles and other cargo in its 9.14m (30ft) long cabin. Its maiden flight was in 1964, but it never entered production.

Other North American companies concerned with tilt-wing projects have been Boeing Vertol and Canadair, the latter company's twin-engined CL-84 having been longest in development. The use of ducted fans or ducted propellers has been yet another concept in the USA's search for a vertical take-off capability. It has been proved feasible by Hiller, Piasecki and others, but is hardly practical for general service. Bell Aerosystems, an associate of the helicopter constructor, developed a project for an aircraft in which four ducted propellers mounted on two stub wings were capable of being tilted through 90 degrees to provide either vertical or horizontal thrust. Powered by twin General Electric T58 shaft turbines of 1,250shp each, the machine was known as the X-22A. A similar aircraft, using four tilting propellers without the ducts, was built by Curtiss-Wright and

designated X-19A. In the 1990s, work on tilting propellers finally paid off with the Bell Boeing V-22, which offers a unique combination of helicopter flexibility, fixed-wing speed and payload/range performance. As the CV-22A, the aircraft is being developed for the US Navy and Air Force as a long-range airlifter with special-operations capability.

Between 1950 and 1970, the US military authorities sponsored the development of almost any apparently feasible VTOL system for practical evaluation. None of the methods, however, was as reliable as the British vectored-thrust principle, which was employed by Bristol Aero Engine (now Rolls-Royce) to design the four-nozzle BE.53 Pegasus 1 turbofan. This was installed in the Hawker P.1127, forerunner of the Harrier, which lifted off for the first time on 21 October 1960. Operational evaluation of the Kestrel military version was undertaken in 1964-65 by a unique squadron with four RAF, one US Air Force, one US Navy, two US Army and two Luftwaffe pilots.

This led to the Hawker Siddeley (now British Aerospace) Harrier GR.1, which entered squadron service with Britain's Royal Air Force on 1 April 1969 to become the world's first operational fixed-wing V/STOL aircraft. Some 105 Harrier GR.1s were ordered for the RAF, followed by 110 for the US Marine Corps and 12 for the Spanish Navy, These export Harriers, called AV-8As, were the first fixed-wing V/STOL aircraft to regularly operate from ships at sea.

RAF Harriers were later upgraded to GR.3 standard with laser nav/attack systems and progressively more powerful versions of the Rolls-Royce Pegasus 11 turbofan, which was developing roughly double the power of the engine used in the P.1127. The US Marine Corps soon became enthusiastic operators of the Harrier. A Marine aviator is thought to have invented thrust vectoring in forward flight (VIFFING) for air combat. But what they really wanted was an improved Harrier which could carry a much greater weight of weapons over a longer range and deliver them bang on target.

The result is the AV-8B or Harrier II, which first flew on 5 November 1981. Designed by McDonnell Douglas, the AV-8B has a new carbon-fibre composite wing with increased span and a deeper, supercritical profile. This enables the aircraft to carry 50 per cent more fuel and 70 per cent more ordnance than the AV-8A using the same engine. The wing has six underwing hardpoints and incorporates single-slotted flaps and leading-edge root extensions to generate more lift, improving manoeuvrability as well as take off performance. Large strakes fitted on the underside of the aircraft help to minimize 'suckdown' effects when hovering near the ground. Advanced avionics ensure that the bombs, missiles, rockets and cannon shells are delivered with amazing precision.

Meanwhile, a more modest redesign of the Harrier was underway in Britain. This was the Sea Harrier, substantially the same as its land-based progenitor but with a completely new raised cockpit, Ferranti Blue Fox nose radar, two Sidewinder missiles (increased to four post-1982) as standard and multimode nav/attack system. The type made its maiden flight in August 1978 and the first of 34 Sea Harrier FRS.1s was delivered to the Royal Navy in June 1979. Designed to operate from small aircraft carriers, the Sea Harrier takes off from a 'ski-jump' without catapult assistance and lands vertically without the need for arrestor gear. The ultimate test for the Sea Harrier came in April 1982 when Argentina invaded the Falkland Islands. Operating from the carriers HMS *Invincible* and HMS *Hermes*, Sea Harriers destroyed a total of 28 enemy aircraft for no loss in air combat, mostly with Sidewinders. Incorporating the lessons learned from that conflict, the F/A.2 can carry up to four Advanced Medium-Range Air-Air Missiles (AMRAAMs), which, when used in conjunction with the much more capable Blue Vixen multi-mode radar, gives the Sea Harrier a look-down/shoot-down capability at ranges far in excess of Blue Fox/Sidewinder.

The first of 328 US Marine Corps AV-8Bs was handed over to VMAT-203 at Cherry Point in January 1984. Many AV-8Bs are special night attack versions, the pilot wearing night vision goggles (NVGs) and using forward-looking infrared (FLIR) to locate and hit targets which would otherwise remain cloaked in darkness or poor visibility. The latest Harrier II Plus (73 of which are being remanufactured for the US Marine Corps from existing AV-8Bs) not only incorporate the night attack systems but also have a higher thrust F402-RR-408 engine and APG-65 multi-mode nose radar, the latter allowing the aircraft to provide beyond visual range (BVR) guidance for both air-to-air and air-to-surface missiles. Although something of a junior partner to McDonnell Douglas, British Aerospace has played an important role in the development of new versions and was contracted to build the RAF's 97 Harrier IIs. The resultant GR.5 is roughly equivalent to the AV-8B, while the GR.7 is comparable with the night attack version. Small numbers of Harrier IIs have been sold to the Spanish and Italian navies.

The first Soviet jet V/STOL aircraft, the Yakovlev Yak-36, did not fly until 1965. This was powered by two R-11V turbojets in the lower part of the forward fuselage fed by a large plain nose inlet. Both nozzles, located under the wing roots, were rotary cascade deflectors of a type patented by Rolls-Royce in 1961. These moved through at least 90 degrees to provide forward thrust after lift off, stability in the hover being maintained by small reaction control jets in the wingtip pods, under the tail and at the end of a prominent pipe on the end of the nose. There were many shortcomings, not least the uncontrollable roll-coupling if one engine failed. But the Yak played an important part in solving control problems, especially the severe pitch instability experienced during an accelerating transition.

First flown on 28 May 1970, the VTOL Yak-38 was quite different. Two lift engines were mounted in tandem just aft of the cockpit, with the main engine providing additional lift and forward thrust from twin rotating nozzles situated behind the wing. Interestingly, the vertical lift engines were fitted with deflector rings to vector thrust over 30 degrees for take-off and landing, but remained fixed during the hover, when the main nozzles at the rear would point down at 95 degrees. In the event of engine failure or a control system malfunction, the pilot would be ejected automatically as soon as the combined altitude and rate of descent exceeded safe limits. More complex and much less versatile than the Harrier, the Yak-38 was designed to give the Soviet navy (AV-MF) operational experience of jet lift and had only a limited attack and interception capability.

RAF Harrier II V/STOL fighters of No 4 Sqn perform at height. Unlike earlier Harrier trainers, the two-seat T.10 nearest the camera is fully combat-capable.

Above left: A formation of the US Marine Corps' AV-8Bs, which are to be rebuilt with new fuselages, multi-mode radars, night attack systems and higher thrust engines.

Above: The world's only supersonic V/STOL combat aircraft, the Yak-141, is helping Britain and America to develop an advanced strike fighter.

Left: The Bell-Boeing V-22 Osprey tilt-rotor is in production for the USAF as a special operations aircraft.

6

UNUSUAL AIRCRAFT

In the early days of flight every aircraft was unusual. More recently <u>these</u> <u>novel</u> <u>designs</u> have enabled man to fly higher, further and faster than ever before, carry unprecedented loads and fly long distances under his own power for the <u>first</u> <u>time</u> <u>in</u> <u>history.</u>

Finished in heat-emissive black, the X-15 flew on the fringes of space and is the fastest aircraft yet built. The No 2 aircraft reached Mach 6.70 in October 1967.

X-15

Many unusual aircraft have been built for high-speed research, but none can equal the achievements of the rocket-powered North American X-15, the fastest aircraft yet built. Constructed under a joint USAF, USN and NACA contract, the first powered flight, by the second aircraft, was made on 17 September 1959. At first sight the small wing of the X-15 looked remarkably unaerodynamic, but the thick wedge shape produced less drag at hypersonic speeds and gave much better directional stability and control. The skin was fabricated in a special nickel-chromium alloy, called Inconel X, while most of the underlying structure was of titanium alloy.

The X-15 was dropped from high altitude by its NB-52 parent aircraft and once clear the pilot fired the engine to climb above the effective atmosphere, where small rockets in the nose and tail kept the vehicle pointing in the right direction on a ballistic trajectory. After being involved in an accident on 9 November 1962, the second aircraft was rebuilt as the X-15A-2, the main modification being the addition of two large jettisonable tanks under the wings. These housed the liquid oxygen (left tank) and ammonia which provided the propellent for the definitive 12-nozzle XLR99 rocket motor with a combined thrust of 253.5kN (57,000lb st). Altogether the three X-15s made 199 flights before the programme was terminated in November 1968. The peak altitude reached was 107.95km (67.08 miles), achieved by Joe Walker on 22 August 1963. 'Pete' Everest flew the X-15A-2 at the peak speed of Mach 6.72 (7,297km/h; 4,534mph) on 3 October 1967.

The S.21 flying boat carried the S.20 *Mercury* seaplane to form the Short-Mayo composite aircraft, which was designed to enable mail to be delivered across great distances in the shortest possible time.

Piggy BacK Aircraft

The Short-Mayo Composite Aircraft experiment involved launching the S.20 Mercury floatplane from the back of the S.21 *Maia*, a modified C-class flying boat. On 20-21 July the *Mercury* made the first commercial crossing of the North Atlantic by a heavier-than-aircraft, when, commanded by Capt D.C.T. Bennett, it flew from Foynes non-stop to Montreal in 20hr 20min carrying mail and newspapers. The power of all eight engines and the lift of both sets of wings was used for take-off, and then at a safe height the fully-fuelled *Mercury* separated from *Maia* before setting off across the Atlantic. This novel, but impractical, method of extending the range of transatlantic aircraft was never used again.

Born of desperate defence, the German Mistel

Both the Fw 190A (as here) and the Bf 109F were used to control the Mistel combination, separating from the lower Ju 88A-4 bomber after aiming it at the target.

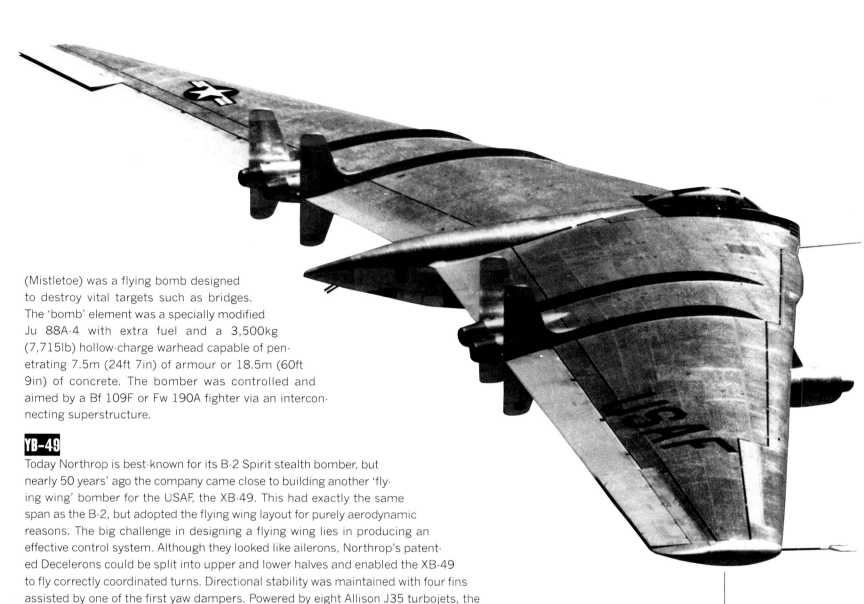

(Mistletoe) was a flying bomb designed
to destroy vital targets such as bridges.
The 'bomb' element was a specially modified
Ju 88A-4 with extra fuel and a 3,500kg
(7,715lb) hollow-charge warhead capable of penetrating 7.5m (24ft 7in) of armour or 18.5m (60ft
9in) of concrete. The bomber was controlled and
aimed by a Bf 109F or Fw 190A fighter via an intercon-
necting superstructure.

YB-49

Today Northrop is best-known for its B-2 Spirit stealth bomber, but
nearly 50 years' ago the company came close to building another 'flying wing' bomber for the USAF, the XB-49. This had exactly the same
span as the B-2, but adopted the flying wing layout for purely aerodynamic
reasons. The big challenge in designing a flying wing lies in producing an
effective control system. Although they looked like ailerons, Northrop's patented Decelerons could be split into upper and lower halves and enabled the XB-49
to fly correctly coordinated turns. Directional stability was maintained with four fins
assisted by one of the first yaw dampers. Powered by eight Allison J35 turbojets, the
prototype YB-49 made its first take-off on 21 October 1947. Flight testing progressed
smoothly until the second aircraft broke up after being overstressed in the recovery from
a high-speed dive. The aircraft was exonorated, but budget cuts led to the cancellation of the
USAF's order for 30 RB-49A reconnaissance bombers.

Gossamer Albatross

On 13 June 1979 it took Bryan Allen 2 hours 49 minutes to pedal the Gossamer Albatross from the
Warren, near Folkestone, to Cap Griz Nez, near Wissant in France and complete the first man-powered
flight across the English Channel. Designed by Californian Dr Paul MacCready, the Albatross combined
strength, lightness and low aerodynamic drag in a brilliantly executed package. Carbon-fibre reinforced plastic (CFRP) was used in hollow tube form for the wing spars, bowsprit and fuselage gondola. The wing ribs, each

Similar in size and shape to the B-2 stealth bomber and made
by the same manufacturer, the Northrop YRB-49A flying wing
of 1950 was designed for reconnaissance.

of which weighed about metric (2oz), were made of expanded poly-styrene and attached to the spar with epoxy adhesive, each joint being locally reinforced with a thin plywood ring; construction of the canard was very similar, and this also incorporated the control cables.

With all that pedalling to do, the Albatross had to be fairly easy to fly. The pilot's left hand grasped a small stick for pitch and direction/roll control, all effected by the canard. The Albatross spanned 141.16m (93ft 10in) and the flying weight was 97.52kg (215lb) including the 63.50kg (140lb) pilot. Its most efficient speed was 18-20km/h (11-12mph).

Voyager

The Voyager was built for the first ever non-stop unrefuelled round-the-world flight. To achieve the required range, designer Burt Rutan produced a 'trimaran' in which the primary structure was formed by 15 integral fuel tanks with a total capacity of 5,636 litres (1,489 US gallons). These were distributed in the tailbooms, centre fuselage, wing and canard, all constructed in lightweight Magnamite graphite/Nomex honeycomb composite. The centre fuselage housed the cabin pod and two Teledyne Continental piston engines of 130/110hp in a centreline thrust arrangement. The handling pilot sat on the right of the pod while the other rested in a bunk located to the rear. A feeder tank forward of the cabin was used to control fuel transfer and had a sight gauge to check the contents. Spanning 33.77m (110ft 9½in), the wing was fitted with winglets to maximize cruise efficiency. After a series of endurance flights to test the systems and perfect the propellers, all was ready.

On 14 December 1986 pilots Dick Rutan (brother of Burt) and Jeana Yeager climbed aboard Voyager at Edwards Air Force Base, California. The take-off was dramatic to say the least. Overburdened with fuel the wings drooped alarmingly, dragging the tips and winglets along the runway as the aircraft struggled to accelerate to flying speed. Finally airborne, what remained of the winglets was soon carried away by the slipstream. But the crew accepted the increased drag and decided to press on. As intended the front engine was shut down for much of the flight to conserve fuel. Nine days later after an epic battle against fatigue and the elements, Voyager reappeared over Edwards having completed a circumnavigation of the world. The precise distance travelled was 40,212.139km (24,986.664 miles).

SATiC A300-600ST Super Transporter

Since 1971, Airbus Industrie had been operating the Aero Spacelines/Boeing 377SGT-201 Super Guppy, a special turboprop transport. By 1983 four of these converted Stratocruisers were hard at work transporting major Airbus components between factories. But as Airbus expanded, its Super Guppies were becoming increasingly costly to maintain. After studying several possible replacements, Airbus decided on a modified version of its own A300-600. Accordingly, the Special Aircraft Transport International Company (SATIC), a joint subsidiary company of Deutsche Aerospace, Airbus and Aerospatiale, was created in 1991 to construct four A300-600STs. The first Super Transporter, soon nicknamed 'Beluga', made its maiden flight on 13 September 1994. The design is dominated by the enlarged, unpressurized upper fuselage. This forms the cargo hold, which is 7.4m (24ft 3 1/4in) high by 7.26m (23ft 93 3/4 in) wide. Stability is maintained by a new tail unit with auxiliary endplate fins and a taller vertical fin from the A340. The huge cargo door allows roll-on/roll-off loading in about 45 minutes, compared to two or three hours for the Super Guppy. The new aircraft is much more efficient, carrying twice the payload, twice as fast at two-thirds the cost.

Ekranoplans

Ekranoplans must rank as one of the most extraordinary achievements of the Soviet aerospace industry. There are many different types but all are designed to ride on the cushion of air created under the wings by the forward motion of a craft travelling close to the surface of the land or sea. The Lun (pronounced 'Lune' and meaning Harrier), is one of the largest Ekranoplans and was delivered to the Soviet Navy in 1987. Its three pairs of cruise missiles are fired from retractable launchers. Powered by eight NK-47 turbofans, the Lun has a maximum speed of 550km/h (342mph) and a range of 3,000km (1,864 miles); loaded weight is 400 tonnes (882,000lb). The Spasatel (Lifesaver) is a rescue version in which the missiles are replaced by three pairs of rescue capsules for 500 people.

Bryan Allen pedalling the Gossamer Albatross, the first pedal-powered aircraft to cross the English Channel.

Opposite: The Grob Strato 2C ultra-high altitude research aircraft is designed to cruise for up to 48 hours at a time while its two scientist passengers study the upper atmosphere.

Left: In 1986 the Voyager became the first aircraft to fly round the world non-stop and unrefuelled.

The A300-600ST 'Beluga' opens wide to reveal its huge unpressurized upper fuselage and cargo door, the latter being the largest fitted to any aircraft.

Antonov An-225

Easily the most powerful and heaviest aircraft ever built, the An-225 Mriya ('Dream') is also the biggest in every respect except wing span, a record still held by the Hughes Hercules flying boat. Maximum take-off weight of the An-225 is quoted at 600 tonnes (1,322,750 lb), the payload contributing an estimated 250 tonnes (551,150lb). The one and only An-225 was built as a transporter for the Buran spacecraft, which it carried pick-a-back, and first flew on 21 December 1988. This gargantuan aircraft bears an obvious family resemblance to the An-124, and many of the major sections are identical. What is not identical is the new centre section, this being the most massive aircraft structure in history. Obvious changes are the additional pair of D-18T turbofans and the new tailplane with twin endplate fins, the latter essential for maintaining directional stability in Buran's turbulent wake. The internal cargo hold is 43m (141ft) long and can accommodate 80 family-sized cars. Sadly, the demise of the Buran programme means that the An-225 is now languishing as a spares source for the An-124 fleet.

Looming over *The Swan* public house on the approach to the Farnborough Airshow in 1992 is the Anotov An-225, currently the world's largest and heaviest aircraft.

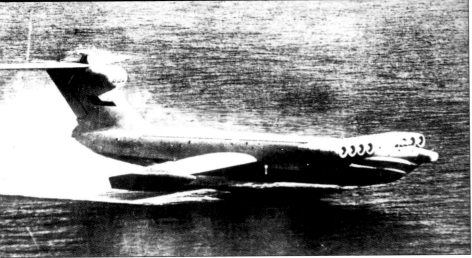

The Lun (pronounced 'Lune' and meaning Harrier) multi-role naval craft was one of the many types of surface-skimming Ekranoplans built by the former Soviet Union.

Photographic acknowledgements

British Aerospace Defence 71 bottom, 85 top, 179 top,
Jeremy Flack/Aviation Photographs International 28 bottom, 36 top, 38 top left, 45
bottom, 50 centre, 53 bottom, 54 top, 61, 64 bottom, 65 top, 65 bottom, 68 right,
71 left, 77 bottom, 78 top right, 81 top left, 81 top right, 82 bottom, 84 bottom, 87
centre, 142 top, 168 left, 171
Tony Holmes 46 centre, 48 centre, 82 top, 82 centre, 175 top left, 175 bottom
Hulton Getty Collection 8, 15 top, 23, 54 bottom, 75 top, 99, 100 /101
Philip Jarrett 9 bottom, 11, 17 top, 27, 34, 36 bottom, 37 top, 37 bottom, 42, 43
bottom, 47, 49 left, 51, 53 top, 58 bottom, 60 bottom, 63 bottom, 66 bottom, 66
top, 74 bottom, 76 bottom, 78 top left, 79 left, 80 top right, 84 top, 84 centre, 86
top right, 91, 93, 94, 97 top, 97 centre, 97 bottom, 98 top, 98 bottom, 102 bottom,
104, 112 /113, 114, 117, 120, 121, 122, 123, 127, 129 top, 132 bottom, 137 top,
142 centre, 148 centre, 158, 160 /161, 181, 182 bottom, 183, /The Bristol
Aeroplane Company Ltd 18
Kamov via Aviation Photographs International 162
Mansell Collection 9 top, 12, 14 /15, 15 bottom
Myers via Aviation Photographs International 141
Photo-Link 19, 20, 21, 29, 30, 35 top left, 40 /41, 45 top, 48 bottom, 50 top, 50
bottom, 52 top, 52 bottom, 53 centre, 65 centre, 67 bottom, 69 top, 69 bottom, 70
bottom, 78 centre right, 81 bottom, 83 top, 83 centre, 83 bottom, 103, 118, 126,
128, 129 bottom, 130 top, 132 top, 133 top, 133 bottom, 134 top, 134 bottom, 138
bottom, 139 top, 140, 142 bottom, 143, 147, 148 top, 150 top, 150 centre, 151
top, 151 centre, 151 bottom, 161, 164, 166 centre, 166 bottom, 167, 168 right,
172 top, 174, 175 top right, 179 centre right, 187 top
Russian Aviation Research Trust 32 /33, 48 top, 60 top, 62 bottom, 67 top, 74 top,
187 bottom

Short Brothers plc 85 bottom, 102 top, 182 top
TRH Pictures 10, 13, 17 bottom, 22, 25, 26 bottom, 26 top, 28 top, 31 top, 31 bottom, 35 top right, 35 bottom, 36 centre, 38 /39, 43 top, 44, 46 top, 46 bottom, 49
right, 55, 56, 57 top, 57 bottom, 58 top, 59 top, 59 bottom, 62 top, 63 top, 63 centre, 64 top, 68 left, 70 top, 71 top right, 72 /73, 75 bottom, 76 top, 77 top, 77 centre, 78 centre left, 78 bottom, 79 right, 80 left, 80 bottom right, 85 centre, 86 top
left, 86 bottom, 87 top, 87 bottom, 92, 95, 106, 107, 108, 109, 110, 111, 116,
119, 124 /125, 130 bottom, 135, 136, 137 bottom, 138 top, 139 bottom, 141 top,
141 centre, 145 top, 145 bottom, 146 top, 146 centre, 146 bottom, 148 bottom,
149, 150 bottom, 153, 154, 155, 156 /157, 159, 163, 165, 166 top, 169, 170, 172
bottom, 173, 176, 177, 179 centre left, 179 bottom, 184, 185 top, 185 bottom, 186

excecutive editor: Julian Brown
design: Martin Topping
picture research: Charlotte Deane
production control: Melanie Frantz
art director: Keith Martin